Boatowner's
Sheet Anchor

NAUTICAL BOOKS BY CARL D. LANE

Boatowner's Sheet Anchor
Cruiser's Manual
How to Sail
The New Boatman's Manual
What the Citizen Should
Know About the Merchant
Marine
Navigation the Easy Way
(WITH JOHN MONTGOMERY)
American Paddle Steamboats

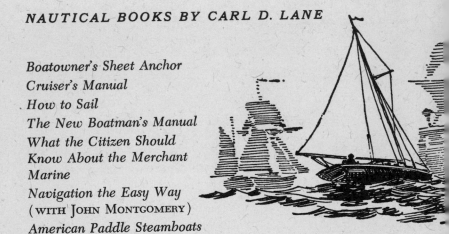

BOATOWNER'S SHEET ANCHOR

A Practical Guide to
Fitting Out, Upkeep, and Alteration
of the Small Wooden Yacht
(Completely revised and updated)

CARL D. LANE

Illustrated by the Author

FUNK & WAGNALLS   NEW YORK   1969

*To the small-boat lovers of the world
who so ably keep alive the traditions
of the sea and the ways of the sailorman,
this book is dedicated.*

Preface

It has always seemed to me that a good book, like a good boat, needs no explanation. They both should sail on their own bottoms. I should much prefer first to taste a handy little packet by the feel of the helm and the song of wind in her rigging, rather than by the excited and prejudiced comment and predictions of her owner. And I hope this is to be a good book, requiring no preliminary diagrams, explanations, or excuses.

Nevertheless, a word as to its *raison d'être* might not only be welcome to the this most inquisitive of mortals, the boatowner and lover, but serve as well ever to remind me of the objectives as the writing of this, the second and modernized edition of this work, progresses.

Really, there is little actually new in the boating field. New bits of hardware, accessories, accommodation and decorative styles, materials—yes, but wooden boatbuilding and maintenance in its fundamentals isn't much different than when practiced by Noah, Argus, Pett, Pook, and Phil Rhodes. These gentlemen had and have—for Mr. Rhodes is very, very much alive today!—the same basic problems to meet and overcome. The laws of ships came only with an understanding of the laws of the seas and the winds, and these things have not changed these centuries since a slope-headed forebear first clung to a log, holding upright a forked branch supporting a skin, and discovered that his rude craft actually moved. From that moment on, this gentleman had his problems. He must keep dry, must keep his log afloat, free of borers and rot, must keep his "sails" drawing and his spars standing. As far horizons, trade, war, and conquest lured, his problems became more complex—and lo! we have a man faced with exactly the same problems that tens of thousands of "boaty" folks face today.

Somehow, we have lost track of the simple, homey "dory-shop" sort of information which our forebears knew and understood so well. This has been through no fault of ours. Without research and much "clamming" about in ancient writings, hoping to fall upon the gem, we have no source to which we may turn. A line in a thousand, a word in a volume, an occasional article in a boating publication (too often not to be found when we actually need it!)—these alone are present sources.

And so, the author—an opinionated tinkerer, incurable romanticist, ever-hopeful experimenter, but loving the smell of Stockholm tar and the ring of a caulking mallet as much as any—presents, under one cover at least, some of the gleanings of his own and others' experience and adventure. A word from Josh Slocum, a "boatshop" sermon by Webster Eldridge who builds modern boats to fare-smack lines hard by, the lesson of a bashed finger, a forgotten owner who once wintered close aboard and had some unique ideas, dreams exploded and dreams come true—all these things shall go to make up this book; all these things, as they apply to the modern yachtsman and owner, shall be presented.

However, a word is here required to take care of that recent giant—the fiberglass, or plastic, hull and boat. This book will make little attempt to become a manual on the art of marine plastics. It is not only far too complex (since almost no brand resin formulaes are the same and each requires its own techniques, usually well explained in an accompanying instruction sheet) but there exist several excellent volumes on the art, and it is recommended that one be added to the hobby book-shelf if more than routine repairs or local coverings are contemplated. After all, whether materials are resins or wood or composites, the basics must still be understood and applied.

It is unnecessary to thank any one particular person or group, for what is presented is, and always has been, the property of all. Each reader will have contributed to some extent by his mere ownership or interest in boats to the perpetuation of the ancient art of preparing to combat, conquer, use, or enjoy the sea. To this group, if to any, should go my thanks, for the art of building and caring for the little ships which live on our pleasant waters and in our hearts is, like religion and language, a universal one.

CARL D. LANE

On board M. V. Penobscot
Ocean Reefs, Key Largo, Florida
March, 1968

Contents

Boatowner's
Sheet Anchor

I *Introduction*

> *"Among the most useful and excellent arts, navigation has always taken first place. In the measure that it is dangerous and perilous, by so much is it honorable and lifted above all other arts, being in no wise suitable for those who lack courage and confidence."*

—SAMUEL DE CHAMPLAIN

Never was the case for the small boatmen and yachtsmen better stated than by this greatest of all cruisers. Samuel de Champlain knew the hardships and joys and rewards of navigating in small boats, in strange waters, along the shores of a continent yet to be explored and conquered. And Champlain, master of many arts, considered navigation lifted above all the others.

The challenge which he found in it, the peril, the glory; the resourcefulness and ability and skill required of the skipper: All these things still make the navigating of a small boat the art above all other arts for thousands of men throughout the world.

On lake and river, on sound and sea, they go forth in their vessels, large and small, with honest canvas or honest power, exploring that four fifths of the surface of the globe which has no frontier, which can never be tamed, which has lured for ages a mighty race of men.

Fortunate is the man who can purchase a suitable vessel, as he does a car, and venture into this fresh new world to feel what Champlain felt so many years ago. Doubly fortunate is the man who cannot purchase a suitable vessel, as he would a used car, but must repair or alter or rebuild—or even build new—for this man tastes of everything that boating can give him. For him boating is more than a pastime or a mere passing hobby.

And it is to this man that this book is directed; to this man who does his own planning, his own work, major and minor, and to the man who, after his dream ship is afloat, by his mastery and understanding of the many skills which make up the art of navigation, must care for his vessel.

The number of yachts which have paid crews and professional skippers, whose owners are busy men of large affairs, wishing perhaps for the simple pleasure of working on a boat, can be counted in the thousands. In the hundred thousands are the boats which must look to their owners for every care and attention, their building and rebuilding, their alteration to suit the purse, locale, and use of their skippers.

Once, in the old Stanley Steamer days, I heard a man solemnly tell my father, grease-covered at the time, that "for every hour you spend on 'em, you spend another hour under 'em."

It is not quite that bad in boating, though careful fitting out and maintenance does take time and effort. However, the boatman has the joy of doing things he likes, out in the open, with his fellows busy round about him, all having the community goal of a thrilling summer afloat with the little ship snugged down, and gleaming alow and aloft to a gouty admiral's fancy. To achieve this, to know, as you set a course for distant ports, that your vessel is tight and able, that the same muscles and brains which now guide her made her fit to be guided, is the true joy of boating.

And aboard a tight and able vessel is the only way to venture offshore, though it be but to cross a stream. Boatmen realize this and have an astounding record of safety behind them. Yet not always can the last dollar be spent upon the boat. Each year during fitting out, for the average man, there is some compromise between what he knows the boat ought to have and what he can afford to give it. He gives it the major requisites of a safe and sane boat, assuring himself comfort, pleasure, and safety, but putting off until next year that replacement which he ought to have now.

But next year a soft plank develops behind the ice chest and once again the replacement must be deferred.

It is deferred because of the cost of the work in a yacht yard or because the owner hasn't the skill to do the work himself. Deep inside, he has been conditioned by the only reading matter he can get on the subject of boats and boating, to the acceptance as truth that boatbuilding and repair is a dark art, not to be attempted by the ordinary mortal.

There is no more to boat work than to building a well house—and few men would shy away from building a well house. Certainly, a boatowner wouldn't, for the very fact that he owns a boat is indication that he must, in some way, have a mechanical twist; that he can reason and use his hands. Without this twist, he could hardly raise his sails or secure his launch to a mooring buoy. Give this man the proper tools, the short cuts, "hows," and professional kinks; let him add his own will to succeed; and the fable dissolves like a lowered spinnaker.

There is this, however, which applies to our well house and doubly so to boat work: the work must be accurate, thorough, and strong enough to do the job it is required to do for a reasonably long time.

In that lies the whole secret of the dark art of boat repair and building. In that lies the difference between the amateur and the professional. A vessel must be well built for lives depend upon it. The well house and the chicken coop, even though jerry-built, will still fulfill their purposes and by means of temporary patches or shorings, not to be tolerated on a boat, remain useful for a reasonably long time.

For the boatman the wire splice MUST hold, the power plant MUST be reliable, the hull MUST have good breeding and good manners.

And to get these "MUSTS," the tradition is that the yachtsman must go to the boatyard where assumedly the dark art is understood and practiced. Also he must pay, frequently much more than he can afford.

This is no indictment of the boatyards. They fill a need and they fill it well, most of them operating under a national organization which assures uniform standards and, to some extent, uniform prices. When the work is done under the supervision of a real naval architect (not to be confused with a yacht broker), it probably will pass the test of the hard usage to which all vessels are put.

But all these services cost money, much more money than a similar operation on a car or a house, and much more money than the budget of three fourths of the men owning boats can afford. These men are universally faced with the choice of spending beyond their means, doing the work themselves, or going boatless. Few of them, these busy men who turn to the water for their relaxation, pleasure, and health, actually go boatless. Most of them stay afloat in whatever they can afford, kept up in whatever manner they can afford.

It is hoped that in the pages of this book will be found the means for this vast class of boat lovers not only to remain afloat but to remain afloat in a safe, sane manner so that their boats, ten-footers to Queen Marys, will not only look but be as fine as the finest which come gleaming and polished from professional yards.

There is an old rule that the cost of yearly boat maintenance, exclusive of crew hire, is the square of the over-all length expressed in dollars. Thus a thirty-foot boat upon which the owner does no work and which is covered by the usual insurance, hauled and stored in the usual boatyard, costs about $900 yearly for upkeep. Not all of this is cash expense, of course, for the full cost is not felt until resale occurs and depreciation is a deduction in the price received. This figure in this year of 1968 is way off, and I expect that double would be about right. I once bought a boat "bargain." Only twenty-six feet she was and pretty as a picture. But she burned sixteen gallons of gas an hour. The first Sunday that I used her cost me $29.20, not including oil. That was also the last Sunday I used her, for I very quickly climbed from under. The next owner perhaps bought a bargain, but actually I sold a headache and never again went near one of these devil boats with a pipeline to my purse.

But even considering only the normal cost of annual upkeep, for the ten or twelve weeks of the boating season in the latitudes where most of our boats are registered, a thirty-foot boat costs $150 to $200 a week to operate and maintain. Not very many boatowners can afford boating at this pace.

The great majority of boatowners spend under $1,000 for the boat, usually a used one or a very small new one; and perhaps $100 yearly for hauling, storage, and only the most necessary repairs, paint, rigging, and replacements. Eventually, these boats catch up with the owners: that is, they need real money spent on them to keep them afloat, and there is a boat on the market, a boat laid up, or a boat abandoned. The process then, glory be to these never-say-die yachtsmen, is repeated, another boat reconditioned, altered, repaired, and placed into commission.

It is not unusual to find old-timers, amateurs, who must earn a living and live chiefly for their annual two weeks' vacation, who have owned twenty or thirty boats in forty years. I just rebuilt my thirty-seventh, and I didn't see the last century, either. I may keep her a few years, let her teach me her lessons, and go joyously on to the next conversion or rebuild or buy a new boat.

"Nut! Ship-jumper!"

Perhaps. But, brother, what fun we have! What fun we have, not only sailing and cruising during those stingy three summer months, but working, dreaming, planning a boat throughout the whole year. We belong to that hardy, lusty tribe of which old Captain Joshua Slocum, doughty lone skipper of the beloved *Spray* is the leader. The old Captain knew the pure joy of sitting in a weed-grown wreck, deep in a Fairhaven cow pasture, perhaps spitting through her gaping seams as he loafed on her paint-hungry decks, there watching his dreams rebuild this ship into a staunch, able vessel.

As the sun dropped low that first day, he must have returned from a brave and thrilling dream voyage on the deep water out beyond the salt marshes, turned joyfully to the old wreck, patted her, and murmured, "Old gal, you an' me is goin' places. A little paint, a mite o' cotton, a dozy plank out an' stout timber in . . . old *Spray*, far horizons is callin' us."

And the Captain's adventure started right there. The planning, the thinking, the bargaining, the ingenuity used—yes, the thumbs pricked and the knuckles skinned—that was the Captain's voyage. Even when, months later, strange lands, leagues from his dear New England, loomed over his homely bowsprit, he could not have forgotten that the deep love he had for the *Spray* started, not when he cast off his dock lines, but when he first found a rusty fastening and decided to replace it with a new one.

That is the way thousands of men love their little ships today.

That is something the man who buys a stock boat, who never lifts iron or marling to help her, will never have.

That is everything boating can give.

The writer, in the following chapters, cannot attempt to deal with the subject in full. There will be much, very much left unsaid; engineering, naval architecture, and scientific data will be hardly recognized, and we shall proceed as most of us must: with the material, knowledge, and experience at hand.

What is here written is the homely, dory-shop sort of information Captain Josh might have given you, gleaned from his experience and observation. Much of it will be highly opinionated (I'm a yachtsman, boys!) and subject to the slide rules, formulae, and slick tabulations of men more educated and professional than the writer.

But let 'em slide, let 'em attack with metacenters and unsheathed versed sines, let 'em gnash their enlightened teeth. There are too many of us still wanting the answers to very simple, common questions.

We don't care why a boat leaks; all we want to do is stop it. We don't care why C.L.R. and C. of E. must be in certain relationship; all we want is a sail rig that will work on our skiff. We don't want to know how to use varnish remover (the directions are on the can anyway); we'd rather know how to make it and save $3 a gallon. Then perhaps we can buy that gadget we can't possibly make. This is *important* and *necessary* information which we must be given or must find out by trial and error—or not get afloat at all.

Perhaps the engineers among you had better stop reading right now—still, Captain Josh didn't know what a curve of versed sines was and look what he did!

II *The Ideal Boat for You*

Every seaport and lakeport, even every river and creek, seems to have its own peculiar type of vessel. Generally speaking, the vessel native to your own port of hail, your own region, is the only vessel ideally suited to you. The experience of years, the controlling depth of water, and the prevailing natural conditions have dictated this peculiar type; and it is probably at the peak of its development in the form in which you see it.

When you go out, boatyard bound in the early spring (though that's not the *best* time to buy a boat), do not take lightly the boat type you find in greater numbers than others. A yard which appears to be a catboat nest, or to have a certain type of powerboat in abundance, is eloquently guiding you in your selection of type. Perhaps nothing determines these types quite so much as the local depth of water. Given a draught limitation, other factors such as beam, rig, power, and construction fall into certain relationships which are fairly common to all boats of that draught. Thus, the Friendship sloops (Bless their gurry-encrusted frames!), long-legged, heel-tappers that they are, suit perfectly parts of the Maine coast and Maine weather. Of course, transplanted to Long Island Sound or the Chesapeake, they will sail, but they will not give 100 per cent usefulness or enjoyment in the generally shallower water of those areas. By the same reasoning, a catboat or high-speed cruiser will not give 100 per cent usefulness or enjoyment in the rips and cross chop of the deep Down East.

It is always pathetic to come upon a fine deepwater craft, designed and fit to cross the big pond, moored deep in an inland sound or bay. She probably doesn't "go to sea" three times in her whole life, yet for the hundreds of week-end cruises and afternoon sails must proceed under the handicap of excessive displacement, heavy rig, and ocean-going deck arrangements. It is almost as pathetic as crossing tacks far offshore with a small centerboarder, with open cockpit, picture-wire standing rigging, and brawn but not brains at her helm.

It is not difficult for the man building a new boat to achieve the ideal for his particular locality. Any naval architect worth his India ink needs to know only three factors to design such an ideal boat: controlling water depths, size, and major uses (i.e., racing, cruising, fishing, etc.). You will, if you don't drop the casual remark that you are thinking of sliding around to Tahiti next fall, get a pretty useful, enjoyable vessel from him. If he is a local man himself so much the better, he's designing from firsthand experience and not research.

But, it is still a fact that most of us are seeking used boats, so our eventual boat must be a compromise between purse, ideal type, and what the local market affords. We find too often that the ideal type boat for a given section maintains a fair value and is not, compared with less well suited sisters near-by, a bargain. Catboats on shallow Barnegat Bay are expensive; utility runabouts on a cottage-studded lake are expensive. It is usually the misfit which is the bargain.

The purchaser of a used boat should approach his problem exactly as if he were acquiring a new boat. His first consideration is size. Size depends upon use, navigational limitations, and operating funds allotted.

Know at the outset that size has very little to do with length. I have cruised with more comfort on a large twenty-six-footer than on a small fifty-footer. Size is usually arrived at by a count of the maximum number of sleeping spaces required or passengers to be carried. This is quite sound, of course, except that we often fail to remember that as hull size increases, so does power requirement, sail area, first cost, and maintenance costs.

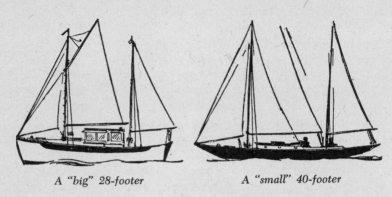

A *"big"* 28-footer   A *"small"* 40-footer

It takes a lot of extra engine horsepower, tankage, and equipment to carry an extra couple. In the case of sailing boats, the increased number or area of sails might easily convert a vessel from a single-hander to one needing a full watch to safely handle her. I shall always remember a cutter which I once owned in this class. Day after day, with no reason for remaining at moorings, I was forced to do just that. The difficulty was getting a crew, another hand or two who had the leisure time I had. Except on week ends, I was compelled to take only short sails after checking the weather most carefully. Alone she was a backbreaker: hard to dock, hard to trim, and hard to enjoy; but she was perfect with a few friends on board.

For perhaps this very reason the large, heavily powered or canvassed vessel is often found on the used-boat market at a tempting price. I believe it a poor investment at any price unless a paid hand can be afforded.

So, it would seem that the wisest course to pursue would be to get the smallest possible vessel for your particular needs. Size, after all, is a matter of layout, a subject upon which later chapters will touch. This is no plea for the tabloid cruiser or the fourteen-foot schooner. One man can handle most boats between twenty and forty feet, reasonable sizes for the average coastal or river port. And it is quite possible to get the requisites of most yachtsmen within the limits of those sizes.

With the offerings defined down to type, the next most important consideration of the boat buyer is the question of cost. To some extent this in itself may determine size, of course. No volume of this sort could possibly give a table of costs for various boat types—so many factors enter into "asking price" and "price paid."

Original cost, age, present condition, and equipment included are all factors which have a bearing on arriving at true value. Stock boats in the last decade have levelled themselves off at fairly steady resale values just as automobiles have. Thus a 1948 Elco of certain model and dimensions is quoted at substantially the same price by all brokers or owners. These values are usually honest and fair, though may again be affected by condition or amount of "extras" an owner includes.

Here are the only formulae for arriving at used-boat value that the writer knows of:

ORIGINAL COST

(less extra equipment, dinghies, etc.)

1 year old	less 40%
2 years old	less 50%
3 years old	less 55%
4 years old	less 60%
5 years old	less 65%
6–10 years old	less 70%
over 10 years old	less 75%

Add to the resultant figures a fair value for extra equipment and deduct cost of major repairs necessary (not annual overhaul or fitting out) as well as yard bills, service bills, etc., standing against the vessel at time of purchase.

For the custom-built vessel, original cost can be determined by adding 33 per cent to the cost of a similarly constructed and powered stock vessel. Another method is to arrive at original cost by following the table below:

	COST PER FOOT
A. Small open sailboats (Snipes, Comets, Bull's-eyes, etc.)	$30–50
B. Small cabin sailboats	$50–100
C. Power cruisers	$500–800
D. Sailing cruisers	$750–1,200

To this must be added TWICE the original cost of the power plant to cover tankage, wiring, and installation. This is far from exact and will serve only as a "jumping-off place" from which to apply the many other factors involved. In practice, we are inclined to let sentiment, racing or cruising record, and just plain human eagerness to "live our dreams" influence the deal. And this is not altogether wrong by any means. It is worth much in joy and contentment to sail the ship which was "love at first sight," come the devil, nailsickness, or stripped gears!

We cannot leave the subject of "value" without mentioning that these days—inflation being with us in abundant measure, like it or not—many boats are sold after a period of use for original or near-to-original prices. This is seemingly fine for the seller—except that he must carefully estimate what he must pay in inflated values when he in turn becomes the buyer, whether of another boat or of other property. And then, too, both Uncle Samuel and possibly your state tax department will want a piece of the inflated price you obtain; and neither will allow depreciation or operating expenses as a counter charge if the vessel is a pleasure boat. So you sold a $3,000 boat for $4,000 and made $1,000. Or did you? Taxes will take $300 of this; broker's fee (if you sell that way) will take another $400; and now you should find a boat of equal value for

$3,300—all that's left for you to spend. It's a good trick if you can do it, mates.

You should check with your state tax bureau as to the status of a used-boat sale and to see if it is subject to a sales tax, or sales tax difference. It would seem that, as sales tax laws have settled down after testing, used boats, like used automobiles, ARE subject to such tax, or to a "use" tax. This charge must be added to the items you deduct from seeming "profit."

Not a little of the real value of any vessel is her breeding: who designed her, who built her, who owned her. The obvious crate, even if purchased at an apparently trifling price, may be difficult to sell again. Odd craft of any type are seldom good investments. To the boatman in the "know" they have no more appeal than an oddly designed automobile.

There are some MUSTS which every prospective boat purchaser should keep well in the foreground as he considers what has been offered.

I would never buy a boat too large or too expensive for my purse. If $1,000 is my limit, that's it, no matter what. I might try to get the owner of a $1,500 outfit down to my price, but I wouldn't nick into any amount not in the boat budget. Nor would I compromise between price and safety. If, by postponing an engine overhaul, a needed suit of sails, or a redecking, I could come within my allowance, I still would not purchase that boat.

I would never buy a boat designed for fresh water for use on salt water, but I would buy one designed for salt water for use on a lake or river. For salt water use I should insist upon *all* underwater metal being of bronze or brass and be greatly influenced in purchasing that boat if deck fittings, rigging, etc., were also of rustproof materials.

I would never buy a boat for salt water use into which an automobile engine, or an engine with an automobile block, had been installed *unless* the engine was fitted with fresh-water cooling. Certain truck and tractor blocks are used as marine blocks and may be slightly more durable by reason of being more thickly walled, but they, too, will eventually rust and corrode through.

I would never buy a boat whose length, beam, or underwater form had been tampered with.

I would never buy a boat which has been suffering for any length of time with dry rot. I am quite sure that I would never effect a real cure and might easily emerge piece by piece with an entirely new hull attached to the original deck hardware. (Of course, I could *sell* it to one who has not read this book.)

I would never buy a boat without:

1. Knowing her complete history.
2. Interviewing people who knew her and had sailed in her.
3. Checking carefully for liens and attachments, in spite of the obvious honesty of her owner or broker.
4. Seeing her bottom, opening her ceiling, and thoroughly exploring her every nook and seam.
5. Taking a trial trip.

Number 5 is, in the case of out-of-season purchase, sometimes an impossibility. In the event that a trial trip (in both hard and soft weather) cannot be arranged, I should call in, for expert advice:

1. A naval architect or marine surveyor (cost $50–$150).
2. An engine mechanic (cost $10–$50).
3. One or more unbiased acquaintances or an owner of a boat of the same general class.

On the other hand I would not refuse to consider a boat because:

1. She had a "jinx" (unless I believed in witches!).
2. She needed reasonable repairs as a result of normal, careful use.
3. She looked "rough." If the "roughness" was merely on the surface and the vessel proved sound underneath, there would be no real reason to condemn her.

4. She was not designed or built by a prominent designer or builder. I would judge her on her merits, performance, and record, knowing full well that some beautiful craft come from the cellars and workshops of boat hobbyists.

The reader will appreciate that the foregoing is one man's opinion but perhaps remember, too, that the almost forty boats that dwelt with the writer at one time or another have taught their lessons.

Every man, driving shoreward with boat in his eyes, has a general idea of the type of boat he wants; that is, straight sail, straight power, cruiser, racer, knockabout, fisherman, or any combination of these. He is usually sure of one thing: the amount of money he plans to spend. Beyond that he is often without prejudice of any kind. Here listed are the several types into which all boats will fall, with a few words about each.

Powerboats

The ideal boat for many is a small open launch or runabout type. But it takes time, what with the romance of sail and the swift beauty of the power cruiser ever luring, for many boatmen to realize that their greatest pleasure can come from a small inexpensive outfit. For the man with limited time or funds, for the man who likes merely to fish the quiet reefs or back eddies, the small cabinless boat is his best bet. Far too many large cruisers never go cruising.

For many, also, the small boat acts as a stopgap or a steppingstone. The launch is a fine type in which to learn navigation, test out for seagoin' constitutions and stomachs, and find out what your next boat should be like.

The problems presented in such ownership are not very complex, with the engine presenting the greatest cost and maintenance problem. Perhaps no type of boat pays such dividends in health and relaxation as the simple open powerboat or sailboat. If the budget will not permit one of the chromium masterpieces of the Boat or Sportsman Show, the boatman need not go boatless. An outboard motor and a good skiff, a runabout, or one-lung launch, approached with the proper attitude, will give an equal amount of fun and keep alive this hankering for the salty horizons far better than reading yachting magazines and sighing for a big .wad.

Get afloat, by all means; that's the watchword, mates! Looking back over the years, small boats have taught me much more than large ones. There was an October cruise once, a week end that stretched into nearly two months. The boat was an old Palmer eighteen-foot fantail launch, the engine a 3.5 h.p. Mianus, and the accommodations a life preserver bed under an overturned skiff. The cruise started in New Jersey and ended in Machias; fun and adventure from the first brush with New York harbor tugs to the last "borrowed" lobster in Maine. I know plenty of men today who wouldn't attempt such a voyage except in a forty-footer with radar, professional skipper, and paid-up insurance!

The cruising yachtsman, may his tribe continue to increase, of necessity must have a boat with some sort of permanent shelter. These range from sixteen-foot top-heavy abortions to eighty-footers which never carry more than two people aft. Once again, the smallest "large" boat for the purpose is here indicated for the average boatman.

Factors in addition to hull and engine design and construction enter into the equation of an ideal cruising boat. Berthing facilities, galley, ice chests, stowing, sanitary arrangements, ventilation, and the dinghy all appear to contribute to or detract from the appeal of a boat or boat design. The eventual boat finally resolves itself into the question of personal likes and dislikes, usually obtainable completely only in the custom-designed-and-build vessel.

The man purchasing a used boat, a stock boat, or knockdown forms must of necessity compromise between needs and actuality. There are certain standards, however, which should be present in any boat before ownership is even mildly contemplated.

A 22-footer with full headroom. In lowering the trunk to 4'2" head-room the seats were also lowered, affording elbowroom under the waterways formerly closed. Leg room was provided by setting the seat risers outboard giving full width floor space. The main hatch was made almost the full width of the trunk for standing room at the galley

Every cruising boat, and this applies to cruising sailboats as well as straight powerboats, should have the following features at least:

1. Sufficient, safe, and economical power.
2. All common safety apparatus, including complete bilge ventilation and a compensated compass.
3. A *comfortable*, full-size berth for every person on board.
4. Either full headroom or full leg room.
5. Reasonable and decent sanitary arrangements.
6. A galley with a safe stove, an ice chest, and reserves of food, water, and fuel.
7. A *sane* dinghy and sane method of towing or carrying it.
8. Protection, alow and aloft, from wind, rain, spray, and sun.

Except in boats of stock build, all of these features can seldom be found in one boat. However, if the major features (Numbers 1, 3, 4) are present, it is not a great matter to incorporate the others. In other parts of this book will be found "helps" and "hows" along these lines.

A boat which cannot be altered or arranged to include *all* of these features would hardly be a wise investment or even an approach to an ideal boat.

Experienced cruising men will tell in no uncertain manner of glorious cruises spoiled by wet bunks, a stubborn stove, or a dinghy that nursed the transom all night and snapped at the ensign staff all day. This sort of thing can be avoided, even in the first boat. It is a matter of viewing the offering coldly, without sentiment or blind enthusiasm. A vessel lacking these features is not necessarily out. A builder may be turned loose on her (and how he'd love it, after duly checking your credit, of course), or you may turn yourself loose on her. The latter course, as has been suggested in Chapter I, would certainly give you the most and fullest enjoyment of your ownership.

Beyond all these things, any boat worth its paint, should *look* good. Her lines should be regular and symmetrical, her deckhouses in proportion and character, and her combinations of paint, varnish, natural wood, and trimmings should be harmonious. Conversions are not necessarily to be frowned on. However, when they take the form of a long-overhang sloop, from which the ballast has been dropped, and a sash-studded porch-type house, complete with geraniums in window boxes and a washline pole added, it is time to put your money in stocks or some other more satisfying scheme for losing it.

So, the ideal powerboat for you is one having, or capable of having installed, at least the features listed and, in addition, is best suited to do the job you require, i.e., sound cruising, ocean cruising, sport fishing, river cruising, etc., ad infinitum.

To be sure, you can discover what appears to be an ideal boat in innumerable boat showrooms, mostly of glass construction. Look into most of these, especially if they are low priced, with care and understanding of what you see. Far, far too many have been created in an advertising agency office and feature—at the expense of genuine sea-going qualities—tested items of eye, woman, or status appeal. Far, far too many are just not practical in terms of what a boat is used for, and many are downright unsafe. The tiny twenty-two-footer that is advertised to sleep six cannot possibly be a safe boat. Imagine her of a pleasant day, steaming out on the bay at top speed (about 60 per cent of her advertised speed)with all hands crowded into the stern in a cockpit five feet long. Can this possibly be fun? Or safe?

The point is that ownership is made so easy (no cash down, best trade-in deal in town, free boating lessons, complementary compass and trading stamps, yet!) that ownership becomes painless and immediate. But few of these low-priced boats, offered like discount home accessories, are worthy of the name after a few months. They do not hold value for any length of time because the man who wants one can buy a new one more readily—just sign here, mister! These low-priced boats cannot be readily repaired because of general lack of plastic technology, and the dealers are seldom true service organizations. Their salesmen are too often former used-car salesmen, and their mechanics limited to outboard motor work—but they'll sell you anything that they can get a 40 to 10 per cent discount on.

This is not an attack on either plastic or stock boats. It is rather an attack on a generally irresponsible group of merchandisers who sell boats with no love for their product or the buyers. Eventually, there will come legislation to control them; and standards of design, building, and selling will be introduced. Meanwhile, there are plenty of fine, handsome, and proud stock boats, mostly of glass, on the market. They are readily recognized, even by the tyro: they cost considerably more than the boats referred to above. They cost as much as a wooden boat, often more. But they are designed by naval architects, built by manufacturers of experience (often enough firms with generations of wooden boat construction experience), and styled by practical people—the same who design campers or trailers or small homes or Pullman car interiors or light planes.

I truly wish that publishing practice would permit me to mention some of these worthy firms. I cannot. However, if you keep your feet on the ground and look beyond price or easy terms and into sound construction and manufacturer's reputation, you will recognize these boats. Their design variations are myriad, and you will have to remember that designs for glass boats cannot be altered, even slightly, on the production line. If you feel that a twenty-four-foot boat will serve, try your darndest to swing a twenty-eight-footer. I'm positive she will serve you better. You can readily manage it—just skip some of the gadgets you or the salesman think you must have. And be realistic if you are a novice. Ask your boating friends for advice. Read this and other books for an answer. Call the local Coast Guard Auxiliary or the United States Power Squadron; they'd love to assist and steer you correctly; and you will find in the advice of the experienced a respect for the power of the sea, an insistence upon safety and quality, and an utter hatred for shoddiness afloat that will go a long way toward making your first boat a safe, proud, and worthy boat.

Sailboats

For the man contemplating first ownership of a small sailboat, the centerboarder of eighteen to twenty-six feet is unquestionably the best. The real problems and "feel" of sailing can hardly be gotten in a hull under this size; and beyond this size, a boat begins to get big and might, under certain conditions, too often unpredictable, need an extra hand or two. The centerboarder, too, gives range. Shallow water presents no hazard with the board sheathed. Indeed, the presence of bottom is often discovered by a tick on the dropped centerboard rather than a sudden inrush of ocean through a hole in the bows. The centerboarder has a marked advantage over keelboats in that it can be easily beached and need seldom carry or tow a dinghy.

Boats of this type are easy to maintain and easy to haul out or move to the family garage on a trailer. It is the least expensive of any type, perhaps the easiest to build, and certainly will pay fat dividends on the investment in the way of fun and adventure.

Keelboats, or those fine combinations of keel and centerboard, have their places in deepwater ports, of course. They are seldom ideal, limiting sailing by their depth, on lake, river, or bay.

I should insist on finding these features, in addition to sound design and construction, in any small sailboat of the open or racing type:

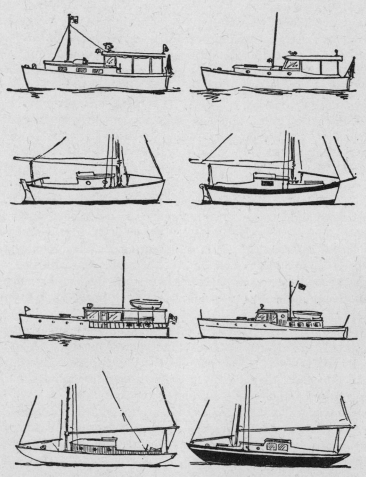

Some old types "modernized." In all cases cabin sizes and interior accommodations have been left the same and only the top camouflaged. Note, in the right-hand sketches, the small details of design, painting, and accessories which contribute to the change

1. Means of floatation in the event of capsizing or filling. Inherent, perhaps, in the centerboarder; by means of air tanks or balsa units in the ballasted keelboat.
2. Sheets and halyards within easy reach of the helmsman.
3. Means of reefing or lessening sail area.
4. Safety devices beyond those required by the Government (for some reason sailing vessels are not *required* to carry life preservers or fire extinguishers).
5. Oars or sweeps, with necessary sockets and rowlocks, with which to move the vessel in calms or tideways.

The small sailboat should be simple in rigging, sparring, and canvassing. Cat or sloop are the most efficient and safest in these sizes. There is no real reason for a twenty-foot schooner, ketch, or yawl. Indeed, they are often so inefficient as to be dangerous and unmanageable.

Small sailboat racing affords one of the real thrills of ownership. There are many classes. The Snipe class has nearly 12,000 boats registered, closely followed by Comets, Whales, Wee Scots, Nationals, Sea Birds, and whatnot. Buying or building into such a class gives an added protection to your boat investment because class boats, well kept up or perhaps with a good racing record, bring more in the resale markets than similar boats not in a class. More about this later.

The large cruising sailboat is becoming more popular yearly, especially around coastal ports, and represents the ultimate to many small-boat men. Ownership should be approached with the realization that it costs more to purchase and to maintain than a powerboat of equal size or accommodations.

As far as hull and accommodation are concerned, the same suggestions as given for the power cruisers hold good. In addition, however, there are these features which I would require of the cruising sailboat:

1. A deck and deckhouse at least as strong and sea-resisting as the hull, with small openings and small strong glass areas.
2. A self-bailing cockpit.

3. The most efficient sail rig for that particular hull, with ample provision for reefing or shortening sail.
4. Some method of below-decks heating and drying.

I believe that Number 3 is where too many sailing cruisers fail; they carry poor sail plans, or at least sail plans which are not as efficient as they might be. The divided rig (ketch, schooner, etc.) all have their places, to be sure, but not on the great majority of our coasting or lake sailing vessels.

Of all rigs, the sloop is the most efficient and surely the simplest. Next in order follow cutter and yawl, with the experts still fighting about the rightful place of schooner and ketch. The ideal inshore boat, unless you value the romance of much cumbersome sparring and rigging, should have a sloop or cutter rig. The ideal boat for ocean passages or racing might ship one of the divided rigs mentioned.

In selecting the ideal type, after satisfaction of the requirements of proper accommodations (which determines size, power, etc.), the next most important consideration is simplicity of deck arrangement, interior, and rigging. The ideal sailing cruiser for you, just as the ideal powerboat, must do the job first; then do it in the simplest, most efficient, and possibly most economical manner.

Since original publication of this work, the catamaran and trimaran have come into full flower and can no longer be ignored as novelties. Both provide excellent day sailing qualities, thrilling high-speed passages, and top racing sport. They are definitely best in glass, or possibly plywood covered with glass. Light weight is essential. They can spell trouble on docking, and if overturned can rapidly wreck their hull because the type goes over full half circle, with the mast straight up and down but *underneath*. Falling tide or a ledge places full weight on the hull structure, and deep damage can result. See nearby sketch for a guard against such capsizing. Every multiple-hull vessel should be so fitted.

These boats do not make good trailer boats, being generally too wide for highway travel without special permit. And I hold no brief for them as cruising boats. The accommodations related to size and cost are definitely substandard, usually two or three tiny

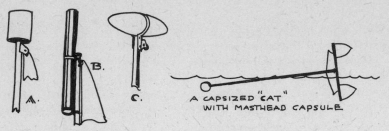

Three types of masthead floaters which keep a cat from turning over completely. Any flotation unit (A. Canister, B. Hollow tube, C. Surplus air force wing fuel tank) as high as possible will prevent a total capsizing—and probably total disaster

spaces, nicely labelled stateroom, galley, etc., on the plans, which make for utterly stupid shipboard living. Even if one of the hulls can sleep two persons, with head and wardrobe, where does the total ship's complement dine or socialize or entertain? On deck? Possibly . . . in pleasant weather only. I would most earnestly advise against a cruising "maran." Just look at the used boat list— they can hardly be given away, it would seem.

Furthermore, at sea these vessels take a terrific drubbing and straining; and not all of them hold together, the marvels of reinforced glass and plywood notwithstanding. No, don't buy one for cruising. And, what's more, even if you did, you couldn't get a night's sleep aboard when under weigh. Sleeping in one of those hulls is like sleeping in a snare drum; just terrible!

Like the powerboat, the stock sailing boat can readily be found in glass boat lines throughout the country. It is a sad sight to see the similarity of hull and rig design, as if one basic design were adequate for the greatly varying sailing conditions all over our hemisphere. Up to twenty feet or thereabouts, or for trailer boats or yacht sailing dinghies, this may be acceptable, for certainly it puts a lot of people afloat who otherwise might still be fated to the crowded highways for relaxation. But it seems to me that we have lost in the great shuffle those admirable local types, so wonderfully suited to their locale and regional uses—the catboats, the Down East clipper-bowed sloops, the sharpies and skipjacks of Long Island Sound and the Chesapeake, the Mackinack boats, those slippery pulling boat types of the Hudson River, and the john boats.

However, the glass boats offered—if you bear the above remarks in mind—are generally good fun boats, reasonably safe, and, if you don't shop for the cheapest, a good investment. I think a mistake often made by novice sailormen is to buy a too-small boat. Sailing is a matter of balance and trim, and the factor of live weight most actively affects this trim. In a small craft the weight of two persons, wrongly placed, can utterly destroy her sailing ability. Avoid eight- and ten-foot "dinks"; they are good for nothing but launch service. To sail with two persons, provided they have free mobility to shift weight over a considerable portion of the midship platform, you will need at least a thirteen by five foot boat. Eighteen by six is much better. For a two-sleeper, you will need at least a twenty-two-foot length and an engine, or a well for an outboard engine. For a family boat, two adults plus two "kids," try for a twenty-eight-footer, enclosed head, and four permanent berths.

There are many glass boats of the type available, almost no wooden stock sailing boats.

Auxiliaries and Motor Sailors

The enjoyment of any sailboat, large or small, not used for racing is much enhanced by the inclusion of auxiliary power in the outfit. Usually, it is not necessary or desirable to seek 100 per cent speed under motor in the sailboat. The motor should be considered as purely auxiliary; a help in tideways and calms and an ace in the hole against the possibility of a week-end cruise ending in light airs far from the office about the time you are due to catch the Monday morning 8:14.

Demand of the auxiliary motor the same standard of condition as you would of the motor of the straight powerboat. When and if used, it is usually sorely needed and for that reason must never be a haphazard installation.

In selecting the auxiliary, I would insist upon finding, or later installing:

1. A feathering propeller.
2. A 100 per cent efficient and safe exhaust line installation, capable of discharging under any angle of heel.

The motor sailor (or 50–50) is a fairly recent type in the yachting field. Generally speaking, the boatman interested in this type, which at first glance seems to provide everything, should know: A, that he is in for the maintenance and expense of probably the most costly type afloat; B, that he will find himself owner of not a 50–50, but a 30–70. Few motor sailors perform well under sail, especially to windward. Indeed, they are usually rigged with 15 or 20 per cent less sail area than a straight sailing or auxiliary vessel and have the added handicap of dragging high topsides and superstructure about.

However, they do provide a happy and healthy combination of sail and power for the man who cruises with his family, offering everything of the powerboat, with the added possibility of pleasant, though not fast, sailing under certain ideal conditions.

Any of these boats, from the launch to the 50–50, can become anything to him its owner wishes. The man with little time and less money can let the wrong type of boat take charge of his life and pocketbook. Too much chromium, power, swank, and brightwork can easily lick the man who must operate his boat on a few hundred dollars a year on an occasional Saturday afternoon. An expensive racing class such as the Star class (which makes rule changes involving almost new boats) can cost an annual sum all out of proportion to the value of the vessel to the owner. The man of means and with leisure can become thoroughly disgusted with and ashamed of the out-of-date boat which he expected would take him to far horizons in safety and comfort.

It is most essential that the eventual boat purchased suit the temperament, standards, and expectation of the owner thoroughly. "Almost the right boat," over a course of time, will not do. One of the reasons that boats are swapped so often is because sufficient care and thought was not applied during the original

purchase. It is extremely expensive to keep swapping boats, trying to achieve the ideal by trial and error. Far better is to define
your wishes and requisites clearly at the outset, then do a real job
of finding, building, or having built the ideal boat.

When you finally decide upon *The Ideal Boat* you will probably
love her faithfully and long. She is very much like the right girl:
until death do us part. But, mate, don't let the boat kill you; you
kill her, it's much more fun!

As this ideal boat takes shape in your mind, as you visit wintry
yacht yards or harass yacht brokers, a certain preparation for
ownership should take place. Whether or not you have owned
a boat before, this new vessel will present certain problems of its
own.

Intelligent ownership and operation will require additional or
supplemental knowledge of operation, rules of the road, and navigation. A more complete enjoyment of yachting, both for yourself
and your guests, will result from a program calculated to place
you afloat well-found.

If your boat measures into a sailing or speedboat class, the
sponsoring organization will probably have a national or series of
local clubs or groups from whom literature, training courses, rules,
etc., may be obtained. Such a class is the Snipe class: fifteen and a
half foot C.B. sloops designed by W. F. Crosby of *The Rudder*.
This organization has several hundred chartered divisional fleets
all over the world. Membership is simply a matter of registering at
a nominal fee and receiving the many benefits of the organization
which include, in addition to Snipe plans, rules, news, etc., the
opportunity of racing in the many regattas held each year. Association with fellow owners, skippers, and builders, adds much both
practical and social to ownership.

There are, of course, many other classes, some of them national
or international in scope. If your boat measures into any one of
them, you would be missing half the sport not to register with the
proper class and to become actively identified with it.

Not a small benefit of owning one of these class boats is the
advantage enjoyed in the purchase of stock parts, sails, spars, and

deck gear. Quantity production has not only placed these items in immediate stock but reduced the cost considerably.

The local yacht club offers the boatowner not only the association with a similar "breed of fish" but sometimes valuable courses as well. A yacht club, strictly within your means, adds fathoms to boat enjoyment.

For the large-boat owner, organizations of a broader character such as the Cruising Club of America, the Off-Sounding Racing Association, the North American Yacht Racing Association, and others offer the companionship and competition of men and boats from an entire region.

For actual training or study in seamanship, navigation, and small boat handling, there is probably no better medium than the United States Power Squadron.

This is an entirely private organization, interested in training boatmen to better appreciate their boats and the sea. It is not necessary to be a boatowner to become a member, though membership takes place only as the result of passing an entrance examination after taking a free elementary course in piloting and small boat handling. Acceptance is a mark of achievement and honor, entitling the member to fly the Squadron's distinctive flag and to apply for more advanced courses dealing with all branches of seamanship and navigation. This training is taken with fellow-yachtsmen at any one of the over one hundred Squadron headquarters located throughout the United States.

Comparable to the United States Power Squadron is the United States Coast Guard Auxiliary, a voluntary service branch of the Coast Guard set up to teach water safety, navigation, small boat handling, vessel operation, and public education in nautical subjects. Call your local Coast Guard base or depot for details or write: The Commandant, United States Coast Guard, Washington, D.C. Membership has no military responsibility, and auxiliary members on Coast Guard business receive no pay. The auxiliary has taken a vast load off the service's shoulders: that of conducting voluntary motorboat inspections for safety standards and vessel condition. So outstanding has been the auxiliary's job that the regular service accepts its inspection as official and valid.

For younger boatowners, an excellent preparatory training, at no charge whatsoever, may be had by joining the Sea Scouts, an older-boy branch of the Boy Scouts of America. Most cities and towns have Sea Scout units (or ships), all uniformed and often owning shore bases and vessels for the practical training. Members must be at least fifteen years of age and pass certain physical and entrance examinations. Further information may be obtained from the nearest Council Office of the Boy Scouts of America, or by addressing the Boy Scouts of America, Senior Scout Service, New Brunswick, New Jersey, 08903.

Certain correspondence and other schools offer courses in advanced navigation for the man contemplating the "big jump." However, in these courses, the social contact so enjoyable and inspiring in the other courses mentioned, is lacking.

The purpose of the writer, in including the foregoing information under the heading of *The Ideal Boat* is to attempt to show that this ideal boat may become more nearly perfect, more nearly *ideal*, by making a serious effort to understand the wide horizons which ownership opens. Ownership goes far beyond an exchange of money for a fast or thrilling ride. A vast hobby is opened: one that carries over through all the seasons, with a perfect balance of physical relaxation, physical labor, mental stimulation, and challenge. Boating does not cease with the winter laying up; there are things to make, things to learn; reading, study, invention. The ideal boat must satisfy beyond mere performance or appearance. Boating is a hobby just as much as stamp collecting and, to be ideal, it must offer complete satisfaction as a hobby.

No matter what size or type your boat is, it can offer you this completeness. As much knowledge of navigation and seamanship (and perhaps more, mates) is required on a sixteen-footer as on a sixty-footer, and the fun of obtaining and using it is equal in both cases.

Here's a slogan of which old Joshua Slocum would have approved:

"A ten–footer is a Yacht!"

Approach any boat in this way and she's an *Ideal Boat*.

III *Acquiring a Boat*

*"Take a purse full of money, mix with enthusiasm (pref-
erably strained), add either salt or fresh water and let bake
in warm April sunshine. If no results, add more money.
Continue baking until a large boat appears, sprinkle with
champagne and serve every weekend. . . ."*

—RECIPE FROM DAVY JONES' CUCK-COOK BOOK

No matter how you go about acquiring this ideal boat of yours,
the "purse full of money" will be absolutely necessary. But large
purse or small, it will build *some kind* of boat. There is only one
really important rule never to lose sight of: the ideal boat must fit
the purse. Small money never yet built large boat. It built long
boats or wide boats or tall boats but never large in the sense of
completeness.

It does not take a great amount of money to build the *hull*, but
too often it is apparent that purse size determined hull size with
no regard to the fact that this item represents only 50 per cent or
less of the *complete* boat cost. Too many boatbuilding or rebuilding projects founder on this reef: a careless and unintelligent estimate of both money and time. If either runs out before the project
is completed, we shortly see in the boating periodicals one of
those pathetic ads: "For Sale. Cheap. Partly finished hull." Worse
than that, we are quite apt to have a disgruntled individual at
large who, being human, maligns the sport and the little vessels
we love.

As far as this writer knows, there is *only one way to acquire a*

32

complete boat: that is, purchase, new, a stock vessel of the type desired. Such a boat has built into it the experience and engineering of many trials and errors and reaches the market a unit as complete as your auto or your refrigerator. It has everything necessary to its operation: government equipment, even name and port of hail, stoves, mattresses, etc., in the case of a cruising boat; and is ready to sail in a safe and comfortable manner. If you are a close trader, you can even get a set of charts, binoculars, and a dinghy thrown in!

But, as pointed out in Chapter I of this book, there is one thing the stock boat can never give—the great adventure of your own association with the boat from the laying down of her lines to the setting of the anchor jack in your first port of call. I firmly believe that most yachtsmen, of inclination rather than necessity, prefer this adventure.

From a crassly commercial viewpoint, buying a stock boat is not the cheapest manner of acquiring a boat. Quantity production may have cut certain manufacturing or assembly operations, but this is largely used up again in an extremely large general overhead made up of advertising costs, experimental building and research, and the considerable cut of both distributor (or agent) and the salesman. A $10,000 cruiser (plus a freight bill which would buy your fuel and gin for a full summer afloat) actually represents about $6,000 to $7,000 of labor and material.

This difference is not a total loss, of course. You have, in a way, bought an insurance, and assurance, that your boat *will* perform as specified, a hidden but real value. You also have purchased a boat which has a definite and standard resale value, though the first year's use may knock off as much as fifty per cent in one fell swoop! Again, the model or appearance of a stock boat may be radically changed within a year or two, and you are in the position of the Model T and later the Model A Ford owners at various periods.

The large stock-boat manufacturers produce a boat as good as, but no better, than the custom yards. Some of the smaller and cheaper stock boats are of a standard far below that of the custom yards or even the rule-of-thumb boat shops in the Down East salt marshes. A fifteen-foot class sailboat for a $600 retail price, with factory and other overhead costs deducted, doesn't leave a large sum for careful selection of materials of first-class workmanship. I believe that Gideon Hanson, who digs clams when he's not busy but *is a real boat builder,* given technical and engineering plans other than his own, would turn out a better-built boat for the same money.

For the man who does purchase, either new or used, a stock boat, I would give this advice:

1. Inspect (or have inspected) while under construction or before delivery, the boat which you have purchased. Do not buy as you would buy an automobile, secure in the knowledge that a responsible, factory-controlled service station, is ready to make good any defects. The split plank or frame or the poor butt will seldom show up until long after the period of guarantee has expired. It is not enough to rely upon the fact that it is a stock boat, built by a large or well-known concern.
2. After ownership, do nothing in the way of *major alterations* which would substantially change the *appearance* of the boat. To do this would most certainly undermine her established resale value.

This ideal boat of yours may be acquired in still another manner. You collect various photos and sketches and drop into the office of a naval architect, selected because he has built a reputation for himself in the general type of vessel you wish. He is always a gentleman, usually a good engineer and designer, and will please you by his immediate enthusiasm for your boat. You will leave him with the impression that for the small fee of 5 to 10 per cent, depending upon how well he likes you or something, he has taken all trouble from your shoulders.

Actually, your trouble is only starting.

The only way, after your general ideas of size, speed, and rig have been revealed, to have the least trouble is to stay away from the naval architect. Then you will have a boat which the *architect* thinks you ought to have, or the one he likes, built by the builder whom he likes. There's nothing particularly wrong with this; your boat will probably be a success. You might find that it has cost considerably more than planned or estimated, that it will be delayed in the building, and that the wheel was placed dead center instead of to starboard. These are minor matters which will be dissipated in your enthusiasm to get afloat and your effort to protect the already large investment you have made.

The builder will say mean things about the architect and the architect about the builder, and you won't get the boat until you pay. Somehow, in spite of specific instructions, blueprints, specifications and contracts, boats never are built without some flaws showing up during construction. These things are nobody's fault —except possibly your own for wanting such a crazy boat in the first place—and you can do nothing about it.

I do not mean to imply that the N.A. is a dunce or a knave or a crook. I do mean to say that he is quite human, with his own reputation to build and maintain, and that he won't and CAN'T give you everything you want in your ideal boat. For this, perhaps you should be thankful!

My plea is that you understand beforehand what you are going to be up against and not calmly assume that building a boat is as simple as drawing it. When "trouble" and "extras" arrive, do not be surprised. They come to every man who has a boat built. One very good, though frightfully expensive, way to minimize building trouble is to place the order on a "time and material" basis. Nobody will bother you until the final payment is due! Rich persons often do this, making changes or additions as they inspect, quite careless of the fact that it costs a trifle more to change a bulkhead of wood than of India ink.

The man who reads this book will probably not fall into this class, and he may even fall into the exact opposite: the man who has estimated and contracted for everything down to the last flag, halyard, and deck mop. Having done this, he is quite liable then to haunt the boatshop until his ship is finally afloat.

It is fun to build this way, though neither architect nor builder would agree, but positively expensive. To actually see the little ship taking form differently than it had been visualized is too much of a temptation. "Stop work," "I'll see the architect," "Hold everything until I write Porthole Pete"—these utterances cost money. And how! The "mistake" actually completed, it often appears not as bad as thinking about it and is allowed to stand, with no real loss to the design or the purse.

So, engage a naval architect or sign a building contract with your eyes open, and do not expect perfection. You will not get it except in very rare cases. I have several friends who have had "perfect" boats, but each has since acquired another boat.

These remarks perhaps appear cynical in the extreme. Nothing is further from the truth. It is simply that I believe it unreasonable to ask a naval designer or a boatbuilder to toy and experiment with your idea of a boat and then hold him to strict account for not achieving the fastest, most beautiful, most commodious vessel afloat. To some extent every new design is an experiment, and the results must be regarded in this light in all fairness.

Many prominent naval architects have evolved and specialized in a few tried-and-true designs. The prospective owner cannot go far wrong in one of these—he may even be given a trial trip—and pet ideas of rig or accommodations can often be incorporated at no risk to success.

When the custom boat is carefully planned on paper and in conference, the builder's estimate will seldom run higher than the cost of a stock boat of equal specification. If neither owner nor architect make changes or additions—and remember that *you* pay for the architect's changes—the boat, a reliable builder having been carefully chosen, will be completed at the contract price.

It has often been stated that boatbuilders make their profit on the extras. This may be true to some extent and providing you authorize the extras (suggested to you one by one but billed en masse—oh, my!). One reason, perhaps, for the builder's doing this (if he does) is because he has too often been forced into an awkward and unprofitable situation by a practice of some types of

A CHEAP YARD.   AN EXPENSIVE YARD.

naval architects. These gentlemen themselves furnish power plant, ship chandlery, cushions, navigational instruments, and other manufactured items, and keep for themselves the 30 or 50 per cent discounts which really belong to the builder.

Insist, if you can get away with it, that the builder purchase and supply these items; you will have a happy builder and a better boat!

A few points now for the man who contemplates a custom boat:

1. Select an architect and builder whose name and reputation will add value to your vessel.
2. Listen carefully to the advice of your N.A. He's an expert on boats *in their entirety,* not merely an engineer to figure the displacements, areas, etc., which you can't do.
3. Design your boat in the summer, build it in the fall—unless you want to lose a season afloat. Many a man's boat trouble is due entirely to the fact that he waited until April to order his boat and *rushed* the builder into slipshod methods in order to get it by July. (One of the reasons for advancement of the annual Motor Boat Show was just to relieve the spring pressure on boat, engine, and accessory manufacturers.)
4. For the sake of the ship as well as the purse, *decide just once.*
5. As this is written, revised to the year 1969, the glass or "plastic" boat has swept the land and taken a great part of the small craft market. I have little practical objection to the

glass hull. I do have serious and deep objections to the utter lack of esthetic values in the type, the sterile repetition of a form often not related in any way to traditional boats and having no recognition of the values beyond, or behind, which seem to me to make up a great part of the pleasures of boat ownership. Or they should. For the buyer of one of these (and they are manufacturing—no longer is the term "build-ing"!—them up to sixty feet and more), acquisition is simply a matter of buying the brand and model that suits best. But you can't change a thing about it, except color. You can't add a shelf or a cleat or remove a bulkhead. You can't put in a different engine or go to twin engines or add tankage *unless* you, or the dealer, undertakes a deep, costly, and most likely unsuccessful alteration. You will have to learn all about glass construction and handling, have special tools, knowl-edge, and experience, and you will end up with a "mess."

So, like a custom-designed boat, the glass one is the most ex-pensive of all. And the least satisfactory. Glass construction, with its necessary wooden form, usually runs higher than the same form in wood. Good glass boats (and there *are* good ones!) must be built in special humidity- and temperature-controlled plants and by trained workmen directed by no less than a chemical engi-neer. Glass construction is not for the wooden-boat shop that has "converted" to glass boats; you will be paying for builders' educa-tion for a long time. Down East, in Maine, we have seen several wooden shops convert to glass, learning as they went; and not one has survived. We simply do not have the climate for successful glass-boat building and have trouble enough in the simple opera-tions of covering decks and trunks with glass! Nor do we have the volume or the available labor to justify a large, modern plant. Nevertheless, eager buyers appear hoping to get a low bid on a modern vessel built by old traditionalists in a relatively low labor and overhead area.

The only solution seems to be to purchase a bare glass hull and custom design the accommodations and superstructure. Such hulls are on the market—and beware of those which are, even if not so described, rejects from a government contract. You probably can't even see what's wrong with such a hull; nor can anybody, including naval architects and boatbuilders, unless they have the technology and proper testing equipment. And thereafter, you are still faced with fitting your ideas and your budget into somebody else's ideas of hull form. Only last summer a neighbor of mine bought a single screw thirty-six-foot glass hull and decided to put in twin engines. This little change, plus beds, shaft alleys, patching the deadwood and later cutting it away, and general beefing up, cost him exactly as much as the hull itself—and he could have had a proper wooden hull, all ready for his engines, at just one half the total cost! And I expect that he has a real dog on his hands. I know the boat doesn't perform well. I doubt that he could find a serious buyer at half his cost.

No, you custom-boat buyers, do not attempt to achieve your ideas in glass unless you are really loaded!

There is no possible means of actually estimating the number of boats acquired each year by owner building. That the number is considerable is certain. There are two ways in which to build a boat: A, working entirely from plans and specifications; B, assembling a knockdown or prefabricated boat. There is no real reason why the careful, conscientious, mechanically inclined man cannot have a successful vessel either way.

Working entirely from plans requires perhaps more skill and certainly more time than assembling a knockdown boat. Heavier tools, steam box, a level floor for a base line, and perhaps an occasional helping hand is needed. Materials will not only have to be selected but also located, sometimes a difficult matter in localities away from boating centers.

Except in a general way, this book cannot attempt to cover these fields in detail. There are many excellent books on boat-building; all knockdown kits and many plans are accompanied by full instructions.

Building a boat is largely a matter of the correct mental approach to the job. It is not a dark art. There are no magic formulae, no short cuts. It is simply a question of self-confidence, plus accurate and thorough workmanship. Research, or a trial operation, should take place beforehand; the builder should resolve that only the best of everything shall go to make up this boat to which he will trust his and others' lives, and it must be thoroughly understood that boatbuilding is, at best, a slow job. The completion of the planking, when the work actually *looks* like a boat, is less than a quarter of the job finished, and there must elapse days of insignificant but important work before the vessel seems actually to grow again.

Perhaps most amateur boatbuilders fail right here, in skipping over the tedious small chores. Resolve, when the keel is first laid, to give just as much thought and care to every dab of paint and every tap of the caulking mallet, and the boat will be a good boat.

The man who builds entirely from plans fixes his chances of success or failure *before* he touches a tool or even purchases the framing timbers. He must do his own laying down, that is, transfer, from a table of offsets and certain sectional hull drawings, the complete form of the boat to a full-size state. The utmost accuracy and patience is required here. *Carelessness* at this point will carry on and on into the design, affecting appearance, seaworthiness, and investment. *Carefulness* here will carry on and on, too, guaranteeing a smooth, pleasurable building experience and a minimum of the too usual amateur's headaches.

The boatbuilder who purchases a knockdown form has purchased a great deal of this preliminary laying down. Reasonable care in assembling and fixing the various hull and other members will assure a true and well-shaped vessel. In a way, the knockdown hull offers assurance of at least a correct start. And that, mate, is something!

Perhaps the greatest hazard which the knockdown boatbuilder faces is the consequences of making a mistake. Inasmuch as most of the hull parts are accurately cut or prefitted, a slight error, say in frame, will necessitate the scrapping of other parts. This is both costly and discouraging, and too often brings unjust blame upon the manufacturer.

The eventual cost of the home-built boat is naturally very much less than the professionally-built boat, quite often as much as 50 per cent. Unfortunately, however, the home-built boat can be sighted when almost hull down on the horizon for what it is. This is seldom the fault of the design or the knockdown hull manufacturer. The trouble is usually the failure of the builder. In resale, this type of boat often shows a profit *on material* but the labor is an economic loss, chargeable to fun, experience, and the grand adventure of building. To command a value equal or near to the custom or stock boat, the complete project *must* be equal to these two types in every respect.

This is a "good trick if you can do it," and the writer hopes that some of the information and "hows" in this book will assist the builder of a new boat as well as the man engaged only in a conversion or refitting.

To the amateur boatbuilder, I would give these few words:

1. DO NOT—oh, please, do NOT—change in any way the plans or any part of the plans of the boat you contemplate building. To do so not only invites but assures failure.
2. Get the BEST of materials only. It will cost more than what seems "just as good," and it may take longer to get—but these are not reasonable reasons for using inferior quality.
3. Forecast your costs and time to complete carefully and honestly. Enthusiasm should play no part in this. There are far too many partly completed boats, in that sad state because the "money ran out" or the builder "lost interest."
4. And—again—decide only ONCE.

I know perhaps five hundred men who own boats. I cannot recall more than twenty of them who have had their boats for five years. I know of only one who has had his boat for ten years. Yet most of these yachtsmen have owned some kind of a boat for the last twenty-five years. The swapping, trading, buying, selling, and building which goes on in a thousand such groups creates the vast used-boat market.

And it is to this market most first-boat owners turn when the bug bites them. It is to this group of boat buyers that this book is largely directed.

Used boats can be found in endless listings at yacht brokers' offices; in endless columns of "Boats for Sale" in magazines and publications devoted to yachting, fishing, sailing, and sport; and in the classified columns of most daily newspapers near a boating center. In addition, the exploration of any boatyard will reveal many boats offered for "Cash or trade. Have bought larger boat. Call Mayback 1128, ask for Eddie."

"Looking for a boat" has become a great American Sunday afternoon sport. In Webster Eldridge's little boatyard which borders my home there are, each weekend, scores of cars from nearby states. The ladies usually sit quietly, resisting the temptation to honk the horn, while the men poke and explore among the little ships which winter in Web's pleasant yard. This is one of the best and most satisfying ways of finding a used boat. Its big danger is in not resisting the many, many types offered; of not holding firmly to the type you want and need in the face of the hypnotic influence of any boat offered. So many of these boats *seem* to be your ideal. So many of them are eloquent in their appeal to be owned. "Come on, mister, just try the feel of my tiller." "Come aboard, mate, you don't find headroom like mine in many boats!"

Visit these boats, love 'em, and wax sentimental about them, but do so only with an empty purse. Make it a hard and fast rule never to look for a used boat with either cash or a checkbook on you. The selection and purchase of an ideal used boat requires cold morning light and a clear head. Many a man wakes up on Monday morning wondering why in blazes he bought the used boat he did!

Firsthand inspection of any boat to be purchased is, of course, necessary. But the boat "discovered" amidst the alluring aroma of Stockholm tar and copper paint, with the sea lapping quietly at the launching ways and the spring marsh peepers taking up the song of the caulker's maul at twilight, may not be the boat for you, however romantic or interesting.

It is, at least for the wirter, far safer with type, length, rig, and cost clearly and sanely defined, to select from printed or other listings the several offerings found which approach nearest to the ideal. Make, then, the necessary arrangements to visit *only* those boats.

From the public prints, vague and overenthusiastic as these ads so often are, a few likely listings should be gleaned. In writing to the owners always request a photo, promising to return it, and secure the following vital information before attempting an inspection:

1. Complete dimensions.
2. Headroom.
3. Number of berths, lockers, toilets, etc.
4. Condition and size of galley.
5. Equipment included.
6. Age, builder, and designer of hull.
7. Age and manufacturer of the motor.
8. Exact location (in commission or stored).
9. Present condition of the boat.
10. Whether free and clear of attachments, liens, or other encumbrances.
11. Whether insured and, if so, by whom.
12. Price and terms.

The answers to all of these queries should thoroughly satisfy you before you take too much time in long-distance inspection trips. Note that "lowest price" is not listed. Every boat deal is subject to a certain amount of bargaining, and the reasons for both sale and purchase are often so acute and complex that sight of the original price asked is completely lost.

Know from the outset, however, that the seller is trying to get the most he can and knows that you are trying to pay the least you can. This in no way affects real value and makes the entire operation of buying a boat a tedious, if delightful, one.

A very satisfactory way of sounding out the used-boat market is to contact one or more of the many yacht brokers who have private listings. Usually, not only full particulars but photographs as well are on file. The one great advantage of this procedure is that you get a pretty straight estimate of the vessel offered right from the broker. His stock in trade is not only the seller but the buyer who, he knows well enough, will himself become a seller in the not too distant future—and the broker will not knowingly jeopardize his position with one by deceiving the other. He will tell you quite frankly perhaps, that he has not even seen the boat, or, if he has, he will give you her true condition whether good or bad. The one thing he will not do is attempt to place a value on the boat other than the one he and the seller have agreed on as an asking price.

If you want an appraisal, which is to be recommended in many cases, go to a naval architect. It is not necessary to tell this man the name of the broker; more than likely the N.A. is himself a broker, and there is undoubtedly some sort of wondrous ethic involved.

A yacht broker exacts a fee (10 per cent of the sale price) from the seller, who has probably passed it along to the buyer in the form of a raised asking price. The old bargaining game, by no means any rarer in boat trading than horse trading, will take care of this, one way or the other.

A word about what the buyer gets by reason of the broker's services. He gets a legally adequate satisfaction piece, duly signed and recorded, showing ownership. He gets an adjustment on any insurance in force at the time of sale, with policies properly transferred, etc. He gets out of a lot of disheartening and disappointing trips all over the seacoast.

If the broker does not have the boat you want, he is in a position to find other listings for you very quickly. The split commission situation then extant in no way affects you or the seller.

Beyond all this, no broker long established will be party to an unfair or crooked deal. He is quite likely, even at the risk of losing a commission, to point out to the buyer a serious fault in a boat.

He does not want to have the responsibility of sending any man to sea except in safety, nor does he want the enmity of the buyer, for obvious reasons.

I would proceed on the basis of trusting the broker, whether I were buyer or seller, if at first glance he appeared to be a gentleman. I think the very nature of his business forces him into the bounds of honesty, fair play, and just dealings.

It is not uncommon to find the same boat, or the same type of boat, offered in several different boat marts. This chronic resale boat; this sloop which appears often (sometimes under the listings of varying brokers or yards) is probably not worth wasting your time on. Either she is too high priced or in too poor condition to interest others and thus keep herself out of the market. Possibly she has sold only to reveal herself a freak or a danger and so appear quickly again in the used-boat lists. I can think of many such boats by name. They appear and reappear like old fraternity brothers who haven't made the grade. It is a good course to regard such a boat with suspicion; better, not to regard her at all.

Another type vessel to watch out for when discovered is the museum piece: the Friendship sloops, the Chesapeake bugeyes, and the Bucksport pinkies.

I am a "sucker" myself for romance, deadeyes, and codfish gurry in a salty little craft. But sad experience has taught me that seldom is strength to be found in "them thar" ancient fastenings

Early Americana. Love 'em but don't own 'em!

and frames. Not that I'm against them as types, though I think all of them greatly overrated as *yachts,* but I'm against their continued use in the condition in which most of them are found today. Even those which have been rebuilt, patch by patch, are hardly fit to go to sea. Remember the *Sea Fox*—lusty, romantic Down Easter that she was, pampered and patched, but never rejuvenated. She sank dozens of times, killed at least five people; and now lies on bottom forever off Watch Hill, her last and wisest owner having swum to shore.

Curiously, but quite understandably, these vessels, thirty to fifty years old, not too well built originally, can still bring a whoop of delight from the man with boat in his eye. Unless extremely carefully rebuilt and refastened, few are safe, and all require a maintenance budget far beyond reason. I know of one twenty-nine foot Friendship sloop. She is in excellent condition—*now.* Her owner has spent over $9,500 on her in three years, has ended many a cruise on a shipway, and proudly points to the only original plank in her: a trail board on which is inscribed the date "1905." Mates, think what John Alden or Rod Stephens could do for you with $9,500!

So you've selected a boat. In fact, you're right in a tight little shipyard, patting her gleaming topsides! You're on the edge, mister—liable to topple, slap-happy and grinning into ownership. But —belay, mate! Pawl the capstan, Johnny Rio!

Is she hauled out or in the water?

You're up against a bit of legal Latin here which translates into "Buyer Beware." The full responsibility of under-hull condition is up to you if you purchase a vessel afloat, unless the owner has expressly warranted its condition. It's a good way to buy a boat— you can see for yourself whether or not she leaks, as well as actually give her a trial run. But on the other hand, you have no comeback, lacking a warrantee, if she's stuck full of canvas patches outside or has half the keel chewed away by teredos. It is up to the buyer to himself ascertain and judge condition and to explore those features which are legally described as (in English) "hidden hazards."

Before buying a floating vessel *always* arrange to have it hauled out or at least beached. Other features being satisfactory, let the condition of the underwater parts constitute the deciding factor for or against purchase.

Now, probably, most boats are bought out of the water, often while in winter storage, and it is almost impossible to have them launched unless at great expense because other neighboring boats block access to the ways. The next chapter will deal with the details of a minute inspection for condition, but, right here, before the winter cover is slipped or a hatch started, is a good time to have a "general" view of the ship which interests you. The careful consideration of the "first look" at a boat will often save the time of looking any further for, from outward evidences alone, she will fall into the class of a "good" boat or a "poor" boat.

SOME SURE SIGNS OF A GOOD BOAT

1. Careful storage, i.e., blocking, covering, and weather protection. The owner who takes pains here probably has taken equal pains in her operation and upkeep.
2. The boat found stored "undercover" or "inside." This costs twice the outside storage, an indication that the owner is not a penny pincher about boat maintenance costs.
3. Evidences of varnishing, painting, and bottom conditioning *before laying up*.
4. Straight keel, fair sheer and other lines; reasonably smooth planking; loose gear carefully stowed or removed entirely; and provision for ventilation.

SOME SURE SIGNS OF A POOR BOAT

1. Careless laying up, no cover, insufficient blocking. (Spars may remain stepped, but running rigging should have been removed and standing rigging well protected from weather.)
2. Evidences of hogging, sagging, twisting, or "nailsickness," indicated by rough or "clapboard" planking; oil showing in seams under engine.

3. Untidiness; gear strewn about; water in bilges or in pools on deck; musty, damp odor.
4. Indication of a flotation line (oil, scum, grass, barnacles, etc.) *higher* than painted water line.
5. Makeshift repair jobs, deck or other gear; cheap or inadequate items of ship chandlery.

Sometimes there is a reasonable excuse for some of the carelessness in the second list, but the discovery of any items mentioned should be followed by a careful inquiry into the causes. View with suspicion such a boat, and purchase her knowing that first cost may represent only a small part of eventual cost.

Naturally, neither list constitutes a complete inspection chart. The first thing a man does when he wishes to purchase a house is to select as possibilities those on the "right side of the track"—and this preliminary classification is designed to do the same thing for the prospective boatowner.

After a certain boat has been definitely decided upon, and price and terms agreed upon, there are still a few things to be done.

If the boat is stored in a yard, a check should be made with the yard owner as to any outstanding bills against the boat and a release secured from him in the form of dated, receipted bills or a statement of account. Unpaid bills should be paid at once and deducted from the sale price. Do not merely "understand" that the seller will do this; do it yourself. After all, the yard man, as long as she is on his property, has control of your boat and no man can blame him for refusing to launch you if bills, even those not your own, are unpaid. The law considers such a bill one against the boat, not against the owner or others, and the boat itself can be libeled for payment.

Hauling and storage charges are usually billed half after hauling and the balance in the early spring. The adjustment or prorationing of this item between buyer and seller should see the yard owner fully paid for any portion of the amount he has already billed.

If a broker has appeared in the transaction as an agent, his charges, unless otherwise agreed, are paid by the seller. I have never found it necessary to check back on this item; these gentlemen are quite capable of arranging for their payment in the early stages of the purchase.

It is not always wise to accept the seller's warranty of clear title as total protection. Both the public records in the County Clerk's office and the Federal Court Clerk's office should be searched, looking under both the name of the owner and name, or former names, of the boat. The owner's warranty to defend the title of the boat may be beyond his ability, and, even should he conscientiously defend it as warranted, the discovery of liens or claims will tie up the vessel and cause the temporary loss of its use.

The searches suggested may be made by mail, enclosing a self-addressed stamped envelope in the letter of inquiry.

Special pains should be exercised in working out the settlement of the boat or parts of the boat, if subject to a chattel mortgage. An engine is frequently bought "on time," and the manufacturer has an interest in it which must be satisfied regardless of change of ownership. Such a chattel mortgage would be on record in the County Clerk's office. By mutual agreement, the unpaid mortgage balance may be assumed by the new owner or the mortgage may be canceled by paying in full and the purchase price adjusted accordingly.

Insurance, if any is in force, should also be discussed and adjusted. Marine coverage is quite complicated and complex, and its adjustment is best advised by an agent of the company. Payment for the unused term of the policy or policies is assumed by the buyer and a refund to the seller arranged. Cancellation is not unusual, with the insurer's refund going to the seller and a new policy being written from the date of transfer, at the cost of the buyer. Quite often the broker will prove to be a marine insurance agent as well and will hardly fail to bring the subject up.

The storage yard, by the way, *does not* carry fire or other insurance on your boat while it is in the yard. This is a matter up to the owner and, in the case of loss or damage to your vessel by fire, water or other causes, is the subject of civil action. Most yard storage contracts especially except and hold free of responsibility the yard owner.

The good yacht broker, if in on the transaction, will bring all the foregoing matters to the attention of the contracting parties, but he is not to be expected to personally take care of them. The later appearance of a lien or attachment is not to be blamed upon the broker.

Having taken care of these preliminaries, actual legal transfer may take place.

Following is a simple but adequate bill of sale form. Note that upon the reverse side is to be listed or inventoried the items included in the transfer. This inventory need not be too detailed but should include such appurtenances as dinghy, government equipment, tools, spare parts, cradle, winter cover, or house, navigational instruments and charts, or any other items not *strictly* necessary to the operation of the boat. A boat to be legally a boat must be capable of being operated as a boat and could logically include engine (if any), rudder, spars, tiller, cabins, etc. The idea of the list suggested is to specifically include or exclude any items suspect of being in the class of "personal belongings" or "extras."

BILL OF SALE

KNOW ALL MEN BY THESE PRESENTS, that I, _____, residing at _____, owner of the boat called the _____, of the burden of _____ tons, or thereabouts, in consideration of the sum of $_____, to me in hand paid, the receipt whereof I hereby acknowledge, have bargained and sold, and by these presents do bargain and sell, unto _____ _____, residing at _____, the said boat, together with the engine, mast, bowsprit, sails, boats, anchors, cables, and other appurtenances thereunto belonging and listed on the reverse hereof, as and where is, without any warranty of condition, express or implied.

TO HAVE AND TO HOLD, the said boat, and appurtenances thereunto belonging, unto him, the said _____, his executors, administrators, and assigns, to his and their sole and only proper use, benefit, and behoof forever.

AND FURTHER, I do hereby warrant that there are no liens or claims whatsoever against said boat, and I do hereby promise, covenant, and agree, for myself, my heirs, executors and administrators, to and with the said _____, his executors, administrators, and assigns, to warrant and defend the title to the said boat, and the appurtenances aforesaid, against all and every person and persons whomsoever.

WITNESS my hand and seal this _____ day of _____, 19__.
Sealed and delivered in presence of: _____(L.S.)

_____

_____

The undersigned hereby certifies that there are no liens or charges against the above boat by this yard.

_____

YARD OWNER

Any state or local sales tax due is paid at this time by the buyer. The seller should assure himself that the tax is actually paid, for if it is not, the state may collect from the buyer. A broker would know about this and provide the appropriate forms.

There remains but one more detail before actual transfer is completed: the report of change of ownership to the proper boat registration agency, now generally a state agency. The procedure varies with our states, but the local tax collector, the Department of Conservation, or Public Boating Commissions can provide the forms and instructions. Most any marine or boat dealer can advise. Should the boat be federally documented, the course will lead to the nearest customshouse. Changing documented ownership is somewhat complex and requires up to a month. If a change in the boat's name is contemplated, this should also be taken care of at this time for it is even more complex! You will be required to post public notice of such intention (at your cost), and there is a small charge as well.

Only the sale of boats subject to registration need be reported. Usually pulling boats, canoes, cartops, etc., etc., are exempt. Dinghies, part of a large vessel's gear, need not be reported.

To undertake legal transfer in a careful and complete manner is, in a way, to insure a happy commencement of ownership. There are many stories rampant of new owners, after spending large sums for refitting or repairs, being faced with some bugaboo of the past which crushes them and turns their ideal boat into a headache and a liability.

I once bought a small cruising yawl carelessly—only to find, in midsummer and on the eve of a cruise eastward, that I didn't own very much of the engine. It took much running about and the services of a state trooper to adjust the situation: small matters compared to some of the prime jams into which other careless purchasers have gotten themselves.

IV *Inspection of Used Boats*

It is curious to observe the behavior of the boat buyer as he comes upon a likely looking ship. Almost immediately he will whip out a pocketknife, take several vicious jabs at planking, keel, and deadwood and emerge with a smear of copper paint between the shoulder blades and the glad tidings that the vessel is sound.

This represents the kind of inspection with which this chapter will not treat. Actually, such a procedure is useless and may dull or break the knife.

There is a way to use the knife or other bladed instrument to determine soundness, but it does not consist of a series of mighty thrusts. A knife of ordinary sharpness will almost pierce even new wood and prove nothing.

So, the seller's boat neatly speared, let us turn to a sane inspection program. It may commence any place you choose, depending perhaps upon the weather, but will divide itself into the following major classifications:

1. Inspection of hull, cabins, decks, etc.
2. Inspection of engine, auxiliaries, plumbing, tankage, etc.
3. Inspection of spars, sails, and rigging.
4. Inspection of equipment.

The Hull

A good hull looks good; a poor hull looks poor. Even after exhaustive inspection and testing this will stand out as true, and the inspection merely serves to indicate the extent of the goodness or poorness which appearance foretells.

Smoothness, flush seams and nail holes, tight butts, and fair uniform lines would be an indication of a sound hull. Roughness,

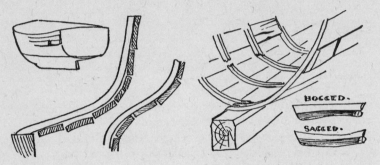

Evidences of nailsickness. Rust spots showing through the paint should send you testing all planking and framing from the INSIDE

Signs of the weakening or aging frame. Open butt blocks one of the first signs

clapboard effect, open butts, and any irregularities in form would indicate a sick condition, but not necessarily a dangerous one.

Old vessels, or vessels with a structurally weak frame, "work" excessively, and this movement is reflected in uneven plank edges or the separation of end matching of planks against each other, the transom, or the stem. It amounts to "loose planks," especially when out of water and dry.

Fastenings, especially iron ones, rust out in time and let go. This is possible even with galvanized fastenings on a comparatively new boat, for in setting the boat nails, the galvanizing is sometimes chipped off and rust gets in its work. Certain types of

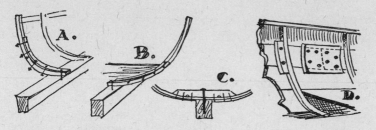

Strengthening weakened frames

A. Backed up with brass strips, riveted through planking and extending to the heel of the frame. B. Siding with either steam bent or sawn oak piece. Screwed into frame and planks then fastened to new piece. C. Hardwood floor over the frame which has rotted and loosened at the keel fastenings. Sawn to shape and drift-rodded to the keel, the planking is through-fastened to the new piece. D. Drawing in the sprung plank with a butt block. Clean old cotton away and be sure that adjacent top and bottom planks are secure. "Soften" with kerosene if the plank won't fit snugly to frame

galvanizing (remember the tinned nails after the war, boys?) offers no real protection. With rust adding to the movement of the plank, a softness occurs, usually in the plank rather than the oak frame to which it is fastened, and "nailsickness" occurs.

A boat need not be turned down because of this. Renailing is not difficult or expensive. Be sure, however, that old nail holes are plugged, with wood or epoxy if possible.

Open butts are not always caused by mere working. Sometimes this is indication of the general collapse of the frame. Many open butts should send you to carefully checking deck beams and frame fastenings at the keel. The letting go of these members will exert a strain or sagging which shows up in the planking.

Bronze fastenings, after long use, will crystallize and become brittle. Gently lift several exposed screwheads with your knife. If too many drop out, parted from the body of the screw, you may be sure that the life has gone out of them and that general refastening will be needed.

The fastenings which have been countersunk and plugged with

a wooden plug have usually been installed with care and patience. Those driven home and puttied, however, are suspect, even in a young vessel.

Splits occurring in the planking are not always dangerous. These, many times, are merely on the curved exterior surface and close tightly when soaking and swelling occurs. Indeed, all boats, once swelled, become very strong and can well survive the failure of a certain percentage of the fastenings. What this percentage is for your boat and for the sea conditions under which she will be used, no one knows, and the safest rule to follow is to strive for 100 per cent perfect fastening.

The keel, deadwood, stern post, stem, etc., should be checked carefully. In the vessel which has been long hauled, shrinkage of the various parts may cause large, gaping cracks. These are not serious and will disappear with swelling, providing the seam is parallel to the grain of the wood. Large seams appearing between end-wood will not close and might be an indication of a weakening of the fastenings holding those parts together.

Beware the boat which has either sagged amidships or hogged. She has probably seen her best days and might prove nigh unfixable. This condition may not be the result of use but of improper shoring up and the consequent loss of shape as drying and loss of structural strength occur. But in either case the result is the same. The keel which has end-dropped, even a little, might be transferring tremendous strains high up in the vicinity of the rail.

There is little cure for the hogged or sagged hull except complete rebuilding. The use of dutchmen, slivers, plugs, butt fillers, and whatnot does not cure the condition; these merely hide it.

Seams should be flush and just as hard as the adjacent wood. Here the knife can come into good use. Cotton rots in time, permitting a knife to be inserted easily into the seam. This does not indicate a leaky vessel or the need for a recaulking job at once. However, if the seam is very wide, say three-sixteenths of an inch or more, or if the cotton hangs out in gay festoons, something is wrong, probably with the plank fastenings themselves. Discovery of such a condition over considerable hull areas would indicate not merely recaulking but refastening of planks, frames, or both.

In salt water, boatyard owners maintain little pets called teredos. These tiny worms attack most woods, entering through a tiny pinhole and eating themselves fat at the cost of the yachtsman's boat, thus forcing him to paint often, or failing that, replace the wood the teredo has eaten.

All spots worn or scraped clean of protective bottom paint should be carefully scraped and inspected. The surface indication of teredos is an area of very tiny holes and a dull sound when struck. Here, the knife jab may be used as a pretty good test, for the wood behind such areas is quite apt to be thoroughly eaten away. Nothing can be seen from the inside, though the eatin' may extend to within one-sixteenth of an inch of the inside surface.

There is no cure for such honeycombing except to replace the affected part. Small teredo-infected areas in a large member such as a heavy keel or deadwood are not always dangerous. In a plank, however, this should mean replacement at once.

Barnacles, grass, and other marine flora and fauna are not dangerous to the hull and are merely to be scraped off.

The garboard strake (the one immediately port and starboard of the keel) is quite apt to be one of the first planks to show age or misuse. The garboard itself is often sound but has pulled away from the keel or out of the rabbit in the keel, leaving a large seam. This should send you inside, for the trouble probably lies in the frames themselves showing an inclination to let go from the keel. Only after thorough refastening of plank and frames should a filler piece be inserted.

The ship with lead patches along this garboard seam is probably so affected and ought to have a little care and dollars applied at this point.

Boats with centerboards should be most carefully checked. The centerboard case logs are favorite hideouts of the teredos, as is the lower edge of the centerboard itself. Any inclination of the boat to change shape will show up along the centerboard case, and knees and posts should be checked for a fair fit.

It is very often difficult to inspect completely the inside of the hull because of the built-in bulkheads, cabin fittings, engine, etc. Removal of the floor boards will show the underbody. Planks should fit closely to the frames, following the curvature of them, and fit wood-to-wood to its adjacent planks. Cotton should not be seen in any inside seam.

Butts should lay fair on the planking and tightly between the frames.

By all means, if the vessel is ceiled, arrange with the owner to remove several of the upper strakes, especially in dark corners not subject to free ventilation. In these corners will be found the greatest enemy of the wooden hull, short of reefs, anchor flukes, and oyster stakes: dry rot.

Dry rot is a fungus, flourishing where there is no change of air. It leaves the wood—any wood—soft and pulpy, in a crumbling condition, very much like the dead sticks picked up in the windfalls of the deep forest. A fresh water leak nearby, or sweating, gives it wonderful encouragement.

There is nothing to do for dry rot but trace it to its limits and *cut out all the affected wood.*

First evidence of it is found by the appearance of small dozy spots or, in its very earliest stages, by tiny black pinpoints in patches. Sounding helps to locate it for the dry-rotted wood will sound flat, dull, and unsound. Look for it all over; it travels like wildfire, into any kind of wood and under paint or varnish. An outward evidence of it is the peeling of paint from the wood, though such peeling does not necessarily mean dry rot.

When it is found, be sure you realize that removal alone will not free the boat of this plague. The causes of dry rot *must* be removed. Look for a leak above, for a condition favorable to sweating or the holding of stale air.

Likely places to look for dry rot are: near and around any built-in feature, behind ice chests, in toilet rooms, around water tanks, under the stern deck, and in bow lockers, particularly if they are used for storage of anchor cables and ground tackle.

Clinker-built hulls should be checked with particular care, for this type of construction is very difficult to repair. Watertightness is achieved by the close fitting and riveting of the overlapping edge seams and any tendency of the boat to twist or warp will usually cause the planks to split along the riveted seam. New planks are indicated then and because of the shingle laying might necessitate the removal of all planking between the split one and the rail.

Sheet lead, peened into such a seam, or a puttying of tar or other mastic, would indicate a leaking condition probably not to be cured without replanking. Clinker or lapstreak construction is very strong in itself, and for that reason the frames are often on the small side. It is wise to check these most carefully for breaks, often at points of quick turn or where joined to the keel.

V-bottom boats show first weakening at the chine, the topside plane drawing away from the dead rise or bilge plane. Weakness, rot, or nailsickness at the chine knees should be examined. The boat with metal angle-plates at this point will probably be found in better condition than the one with wooden knees, or none. Otherwise V-bottom construction might be found quite free of some of the roughness of round bilge construction because plank faces are either on a straight or concave sectional line and free of strains tending to pull away from the ribs or frames. Seam batten construction, in this type, makes for a strong, sound hull.

In the case of a keel sailboat, the keel bolts should always be carefully inspected. If of bronze, they probably will be in fairly good shape, even though quite old. Iron bolts subject to rusting will show evidences of weakening in the way of the keel, the top washer and nut sometimes being entirely eaten away. There is no positive way of testing, however, unless a bolt is actually driven out and examined.

The metal keel which has been strapped to its adjacent deadwood members, obviously at a time later than her original build, should be viewed with active suspicion: The bolts are probably gone. Generally, it is a poor practice to go to sea with this weight supported by framing members other than the keel or backbone. The discovery of this condition need not condemn a boat, but the buyer should certainly plan to restore the original hanging method as soon as possible.

The vessel which carries her ballast inside is often a "mess" in the bilges. This mess may not mean danger. Iron pigs or scrap iron is perfectly good ballast. It should be stowed in such a manner (battened or cleated down in the bays) as not to shift and, if kept on board while the boat is hauled, to rest upon the frames or the top of the keel, not on the planking.

Examine for evidences of ballast having worn the planking thin from the inside and also chafing against plumbing or other outlets.

Ballast in the form of cast-in cement has ever been a bone of contention for the boatmen. I know of several ancient craft, proudly lugging cement or cement and boiler-punchings ballast, apparently in sound condition. I know of several new boats doing the same with not such good success. It probably depends to a large extent upon the cement mix, how and when it was stowed, and other factors. I believe that if the cement ballast is supported by the frame and not the planking and has been in the boat for at least three years without showing any signs of rot in the adjoining wood, it would not count seriously against a boat.

Certainly, if I did find cement ballast I would bore ¾" or 1" holes in several places *under the ballast,* from the outside, to test the condition of the nearby wood. If it is sound after three years, I wouldn't worry about the next ten years. (I would also plug the holes again with a soft pine stopper, sawn off flush.)

This is entirely one man's opinion. It may be quite untrue on fresh water on in warm climates. A most thorough examination is the only way to be safe on the particular vessel you are buying.

Dangerous and annoying leaks are not to be found only below the water line. The deck, deckhouses, and cabins need careful inspection. Dry rot is often to be found where superstructure enters or joins the main deck, under the bed moldings and quarter rounds between canvas and vertical members. Any signs of standing water (such as near scuppers, corners of cockpit, or on the high side of deck fittings) should be viewed as a possible location of rot.

Canvas decks, the paint of which is cracked, will not last very much longer and will probably be found to have lost their bond to the surface below. Actual rot of the canvas itself should be looked for first where it laps under rails, etc., or near a spot which has been tacked. Possibly, temporary patches can serve for a season, but the rotten canvas deck will have to be replaced eventually, a costly and fussy job.

A word about paint:

Almost any boat purchased in the off season will need the usual spring repainting, and buyers expect this cost. It is a question of cleaning, sanding, and repainting only. However, the boat which is a chronic peeler, showing areas of bare wood, should be viewed with alarm. Behind the bare spots there is likely to be a moist condition due to sweating, leaking, or dry rot's having established itself. Always look *behind* the peeling paint!

Sometimes certain woods, notably pine and fir, have grains to which paint does not readily bond, and this may be the cause of peeling. A priming coat of shellac, or in extreme cases, a surface burning with a blowtorch, will usually give paint the opportunity to cling. Of course, poor paint, or paint applied under unfavorable weather and moisture conditions, or "inside paint," may be the cause.

The hull which is crazy-cracked or shows blotches of thick and thin coatings of varying thickness, will need "wooding" to make it smooth and fair. This is an expensive operation but one needed several times in the life of every vessel if it is to be kept up in yacht style.

Revarnishing of brightwork is not serious if the existing varnish surface is smooth and even. However, if the wood underneath has been water stained or weathered, complete varnish removal, scraping, bleaching, and revarnishing is necessary. Oak is the foremost offender in this respect and presents a large restoration problem.

The ultimate appearance, and indeed the value of the boat, depends much upon how well her paint and varnish looks. Poor paint work is not always a reason for turning a boat down, but its restoration represents a cost which may well run the total beyond the budget.

Mere looking will seldom give the true hull condition. Seams can be puttied flush, dry rot painted over, worm holes filled with plastic, bilges brightly red-leaded, and a loose keel left loose, the weight of the vessel making it appear secure. Inspection is a job to be done with plenty of time, tools, a flashlight, and overalls.

The inspection of glass boats is far easier; here appearance is a fairly accurate gauge of condition. You should search carefully for cracks, however "hairline," for they may spread and become dangerous. Most glass hulls have certain unavoidable stresses and strains fabricated into them, and as the glass cures, or becomes brittle with age, these factors cause cracks which creep in an unpredictable manner throughout the hull. The spread is somewhat aggravated by the vibration of motors, especially outboard motors. It is these boats which sometimes separate into two or more pieces while in service and drown people.

Surface or "crazy cracking" is not necessarily an indication of general hull failure. This may mean only the breaking down of the finish or jell coats. You can do nothing about it save paint with one of the many plastic-base paints and hope to hide the crack. Light sanding will help, of course. If there is indication of a large repair job, more than a mere patch, look deeply into the situation. Such a repair should be heavily backed up by laminations *inside*, and you should have positive evidence of the bonding of the repair laminates.

Dry rot does not affect plastic hulls. It may, however, affect trim, coamings, trunks, spars, and especially wooden backing blocks for cleats and other deck fittings. Look carefully at the glass hull which has been heavily painted: it may conceal a deteriorating surface. Certainly avoid the vessel which shows even the slightest inclination to hog or to buckle or which seems twisted. You see, most plastics cure into a brittle hard substance, much like porcelain, and manufacturers attempt, by formula, to delay and control the curing period, sometimes successfully for five or more years. But eventually, the material surrenders flexibility and resists change or impact, and so a glass boat of more than, say, four years of age, should be viewed with considerable care. A limber new boat will withstand much more punishment than the same boat after a number of years. This is why engine vibration or extreme and rapid temperature changes frequently cause a hull, untouched, to suddenly split or fracture.

Plastics are essentially chemistry, and as such deserve the attention of a chemist in evaluating condition after a period of time. The average boatbuilder, or boat surveyor or naval architect knows nothing about the subject firsthand. I do not know if you can get a chemical engineer to conduct tests, or if it would pay; but I do know that I would not trust my own judgment, nor that of another, especially were he a boat dealer or distributor, in evaluating a glass boat. It might be all right to take a chance on a small utility boat, but were a sixty-foot yawl involved, I surely would obtain, and expect to pay a substantial fee for, an expert's opinion.

The Engine and Auxiliaries

A good engine, like a good hull, *looks* good.

There is only one real test for an engine, however, and that is to run it. If at all possible, the vessel being hauled up, ask the owner and the yard man for permission to turn over the engine under its own power. Ninety per cent of the examination will have been completed. If this is done with an engine mechanic at hand, the test will be quite conclusive.

Lacking the opportunity actually to run the power plant, the prospective boat buyer, unless he is thoroughly familiar with motors and therefore will not need to read this chapter, should by all means, *call in the expert.* For a gas engine, an automobile mechanic is good; so is a marine engine mechanic. For a diesel power plant, by all means get in a diesel man . . . he's quite a different breed than a gas engine man. And neither knows much about the outboard motor, so call in an outboard mechanic; preferably one factory-trained at the builder of the particular engine involved.

Preliminary examination might be made by the boat purchaser himself. This would certainly include the following:

1. Flashlight search for cracks in the cylinder block.
2. Examination of the sludge or oil in the crankcase.
3. Rocking—to test for worn internal bearings.
4. Use of a pry bar (or wooden stave) under flywheel and stub shaft to test for worn main bearings.
5. Examination of valve action, springs, and seating.
6. Examination of hold-down bolts and checking of alignment.
7. Checking of wiring, gas lines, strainers, and fuel pumps.

In the good motor, there will be ample evidence of care. I should view with suspicion the engine's showing signs of leaking oil or circulating water or a dirty deposit of grease in the bilges underneath. An examination of the spare-part kit (or the various lockers and bins roundabout) would indicate chronic troubles. A collection of dead spark plugs might indicate oil-shooting; iron cement, the need of it for patching purposes; or brass shims, recent bearing trouble. I once found a logbook on a boat I was pur-

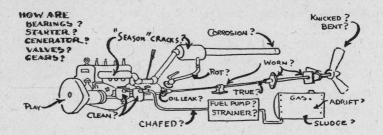

Engine "Top" inspection

chasing in which some revealing remarks were made about the engine which had been represented to me as perfect.

By and large, the say-so on an engine, perhaps even with an actual demonstration, is for the expert to give. Abide by his opinion; he has no reason to mislead you if he has been chosen wisely.

The storage battery found on board in the off season should be regarded as misplaced—it belongs in the junk pile. Dry cells, too, after wintering, while possibly testing all right, will not give long service. Check all electric outlets, especially those on deck, and resolve that if you purchase, you will at once correct the defects you find. Faulty wiring on shipboard is a very real danger, and no sane man wants to be shipmates with it.

The exhaust line is subject to corrosion and should be examined, especially in its most inaccessible reaches. Shafts out of line will usually show undue wear at the stern bearing, intermediate bearings, or stuffing box. Apparent misalignment of the engine while hauled may mean nothing, for all boats take their true shape only when water-borne. Propellers obviously bent or savagely nicked will need repitching—a factory job. Gasoline tanks and lines should be traced, searching for wear at places where supported or strapped. (Do not do this under match light, please!) The galvanized tank should be "stuck" and the finding of much scale or sludge be warning that only a new tank will insure free-running feed lines in the future. Small tanks which can be removed may be cleaned, using gasoline and a few pounds of shot, violently agitated, and then carefully cleaned. At best this is but a temporary measure.

Tiller cables, the steering mechanism, and engine controls will tell their own story. Look for cable wear near the sheaves and where it passes through bulkheads or decks. The slightly worn cable, reversed, will often last a while longer.

Plumbing needs checking, too. Toilets and lavatories, carelessly laid up, may have become frost split because water was not drawn off. Galvanized piping, deep in the bilges, rusts out very quickly, usually at the most inaccessible point. Outboard connections need special inspection as they are usually of bronze and may have become quite brittle. The weakest point is usually at the threads. Do not hesitate to slip off connecting hoses or pipes and apply the test of real force. Be encouraged when you find all outboard connections protected by a sea cock.

I would not compromise one iota with the power plant of a boat—it MUST be good! There can be no halfway measure, for lives may some day depend upon its reliability.

The motor which needs an overhauling, rebuilding, or replacement must be attended to. No matter how fine the hull or accommodations, if the budget does not allow for 100 per cent conditioning of the power plant, I would not buy that boat. The placing of it in the best possible condition would be my first concern, perhaps even beyond needed repairs to other parts of the vessel.

Spars, Sails, and Rigging

Masts found standing should be most carefully inspected (and pulled if possible), for the most likely places to find weakness are at the partners (deck line) and the heel. Here dry rot does its work, and masts may have been further weakened by various cleats and mast coat fastenings. Seasoning cracks are not necessarily dangerous. If they show evidences of puttying or of having been filled with wood dutchmen they are probably good for many seasons yet. The split or cracked mast, not so treated, however, is very liable to be rotted in the center heartwood. Excessive chafing and chewing where the gaff jaws rest might condemn a mast, or a similar wearing by the after shrouds on the main boom. Sighted, the spar should be fair and straight, without twists or kinks.

The hollow mast or spar should have all seams tight, especially if glued-up only, and its furnishings through-bolted, not merely screwed on.

Any spar which has actually started to split apart needs replacement. No amount of banding or strapping will save it. I should count it the sign of a passable stick if I found it stored indoors, carefully blocked for its full length and possibly newly varnished.

There is only one test for standing rigging: actually to pick it open at its splices, at least at the deck end. A marlingspike will soon show the rustiness and disintegration which condemns it. If the wire is bent at a given point and several of the small wires of which it is formed snap, it is time to replace it. Painting, after rusting has commenced, would come too late to preserve the strength of the wire. It often seems a waste to scrap a full length of wire because of a small rusted spot near the lower thimble, but the shorter remaining lengths can often be used on other parts of the vessel or a new splice turned in and a few links of chain inserted to make up the length.

It is best to be able to regard running rigging as so much spare rope—to be able to forget about it and sail with assurance. On poor ships odd parts can be utilized or a line turned end for end with some success, but running rigging is too vital a part of the ship to have fail. Rope which does not show clean, glossy fibers when back-rolled is of very little use for the strain of big wind and must be replaced. Look for fatigue, always, near the point where a block or fair-lead has changed the direction of lead or hoist; also at eye splices or joining splices.

Old canvas is gray and easily torn; there is little difficulty in spotting it. Except as a possible winter covering or chafing gear, it has no value when represented as a sail. All sails should be laid out flat, and canvas, bright and clean, inspected for excess "nigger-heeling" or bagging. This is a common fault with sails, robbing the boat of speed and maneuverability, but not too important except in the racing classes. By all means, if your proposed vessel is in a class, have an experienced fellow skipper examine the canvas. His experience will best tell the condition of the sails for racing use.

Dirty sails can be bleached and laundered very easily, and many commercial laundries have such a service at no great cost.

One of the best methods of finding how the sails "set" is to look over carefully photos of the vessel on various points of sailing. "Nigger-heeling," undue bagging, bellying, drag, or wrinkling will show up at once. The racing record of a class boat may be an indication of how well her sails perform.

Modern sail materials, the nylons and dacrons, are almost everlasting. Look for fatigue, not in the material, but in the stitching, especially in the way of abrasion points. Even if dirty they wash up very well and will withstand heavy removal agents if paint stained or otherwise deeply stained. If you plan to race, the sails should be surveyed by a qualified sailmaker or a member of the class, for sails with bunts, stretched sails, or poorly cut sails cannot win races.

Equipment

This item varies so greatly with the many types of vessels offered that no one book could do real service in giving inspection instructions.

The buyer should know, however, that the vast array of items coming under the general heading of equipment for his boat represents a considerable outlay of money, and equipment is not to be regarded as so much junk thrown in with the deal. The equipment included, while it will undoubtedly show signs of use (or misuse), should nevertheless be in a condition to warrant its continued use for a reasonably long period. Under general headings, the equipment common to all boats will be discussed.

Ground Tackle:

Anchors adequate. (Navy type anchors do not count, except in unusual circumstances.) Rope warps discounted; figure a new one. Chain not rusted. Moorings up for inspection and new end links. Rope warps and fasts to be renewed.

Navigating Instruments:

Compass checked for bubbles and liveliness. Remagnetize (by professionals) if required. Compensating magnets to be relocated if any major changes to engine, tanks, ballast, etc., are contemplated.

Government Equipment:

Life preservers, passable by inspectors and stowed where they can be quickly reached. Horn, whistle, lights, bell in working order and of correct character to meet requirements of the class.

Fire extinguisher filled and working, with spare liquid on hand

and of approved make. Built-in fire suppression apparatus inspected and passed by manufacturer's agent.

Small Boats:

Examined for condition and equipment. Davits and boat skids checked. Sails or outboard motor, if included, checked.

Deck Gear:

Check for fenders, dock lines, boat hook, ensign and signal flags; bilge pump, mop, deck plate keys, covers for boat, sail, and hatch; tank gauge-sticks, boarding ladders, etc.

Interior:

Check for cushions, mattresses, carpets, curtains, screens, galley gear, engine parts, and hand crank; ventilators, sea cock handles, etc.

The stove should be safe and sane, with the fuel tank removed from any possibility of being reached by flame, and in gimbals on a sailing vessel. Coal stoves strapped or bolted securely to *frame* of vessel.

Ice chest should drain overboard or into a pan, not into bilges.

Lockers, especially clothes lockers, to be well ventilated.

General:

Check winter covers, cradles, trailers, moorings, and other items not expected to be found on board.

An extremely important area for examination is that of fastenings and exterior metal fittings. Modern pleasure vessels carry considerable electrical equipment, are often wired for 110-volt a.c. "shore" current, have high-powered generators, and large, heavy-duty storage battery banks. There is bound to be some current leakage, even through merely damp wood; and in seeking a ground, this current streams into the water via any convenient metallic surface. In so doing it creates electrolysis, which is the

Compensating magnets from a steel file, shocked with a storage battery and peened into a copper fuel line. Run known courses, with all equipment on board, place magnets under deck around binnacle until compass bears correctly

eating away of tins and zincs in brass or bronze fittings and the galvanizing of coated iron fittings. Direct current is the worst offender. Alternating current is more easily controlled, because it has a controllable polarity. In time, a remarkably short time in some cases, such fittings as through-hulls, sea cocks, strainers, shafts, wheels and stern bearings, rudder posts and heel plates, and, indeed, bronze fastenings themselves, are reduced to a strengthless porous shell of base metal and will soon fail.

If the boat has a system whereby all these exterior fittings are grounded to each other and to the engine itself, or to the keel casting, and the connections are electrically sound, there probably is no great trouble. However, look for a reddish cast to suspect bronze fittings and test them by tapping with a small ball peen hammer. A mushy sound or an unduly deep indentation or the fracture of the metal itself means electrolysis has done its work and that the fittings must be replaced. Bronze fastenings, buried in the wood, behind putty or bungs, are less apt to be affected. However, bolt heads, exposed to water, especially salt water, should be most carefully checked. Iron fastenings will indicate electrolysis by showing not only rust but disintegration of the metal.

There is no cure save replacement, and thereafter be certain that there is a continuous grounding system and that any shore lines or generator lines are fitted with polarity indicators (buzzer or light) so that the boat and the supply line can be given a common ground. A three-wire internal electrical system will not

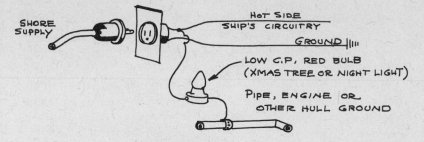

HOT SIDE
SHIP'S CIRCUITRY
GROUND |||||

SHORE SUPPLY

LOW C.P., RED BULB
(XMAS TREE OR NIGHT LIGHT)

PIPE, ENGINE OR
OTHER HULL GROUND

A homemade polarity indicator

Wired in as shown, this device will indicate, by lighting, if you have crossed the circuit and are leaking current into the ground and inviting electrolysis. If the lamp lights, merely reverse the plug; if it does not light, it is plugged in correctly. Mount the lamp where it can be seen from your electric entrance

offend since all sides are grounded and there can be no leakage through hull fastenings.

The results of a careful inspection such as suggested in the foregoing pages are twofold. The prospective purchaser knows the exact condition of the vessel he is considering, and he has an exact basis upon which to make the estimates of the costs and time involved to bring the vessel up to the standards he wishes. Usually at this point a compromise occurs, for almost any vessel can double her cost by receiving *all* the work she seems to need. Such a compromise can be sanely approached and a refitting schedule arrived at which will spread the time and costs over several years. There is one compromise, however, that cannot be made, and that is between purse and safety. A tight and sound hull and a reliable engine are far more important than new mattresses or the chromium plating of deck hardware.

As the inspection proceeds, notes may be jotted down and upon arrival at home, away from this little ship which is trying so hard to worm its way into your heart, a list of the needed operations made. It is now up to the purchaser to decide who, how, and when this rejuvenating is to be done.

One way, of course, is to call in the professional boatbuilder or engine mechanic; this is a good trick if you are one of the fortunate ones who can do it.

Another way, and the way with which this book is most concerned, is to do the work yourself.

List out then, in detail, everything you believe the boat needs. Estimate carefully the time and, with the aid of sundry marine catalogues, forecast the cost. At this point the writer would not wish to be present as he himself is very cautious of blasphemy.

The amount, shipmate, is staggering, isn't it?

But try as you might, this is what your eventual cost will be. Nothing can change it except your own elbow grease, your own ingenuity, and the possible help over the rough spots which it is hoped this book will give you.

It has been assumed that the reader of this book is a mechanic, indeed that most owners of boats are mechanics. This cannot possibly be true, of course, yet for even the man who has his work professionally done, there may be an idea or two that will reveal themselves as money- or time-savers.

Let it be well understood that the writer does not recommend that any but the man with some degree of mechanical skill be encouraged to tackle this "job of work" which shipfitting is. To the man willing to learn and eager to enjoy *all* the thrills of boat ownership, the pure fun of working on your own boat is an absorbing hobby, an all-year-round interest.

This work which you contemplate is not to be regarded entirely as expense. Replacement or renewing of worn parts will hardly increase the value of your boat investment. However, when this work takes the form of improvement—new engine, new fittings or sails, for example—a man is converting his time into a valuable asset which will be reflected in the higher value of his boat.

So, matey, buy this boat which you are set on; don't worry too much about her present condition. Joshua Slocum, after he had commenced tearing down his dear old *Spray*, emerged with very little of the original vessel except a keel and a pole mast, yet name me a man who loved his vessel more or sailed her to greater triumphs!

V Conversions

Conversions have ever lured the boat-minded man. I am just impractical enough to want to believe that this lure is because conversion offers the glorious fun of creating, of working on and for, the long-planned little ship and not because it is a "cheap" way of acquiring a boat.

Actually, the purchase of a used hull, or part of a hull, seems like a mighty economical way of getting afloat. Soberly considered, however, it is not economical, nor, in most cases, is it a proposition in which money or labor should be very heavily invested. But conversion will go on forever; as long as men love the sea and its little ships, as long as they must respond to the beckoning call of summer winds and far horizons, as long as there is a drop of red blood in them, they will want to get afloat. If conversion seems to be the only manner in which this call can be answered, they will convert. Whaleboats, ship's boats, ancient craft, insurance losses, and storm-wrecked vessels, or almost anything faintly resembling in shape a boat, offers itself as a foundation from which to commence the dream boat.

So this chapter will be concerned not with pointing out the reasons against conversion, but rather, with how best to attack the problem if convert you must: what you may expect; and how you might, in spite of the many obstacles in your way, actually emerge with an able, seaworthy, and proud boat.

One warning only will be sounded. The converted boat will never be what it should be; it cannot possibly be made so, not with the combined talents of Nehemiah Bourne, Webb, Donald MacKay, the U. S. Navy, and Joshua Slocum himself! The ship's lifeboat will always be an ideal ship's lifeboat—no amount of top-hamper, bilge keels, decking over, power or sailing gear will make her into an ideal cruiser. Know this—and remember that it is your money and time going into it (and possibly not coming out!) and listen to one who has converted, while well aware of all this, a dozen or so boats anyway!

One of the great sources of hulls, offering conversion possibilities, is the steamship lines which periodically must renew their lifeboats after government inspection has condemned those in use. These boats find their way singly to various fitting-out yards or to the steamship docks along any seaport town, or, in groups, to the public advertising columns for sale on an asking-price or bid basis. There are concerns which make a practice of buying these grouped offerings and offering them for resale singly to the public at greatly advanced prices. Depending upon condition, the boats can be bought for from $50 to several hundreds of dollars. However, the man who is willing to explore, or who has a connection in a steamship or shipyard company, might find the odd boat and pick up a fairly good hull for $25 or less.

The wooden boat, difficult to find of course, offers the greatest opportunity to do a thorough rebuilding job. These are often found to be affected by dry rot, or to have suffered structurally in a storm or from fire. More easily found is that curse of the boating world, the metal lifeboat. Its discarding is almost surely due to weaknesses caused by rust, or possibly crushing or stoving. Either way, it's the devil's own job to make one seaworthy again. Of all types, the metal lifeboat is the least desirable. Possibly a man whose trade is welding might prefer it to a wooden boat—but, mates, he'd have to be a damn good welder!

Another great source is the surveyed boats of the U. S. Navy, Coast Guard, or Department of Commerce. Here it is more likely that the wooden boat will be found. Generally, the boat which the government surveys out of service is not a condemned boat in the ordinary sense. If actually wrecked, it is more apt to be ordered destroyed. However, many of the boats, while perfectly sound, are no longer considered safe to be subjected to the strains of hoisting and daviting on sea duty. Relief from this handling, before failure has actually occurred, places on the market many boats with a long and useful life under ordinary demands of service.

Such boats are, by law, offered at auction or bid, in the public prints. The Navy Department, or the commanding officer of a nearby Naval or Coast Guard base, will give information. Your congressman in Washington can also supply lists of surveyed boats and the dates on which they will be disposed of. Public notice of auction is often posted in the U. S. Post Office of seaport or lake towns. Bidding is sealed and must be accompanied by a certified check for a portion (usually 25 per cent) of the amount bid and made out to the Treasurer of the United States. The successful bidder must pay the balance at once and remove the boat within a stated number of days. Occasionally, equipment, power plant, or sails are included.

The great difficulty in obtaining such a boat is that other organizations are constantly on the watch for these sales and are better able, because of experience, to bid successfully or to bid on a group of boats than is the lone boatman. Indeed, by special act of Congress, a certain proportion of the less valuable of such boats are first offered to the Boy Scouts of America for use in their Sea Scout program. If such a boat is accepted, it is on a loan basis and may again find its way to the open market.

Government boats bring prices, depending upon condition, of from $15 to $35 for a Monomoy surf boat, lifeboat, or barge; of from $50 to $400 for a power launch or motor sailer. To this must be added the cost of removal and possible launching or handling.

Work on the boat cannot be ordinarily done upon the government reservation.

Insurance companies, particularly after a hurricane or bad storm, will have wrecked vessels on their hands. These, in the process of rebuilding, often become "conversions" and are mentioned here for that reason. A bid is made, usually at about the cost of removing the hull from its present location, which is now the task of the insurance company. There is no way to arrive at fair value, and the price depends chiefly upon how many persons are seriously bidding for it. A large wrecked ketch, costing $8,000 when built, I once bought on the beach for $40 in this manner. Meantime, my own vessel, also wrecked and costing only about $3,500, was bought from the same company for $625. In both cases the insurance company had paid full loss. This was after the New England hurricane of 1938.

Yacht yards, particularly the smaller ones deep in the salt marshes, often yield small boats suited for conversion. Marine salvage, wrecking, and towing companies sometimes have such boats; also laid-up sound or river steamers, the U. S. Army (island bases), and the U. S. Coast Guard.

Still another type of vessel is the racing sailboat which has, because of outclassing or years of the strain of racing, been relegated to a less picturesque life afloat. In many ways such a boat, because its use is not being essentially changed, will serve for a long time as a cruiser or auxiliary. The open launch, itself a good seaworthy design, will often stand the addition of cruising accommodations or other weight and bulk. Seldom will the powerboat convert into a satisfactory sailboat or the straight sailboat into a satisfactory powerboat. The essentials of the two designs are too far apart for conversion ever to be 100 per cent successful.

There is one type of boat with which I would not fool: the boat which the other fellow had already converted. One conversion seems to me enough for any boat!

If all the converted boats were laid end to end they would reach from the Statue of Liberty to Umpty-whosis Land. Now, if all the conversions of *double-enders* were removed from the line, it would be quite a normal-size little fleet. Somehow—but for a very obvious reason—the lifeboat, the seine boat, the dory, the surfboat, double-enders all, form the bulk of the conversion fleet; they tail off their last years as ketches, yawls, cruisers, powerboats, and whatnot.

There is probably no type less suited for the installation of power, sail, or both than the double-ender. Now, mind there can be good double-enders but these are without exception deep-draught keelboats, developed in many world ports to meet a certain local condition or use, not a shallow-draught, lightly-built boat which spends most of its life ignominiously lashed to a pair of boat skids.

The lifeboat type is too low amidships, for one thing. This is as it should be (remember she has been designed to be rowed), but it can be dangerous, or at least very wet, when the same hull is moved by sail. It has not the end bearing (having been designed to carry weight concentrated amidships) necessary for the power-driven hull. It is often a roller in a seaway; seldom dangerously so, but most times quite uncomfortably so. It is quite apt to be very wet, throwing spray clear to the stern sheets, at anything over three or four miles an hour. It is narrow and small for the length. It hasn't the depth to provide either headroom or leg room. It is usually so lightly built that the installation of a centerboard or shaft log or engine beds presents major problems. It is anything but the boat it ought to be for either power or sail.

In spite of which, each year, hundreds of such boats are, and will continue to be, converted. So, if the paragraph above hasn't discouraged you, let's get along to thinking about the actual detailed steps to be taken. Remember, however, that you will not have an ideal boat from the point of performance. All the horsepower in Boulder Dam will not drive her over seven or eight miles an hour, and she'll scare the daylights out of you under anything like near enough sail to make her move. Bilge keels won't stop her rolling, and you'll have a hard time getting your money back on her. So let's go!

Converting to Sail

A naval architect could measure up your boat; oil up his slide rule; and pretty soon tell you all about bearing, inherent stability, displacement, moment of roll, etc., ad infinitum. He'd also tell you where to place your sails and how large they should be.

But you are not going to a naval architect, nor even going mildly into his fascinating profession to figure it out for yourself. Trial and error is good enough. The following paragraphs offer some guidelines.

For the most part, especially in the cases of the surfboats and seine boats, these double-enders are narrow and without great stability. Any sail rig installed should therefore have its center of effort fairly low down. The gaff-headed rig is most certainly indicated for this reason. The divided rig, especially the ketch rig, will help achieve this and have the added advantage of *making* you provide mizzen partners, thus strengthening the boat in a place you would most assuredly try to keep open for deck or cockpit room.

The placing, balancing, and relation to the various hull factors of the sail plan can be determined by referring to the text of Chapter XI. That chapter, as all others, has been purposely kept free from engineering formulae beyond the grasp of the ordinary boatowner; and the methods suggested, while quite primitive, are practical and accurate. By all means, the exact and correct positions of the mast or masts must be fixed before cabins, power plant, or deck arrangements can be decided upon.

Following is a table (not flawless, by any means!) of the sail areas recommended for several sizes of double-ended hulls. These are calculated to provide ordinary cruising speeds and are not in any way speed rigs. In every case, provision for shortening sail should be made by either dousing part of the area, reefing, or both.

TOTAL SAIL AREAS RECOMMENDED FOR
DOUBLE-ENDED BOATS

W. L. LENGTH	SLOOP RIG	DIVIDED RIG
20–22 ft.	160	180
24–26 ft.	220	250
28–30 ft.	270	300

For lifeboats (or others of beams over 7 feet) add 10 per cent to these figures.

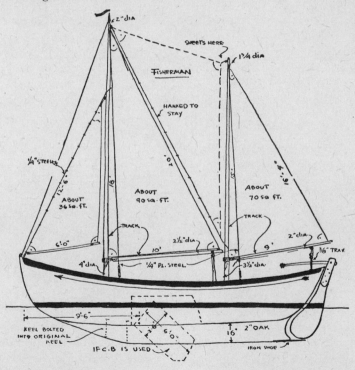

*Keel, centerboard, and sail plan suited for a 24- to 26-foot ship's boat
(Plan shows how to use either keel or centerboard; not both together)*

In all cases, a means of obtaining additional lateral resistance will have to be provided. Some of the boats, of course, have a centerboard built in, and there is no further problem.

Perhaps the easiest method of giving the type more keel is merely to attach additional depth to the present keel. This might make beaching and hauling difficult; on the other hand, it does not structurally weaken the boat—indeed, it strengthens it. A keel of this kind will take some of the snap and zip out of a boat. The boat will not come about quickly and, under certain tide or sea conditions, might even have to be driven around by the jib or mizzen. This condition can be helped somewhat by making the keel fairly deep and cutting away both forefoot and stern, allowing the boat to pivot more readily when tacking. The area of such a keel should be approximately enough, when added to the area provided by other immersed parts exclusive of rudder, to be about 15 per cent of the total sail area.

Total area of lateral resistance is the total of the fore-and-aft plane of hull and keel *below the water line*. The rudder should be, in area, about 10 to 12 per cent of the total area of lateral resistance and deep enough so that, when heeled down and rolled out of water, the area is not substantially lessened.

The centerboard, while much more difficult to install, has the great advantages of sheathing for beaching and hauling; opening up shallow waters for sailing; and concentrating of lateral resistance in a small local center, thus affording a lively boat, easily tacked and spun about. Also, while sailing on a reach or before the wind, the centerboard can be partly or completely sheathed, the skin friction reduced, and better speed obtained.

A metal centerboard will often provide enough low down-weight to act as the much-needed ballast in this type of boat. Either wooden or metal centerboards should be of an area to preserve the relationship to sail area of about 15 per cent when dropped to its deepest position.

The installation of a centerboard is too often a job that calls for the weakening of the light keel. The plank keel can probably be slotted and long hardwood logs bolted alongside and extending well fore-and-aft without marked weakening. But the narrow edge-keel, often itself nearly the thickness of the proposed center-board, is a real problem. There is no reason, however, for the centerboard not being placed off-center this inch or so, leaving the keel undisturbed. Of course, adequate framing to the keel will have to be provided to tie securely to the frames which have been cut adrift. A method of doing this is suggested in the sketch.

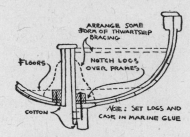 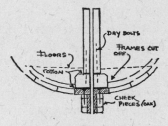

Off-center installation. Logs are carefully notched over frame heels and bolted to plank keel at center directly to planking and frames off-center. The case is left to project to the face of the planking in order to get a caulking seam easy to keep tight

Center-line installation for metal (¼" steel) board. Frames are cut off at logs and secured to floors which are fastened to logs by corner angles of brass. Long cheeks either side of the keel, faired off at ends, help strengthen the keel in the way of the slot

In general, the sail rig should be designed to be light aloft. Heavy rigging, spars, spreaders, or a welter of blocks, mast withes, turnbuckles, or other hardware aloft tend to make the boat skittish and slow on the comeback from a roll. Canvas should be fairly light, thus cutting down on heavy halyards and the necessity of too many tackles.

Weight in such an outfit, and most of them will require some ballast other than live weight, must be kept as low as possible. Ballast in the form of lead or iron pigs will usually be found best placed port and starboard of the centerboard case, as close to the center line as possible. Trimming ballast in the ends should be very gingerly carried, for the ends are the weakness of the double-ender, and too much weight here will cause them to further plunge or bury. A regular cast shoe, hung outside, as low as possible, will provide the most satisfactory form of ballast. A twenty-six footer will be a much more well-behaved vessel for about 800 pounds so placed.

Converting to Power

I have never seen a converted lifeboat or double-ender capable of speeds over eight miles per hour. Most of them do a leisurely six, and not too economically at that. All of them spend much power in churning out a large hole in the water astern and promptly sitting in it and being mighty stubborn about climbing out again. This is the nature of the beast. The weird arrangements of planing fins, anti-squatting boards, and other alleged cures sometimes seen are, one and all, worthless.

So, if it's set on power you are, don't for Heaven's sake install the same amount of power you would for a straight power design of equal length, breadth, and depth. Fifteen horsepower is enough for a twenty-six footer, and I'd personally prefer a slow-speed motor, turning a large wheel. I once owned a double-ended twenty-four foot seine boat, duly decorated with trunk cabin and other trivia calculated to make her into a cruiser. She had a 5 h.p. Palmer 2-cycle motor and—so help me!—she gave me an honest day-long five and a half miles an hour. The new owner put in, upon the advice of an engine salesman who worked out his wheel size, etc., a 25 h.p. modern 4-cycle job. Switch wheels and rev up as he might, the best he could get was six and a half miles per hour. He got a beautiful wake and right picturesque fore-and-aft trim, but he couldn't get twenty additional horsepower to give more than one mile per hour increase in speed. Such boatmen are cultivated by the gasoline dealers.

Now, for auxiliary power in the average size, I'd advise an engine, small and compact, of five to eight horsepower. For straight power, perhaps one of the modern machines of 10 to 15 h.p., preferably with a reduction gear to provide a shaft speed of not over 600 r.p.m. The slow wheel, I believe best for the double-ender—and don't ask me why.

No matter what the engine, it and its auxiliaries should be concentrated at or slightly aft of the fore-and-aft center line. This center line will be found to be, in this type boat, substantially the

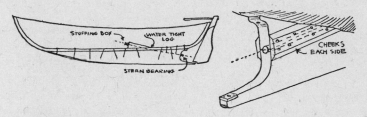

Installing keel with shaft hole for the conversion to auxiliary. The keel is cut along the shaft line and each side routed out instead of bored. Oak cheek pieces, riveted through, make this a very strong method. There are no bothersome outside caulking joints. A log is bolted to the plank keel inside and a stuffing box placed here

center of balance of the hull displacement. To achieve good design and good manners, the center of gravity (or the center of all the weight) should coincide with the center of balance without force in the form of excessive trimming ballast. Actual weight at this point, rather than an imaginary mean of weights fore-and-aft of it, is bound to make the boat a better sea boat; dryer and less apt to head-plunge or stern-settle unduly.

Preparation of the hull for the engine and shafting sometimes presents peculiar difficulties. Because of the general lightness of the construction, a long engine-bed should be installed. Its floors should be fitted very carefully, one at each frame and most securely through-bolted into the keel. The bearers should in turn be drift-rodded to each floor, tying the entire assembly together and distributing the thrust, torque, and vibration it will receive later over as much of the boat frame as possible. The iron straps, en-

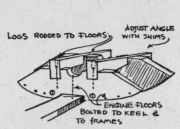

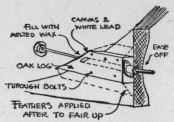

A typical engine bed for the converted ship's boat. Must be of oak carefully fitted to frames and logs notched in

An off-center engine installation. Only a small shaft hole necessary in hull. After the log has been lined and secured, the planking is screwed to it from inside and, with the shaft in place, the alley filled with beeswax. Note how the keel has been faired to allow a free passage of water to the wheel

gine-head to outboard frame-ends or clamp, so often seen, does little to take the place of sound, secure engine bedding.

The extension of the shaft through the hull can be done in the usual manner of boring through the keel, providing the long alley will not weaken it too much. The plank keel offers no problem here. But the edge keel does. By far the best way seems to be to set the entire power installation slightly off-center, balancing this thwartship shifting of weight by either moving the engine in the direction of its *light* side (opposite the heavy manifolds) or by placing ballast, tankage, ice chest, or other heavy installation on the side opposite that to which the engine has been shifted.

In the size engines recommended, this off-center installation will not create a serious off-balance condition or one that will be reflected in lopsidedness.

The propeller is best located *under the hull*. This necessitates the building up of a deadwood and shaft-log, further complicating hauling and beaching and also makes it necessary to install the engine at a steep pitch. But remember that a slow-speed engine was recommended, and slow-speed engines, especially 2-cyclers, with their simple oiling problems, will run thus installed as well as plumb.

To get the engine setting at a more nearly level angle, the steeve of the shaft alley must be lessened. This will either put the engine far forward (Bad!) or put the propeller far aft (Just as bad!). There is probably no real objection to the wheel being placed far aft (though it *will* complicate the steering apparatus) except that, in the shallow hull of the double-ended type, the wheel turning so near the surface, without a "roof" over it, is quite liable to cause cavitation; that is, sucking air from the surface. This cuts efficiency in still water and makes for racing and excess vibration in any kind of a sea.

A universal joint in the shaft will take care of *slight* changes in angle only. This piece of mechanism is not designed to handle great power or large angles of direction change, also—lurking deep in the bilges, under floor hatches, subject to rust and corrosion—it seldom gets the lubrication attention it requires and too often fails when most needed. Any acute change of shaft direction should be attempted only by the use of a self-lubricated gearbox assembly—an expensive piece of machinery, mates!

The rudder for the double-ended powerboat need not be of as great an area as for a sailing boat. A rudder of about 6 to 8 per

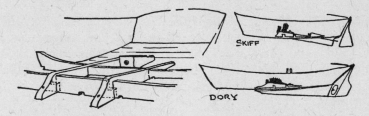

Engine beds for flat-bottomed boats planked athwartships should have very long fore-and-aft beds. Cross members secured to the lower strake of the topsides to take weight off planking. An inside log is easiest and best

cent of the total area of lateral plane is sufficient; say, for the average size boat, 18″ × 18″ square. Plank keelboats can easily take a rudder-pipe and metal rudder, well under the hull. This is the most satisfactory installation for a boat steering by wheel as the trident or tiller can be kept inboard, under a stern locker or deck. For a sailing outfit, the outboard or barn-door rudder and long tiller is indicated. For the powerboat, use a balanced rudder, i.e., one with 20 per cent of its area *forward* of the center of pivot.

The exhaust line should *positively* lead to an exhaust at the *stern*. This may cause some mean pipe-fitting or bending, but is essential to good performance. The double-ender is usually a roller, and side exhausts (besides being annoying under beam wind conditions) are apt to bury and cause motor pounding and loss of power. The exhaust outlet should, remembering the squatting of this type, be as high as practical; not just inches above the water line when idle.

Gasoline tanks, again because of the squatting, should not be too far astern. Gas will not run uphill, and fuel pumps for this size outfit are unnecessary. Tanks, near the engine, one port and one starboard and connected by a levelling loop, are the best. Filler ports to these, *of course,* outboard of the cockpit so that spilled gas scuppers overboard and not into the bilges.

Accommodation Plans for Conversions

Very—oh very—seldom does the lifeboat type afford a cabin with full headroom. Of course, it can be done, and, unfortunately, has been done. There is no doubt in my mind that the amateur muffs in this matter of adding ungainly, top-heavy, and dangerous houses, cabins, and shelters more than in anything else when he converts.

Before ever lifting a hammer, I should most certainly take off and draw, in scale, the profile of the boat as it is. I should then sketch in the limits of the cabin or top-hamper with an eye to good looks and fair lines, and *nothing* could make me go outside

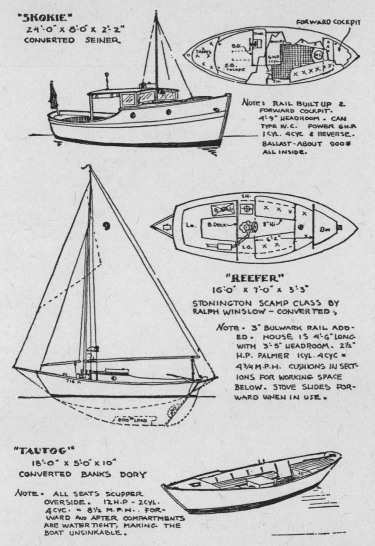

"SKOKIE."
24'-0" x 8'-0" x 2'-2"
CONVERTED SEINER

FORWARD COCKPIT

NOTE: RAIL BUILT UP &
FORWARD COCKPIT.
4'-9" HEADROOM. CAN
TYPE W.C. POWER 6 H.P.
I CYL. 4 CYC & REVERSE.
BALLAST-ABOUT 900#
ALL INSIDE.

"REEFER"
16'-0" x 7'-0" x 3'-3"

STONINGTON SCAMP CLASS BY
RALPH WINSLOW — CONVERTED.

NOTE. 3" BULWARK RAIL ADD-
ED. HOUSE IS 4'-6" LONG
WITH 3'-5" HEADROOM. 2½"
H.P. PALMER 1 CYL. 4 CYC =
4¾ M.P.H. CUSHIONS IN SECT-
IONS FOR WORKING SPACE
BELOW. STOVE SLIDES FOR-
WARD WHEN IN USE.

"TAUTOG"
18'-0" x 5'-0" x 10"
CONVERTED BANKS DORY

NOTE. ALL SEATS SCUPPER
OVERSIDE. 12 H.P. - 2 CYL.
4 CYC. = 8½ M.P.H.. FOR-
WARD AND AFTER COMPARTMENTS
ARE WATERTIGHT, MAKING THE
BOAT UNSINKABLE.

SOME CONVERSIONS BY THE AUTHOR

of those limits. These limits will *always* preclude full headroom, so I should concentrate my efforts on getting leg room and elbow-room. Sailboat men have long ago learned how to do this, and six feet, floor to carlins, is not expected by them in much under thirty feet.

The conversion to sail, perforce, dictates the truck cabin in order to provide the necessary deck room and a minimum of windage. By all means, it should also include wide waterways and a self-bailing cockpit. The addition of a low bulwark rail (three to five inches high) lessens the apparent sticking in the air of cabins and trunks. This should always be equi-width for its full length and never used to flatten sheer on the outside elevation and fake the low midship sections.

Deck, trunk, and cockpit of the sailing conversion should be made at least as heavy and substantial in construction as the hull itself. Boarding seas are more powerful in sheer weight than the growler which attacks at the water line. (See Chapter VII for detailed helps.)

The weight of spars, rigging gear, cabins, deck, and bracing members is considerable in the sailboat. While lightness must be ever kept in mind and weights concentrated as low as possible, strength cannot be sacrificed in the sailing conversion. Design for strength first. Weight should be kept at a safe minimum only by omission. Conserve weight, not in sparring, decking, or rigging, but in cruising gear, interior accommodations, and the great amount of junk the average vessel lugs around and never uses. Cut out a bulkhead, use waterproof plywood; forget the iron coal-stove or the auxiliary engine itself; this is the only way to preserve safe sailing lines and have a safe boat.

It is a tremendous temptation to cut loose on the lifeboat conversion and design into it all the features an equal-sized boat of conventional design would have. It can be argued that these boats are designed to carry much weight in the form of passengers, perhaps a weight equal to what is being added. But the great difference lies in where this weight is being carried. The center of the weight of twenty people, totalling perhaps three thousand

pounds, is *low;* probably at or very near the water line. The center
of weight represented in a conversion is far, far above this—too
far above it in most cases to be safe. Of course, ballast helps, but it
is not a cure-all. Placed inside as it necessarily is, it requires a lot
of ballast to counteract the top-heaviness of high cabins and tall
spars; and it will, by setting the vessel far below her natural water
line, destroy what might be left of her sailing lines.

So, keep the entire conversion simple. Fight for ounces! A single
shroud three-eighths inch in diameter is equal in strength to two
shrouds one-fourth inch in diameter, and weight is saved in the
extra turnbuckles, splices, mast fittings, chain plates, windage, and
the wire itself. More important, it is saved where most needed—
high up!

Following through in all phases of the conversion: plywood for
cabin trunks (a grand material, light, strong, and cheap!), a modern 15# anchor that will do the work of a 50# old type, hollow
spars instead of pine log, etc. Only in this way will you have a
boat, already tremendously handicapped by not being an ideal
design, which will give you some measure of pleasure and pride.

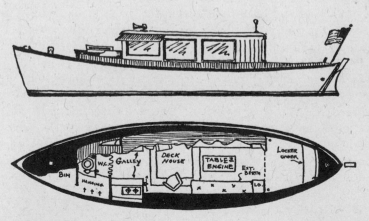

*A 26-foot double-end conversion. Sleeps four, has 6'3" headroom except
in toilet room and still looks long and low*

The conversion to power presents a less complex problem. Weights here are centered lower, especially the useful weight of the power plant. Once again scale off the profile and be most careful with that shelter or awning you want over the cockpit. Omit it entirely if you want a self-bailing cockpit (not so essential in straight power)—its top will be seven or more feet above the water line!

The raised deck is quite practical here and gives the maximum interior room, but not for one's head! Five-foot headroom is almost the limit to be expected. Not bad, if the layout permits you to spread instead of stretch. And to do this means to forget bulkheads, partitions, separate galley, and toilet rooms.

The small stock cruisers have taught a lesson that could well be heeded here: the fine use as living space they make of the deckhouse or shelter where it is not difficult to achieve *full headroom.* Toilet room and even galley can be located under a forward space not having full headroom, and the wide midship space immediately aft, securely closed against weather, can be used as steering station, living room, dining room, and stateroom. The Pullman type berth, a great space saver and of double utility, fits beautifully into such an arrangement.

Another advantage of such a layout is that weights, both static and live, are concentrated near the center of buoyancy where they belong. Cruising accommodations in the bow will certainly result in the need for ballast in the open and lightweight stern.

Fight against weight in the straight power conversion, also. Keep everything as light as possible for the great weight of engine and tankage will alone raise the water line considerably. Deck strength is not so important here, and raised-deck construction is much lighter than trunk-cabin construction. However, crossties or thwartship bracing becomes of more importance, and the bulkheads dividing the cabin from the outdoors should be made strong and treated as a structural member.

The double-ended boat, afloat and light, is not down to her designed safe water line. Reasonable weight *in the right place* is not going to spoil her sailing lines. Indeed, it is going to stiffen her very much. But still, she is going to roll.

Nothing much can be done about this; it is chiefly a matter of inherent stability or beam. Bilge keels are sometimes used, but the writer has never had any marked success with them. To be large enough in area to really lessen roll they are so large that speed is sacrificed. On paper, they can be streamlined and given a fair swing that seemingly presents only the leading edge to the water. Actually, under sea conditions, with the vessel constantly presenting herself to the water in ever-varying angles, these bilge keels form pockets and back eddies that retard speed. The skin friction alone of wide, long bilge keels is considerable, often, in the bilge keels that work, as much as 25 per cent of the hull skin area.

At best, bilge keels only ease the roll; they do not stop it. I have had far better luck by extending the regular keel a few inches by the addition of a shoe. Once this was in the form of a length of steel railroad track, faired off fore-and-aft with wood fillers. I'm not recommending it from the esthetic viewpoint, but it did lessen the roll. Naturally, any such weight should be hung about amidships and not extended to the extreme ends lest excessive pitching be encouraged.

Many times the converted ship's boat needs only to be set into the water. They are remarkably buoyant, and the full factors which determine their inherent stability are not brought into force until a certain displacement is reached.

There's your double-ender, sailor! A lot of fun thinking about; a lot of fun working on; perhaps cheap; but a tough baby to get rid of. And you'll want to get rid of her, there's no doubt of that!

Not all boats in the "conversion" class are double-enders. The Navy boats, primarily designed for power, are still good for powerboats. But I wouldn't depend too much upon them as ideal sailboats, even though classed as motor sailers. The big thirty- and forty-footers make husky hulls, quite able to carry the weight of cabins and top-hamper. They are fair sea-boats and by the addition of a top strake or rail are quite dry. They *cannot* be driven fast—nothing like the fifteen knots modern yachtsmen want. Look, in this type, for cracked frames at the sharper turns of the midship sections and for keel-springing. The Navy keeps its boats

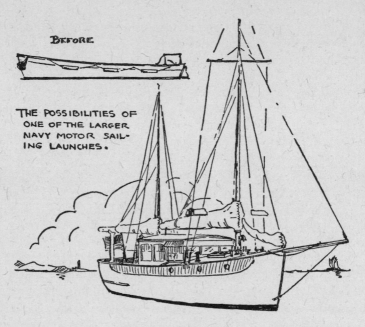

BEFORE

THE POSSIBILITIES OF
ONE OF THE LARGER
NAVY MOTOR SAIL-
ING LAUNCHES.

up well; they are probably not nailsick or rotten; but the constant handling by cranes, or the accidental crash against the steel topsides of the mother vessel, in time will send even these husky boats off the lists.

The small open racing sailboat can often be converted into a handy little overnighter at no great cost or effort. Here, too, a minimum of additional weight is indicated. Unlike the double-ender, the sailboat is *now* in true and designed trim. Any addition of weight is going to tend to throw her out of trim. So add lightly in construction, gear, and passengers! At best, the cabin will be a cuddy; strive only to make it a comfortable cuddy.

Shore-going luxuries such as plumbing, heat, electric lights, etc., are not for the eighteen-foot converted Comet or Cape Cod—they just won't take it and sail. If I were looking for a boat of this size to fool around with, I'd try to find a cat. They are husky, beamy, and roomy for their size and will provide reasonable space for the all-important full-width berth. Look over any small sailboat with

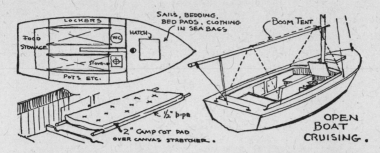

an eye to headroom. I think three feet eight inches, with berths (or seats) not more than six inches high an absolute minimum. Sometimes, it is not necessary to go up to achieve this. The floors can sometimes be skinned down an inch or two without weakening. Lay the new floor boards, not over them, but between them, cover with linoleum, and save another inch. The three inches gained here would look like ten inches above the rail.

The cabin will probably necessitate the raising of the boom to permit clearance. If this is a matter of only inches, it can be gained at the head of the sail by the cutting and sewing in of a new and wider headboard. Sometimes main halyard blocks can be moved or replaced, gaining part of the needed extra hoist. A shim on the mast step and the insertion of a few chain links in the standing rigging will help, too. However, if this raising is a matter of a foot or more, the center of effort of the sail plan might be thrown dangerously out of adjustment. In that case, the sails might have to be recut, the mast moved or given a different rake, or both. Under no circumstances should the safe relationships of hull to sail plan be altered. These ratios are given in Chapter XI.

It seems, to me that these small conversions are too often spoiled by the installation of inboard power plants. The centerboarder will hardly take an inboard engine of any kind where it belongs, thus necessitating its installation too far forward or too far aft. Off-center installation is not good practice in the small boat and the then necessary strut is a poor shipmate, affecting speed, handling, and beaching.

Yes—you guessed it! The outboard motor. I, personally, don't like 'em, but I honestly believe that they are the real solution of the small class auxiliary. They are light, cheap, reliable, easily stowed or removed for racing—they are everything a man could ask but, mates, they sure look lubberly!

Sketched here is a device I have used with success on two boats. It removes my foremost objection to the outboard motor as auxiliary power.

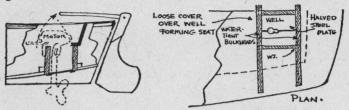

Outboard motor well on the 21-foot sloop "Williwaw." Note the halved steel plates which fit snugly around the motor shaft when under power or sail, retaining fair underwater surface. These are held by hinges and drop against pins or other stoppers. The boat is steered by the rudder, not the motor, and the steering handle may be removed to give more cockpit space

Outboard motors are designed to run fast and drive light boats. Generally, they can be made very much more efficient by changing wheels to the size and pitch more nearly suited to your boat. You probably can't reach 100 per cent efficiency here because of the limiting structural features of the underwater parts. Your motor dealer, or (remembering that this guy is too often only a salesman) the motor manufacturer can best recommend the right wheel. He'll need water line length, beam, depth, and general type of the boat as well as motor size and serial number. He'll also be able to advise on extension shafts for the motor. If the wheel shows signs of cavitating, racing, or bubble-throwing in the wake, it is important to get it down deeper in the water.

Such an installation requires the boat to be registered as a powerboat and to carry full government equipment of its class.

SAIL RIG FOR A 12FT. SHARPIE ★

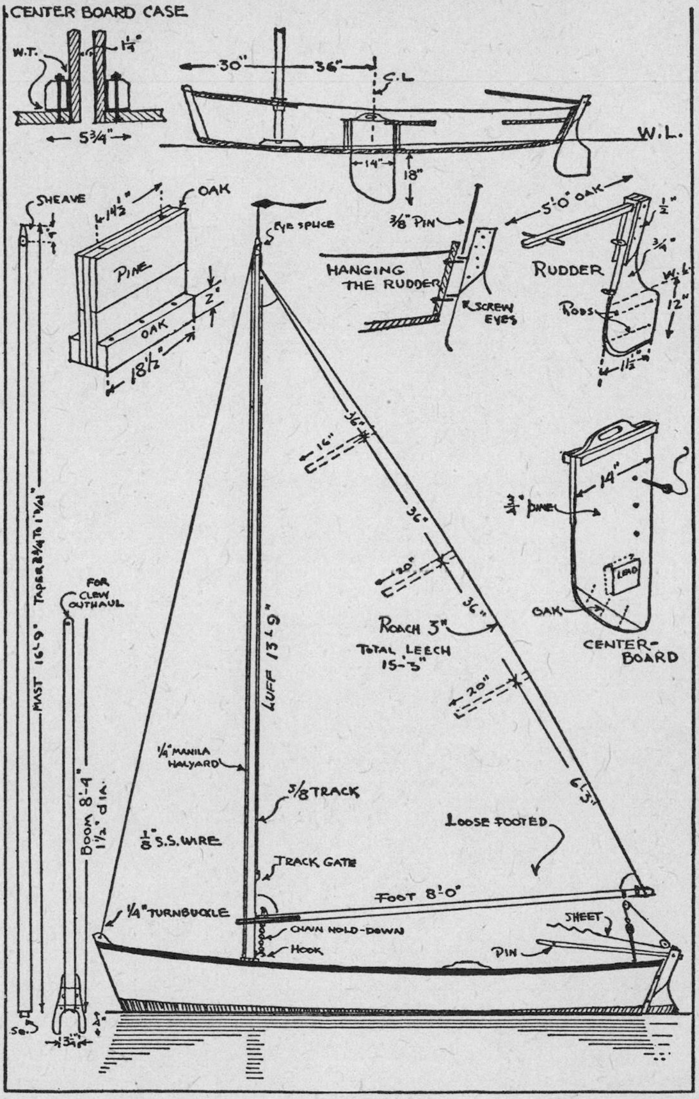

CENTER BOARD CASE

W.T.   1¼"

← 5¾" →

← 30" → ← 36" → C.L.

W.L.

14"   18"

⅜" PIN

SHEAVE   1½"   OAK

PINE

OAK

18½"   2"

EYE SPLICE

HANGING THE RUDDER

R. SCREW EYES

5'-0" OAK   1½"

RUDDER   ¾"

RODS   W.L.   12"

← 1½"

MAST 16'-9" TAPER 8¾" TO 1¼"

FOR CLEW OUTHAUL

BOOM 8'-4 1½" DIA.

Se.

3¼"

← 16" →

36"

LUFF 13'-9"

⅛" MANILA HALYARD

36"

← 20" →

36"

ROACH 3"
TOTAL LEECH 15'-3"

⅛" S.S. WIRE

⅜" TRACK

TRACK GATE

← 20" →

LOOSE FOOTED

¼" TURNBUCKLE

CHAIN HOLD-DOWN

HOOK

FOOT 8'-0"

PIN

SHEET

6'-3"

14"

1¾" PINE

LEAD

OAK

CENTER BOARD

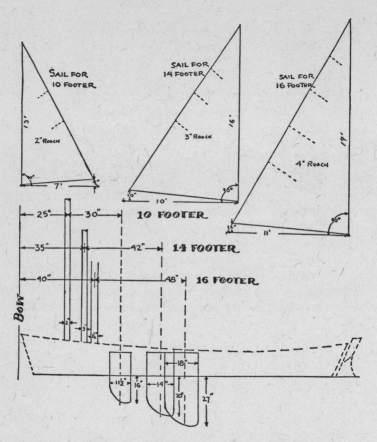

Using the details shown on the drawing of the 12-foot sharpie conversion, the 10-, 14-, and 16-foot hulls need masts, centerboard locations, and areas and sail size adjusted as per the above chart

All types of conversions cannot possibly be covered here. However, drawings are included showing the conversion steps for small rowboats and dinghies (sizes 10, 12, and 14 feet) into sailboats. This is not difficult work and puts any rowboat into the class of a well-balanced, safe sailer which will greatly add to water enjoyment.

It is not necessary to stay the mast, but a pin through the mast step will keep it from jumping out. A wooden centerboard, weighted with lead is shown, but ⅛″ sheet iron or steel will do as well. The addition of a lightly built waterway and a 2½″ combing between small fore- and afterdecks will take it out of the open boat class and permit sailing in real blows and sea conditions. I would make all seats except the midship one removable and include a floor grating. Having the live weight low will help the sailing of the boat and give much more room and comfort than being perched on a narrow seat exposed to the weather and the world at large.

Conversion has no limits. I know of a brig-rigged Snipe; 15½ feet of handkerchiefs and spars and no doubt lots of fun to her romantic owner; I know of a beautiful slim cup-defender model, now the foundation for a small bungalow and twin-automobile motors; I know of a paddle wheel scow-type houseboat that was once a tender to a deep-sea salvage ship, etc., *ad nauseam.* Phooey, on 'em all!

There is no reason why conversion cannot be a sane, happy matter of ingenuity and engineering. Ideal boat it will never be (well, seldom anyway!)—but, at least a conversion need not look like, and be, a monstrosity.

VI *The Hull*

I was recently much amused at the question propounded upon one of the eternal quiz programs. "If you were to build a ship," the announcer asked, "in what handy book would you find specifications?" Answer (and five bucks to Luke McGluke, 29 Gleep Street): "In the Bible. It tells how Noah's Ark was built."

Okay! But shipmate, don't you take your specifications from the ark. As I remember my Sunday School lithographs, she was a pretty short-ended crate, with no more sheer than a Pilgrim father, and she ended her forty days on a mountaintop all standing.

I wish I could approach the subject of "hull" with the *élan* of Luke McGluke. Actually, it is (and has been) the subject of countless books and articles. So let's, once again, just hit the high spots, treat the subject very generally, and delve only into the matters which so many authorities have taken for granted that the amateur knows. "Frames will have to be steam bent," says the authority, quite forgetting that you and I don't even know how to make a steam box, much less actually feel confident of our ability to soften and shape hard oak.

Hull Design

I am going to duck this one completely. In so doing, I am not cheating the reader one iota. On the contrary, I am doing him a real favor. Hull design positively is not for the average amateur. Even many naval architects designing boats today do not, after extensive training and years of experience, know how to design a hull. If they did, there would be no need for the great testing tank outside of Washington, D.C., or the sailing class rules which are framed to encourage experiments on hull design within certain limitations; nor would we have the occasional failure or dud which drops from his board.

The entire subject is hidden deep in engineering of the most complex sort, the slide rule representing only a short cut and not a

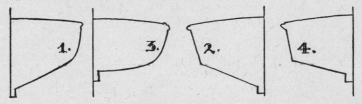

Midship sections
1 and 2 are better sea boats than 3 and 4

formula. To those readers who are engineering-minded, who have a thorough grounding in mathematics, I would say that self-design might be possible and perhaps even successful. I must refer them to other works for the "hows." No better work, as an introduction and very practical start in the subject, can be found than *Yacht Designing and Planning* by Howard I. Chapelle. I most enthusiastically recommend it.

However, by eye alone, the design of a boat impresses itself upon the observer. A look at her or her model or her lines as drawn out immediately classifies her as generally good, bad, or indifferent.

The hull in motion will indicate a lot about her design. The good hull, in smooth water, should proceed without fuss. There will be, of course, a bow wave passing smoothly aft rather than spreading away from the hull at a sharp angle. There should be no marked inclination to squat or stern-bury. The bow will rise slightly, not enough to affect seriously the fore-and-aft trim. The wake will be clean and flowing, showing no inclination to drag huge amounts of dead water along with the boat. In a seaway, the well-designed hull should take it without excessive roll and with no quick jerking motion. While slamming into the sea, the good sea-boat will jump plenty, but she will fall smoothly into the water, without excess spray-throwing, and there will be a feeling of increasing buoyancy as she plunges. The shallow or too-flat boat, on the other hand, will pound, striking the water with a sudden jar and pitching spray unmercifully. The good sea-boat is a 100 per cent displacement model, that is, not designed to plane in the least.

This is all rule of thumb judgment and becomes exact only after much experience with various types of boats under various conditions. But when the amateur, looking at a hull, remarks that she seems "kind of quick in the bilges" he is already beginning to sense design, to get the "feel" of the boat. Broadly, he can sense that this hull will or will not be suitable for the purposes he has in mind. Confirmation of his opinions can be verified from surrounding boats, especially the commercial and fishing boats. These latter are almost always true reflections of the design best suited for the adjacent waters. Down East here, where we can seldom sail very far without having to enter or cross the furious rips of numerous entering sounds and bold headlands, we have evolved certain design features best suited to our local waters. Jonesport, Barnegat, and Monomoy Point have their own favorite models. Each, being a sea model, has something in common with the others, yet differs in slight underwater and topside details too infinitesimal to be discovered except by the trained eye or by measurement.

Study of the usual sectional lines as shown on the drawn plans of a boat will place it easily into a well-defined classification. Cer-

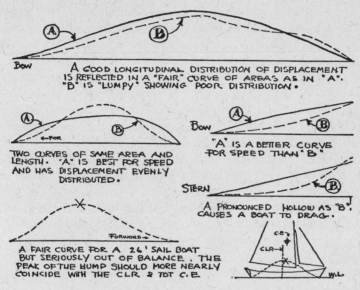

The curve of areas as a check on hull design

tainly, it is easily distinguished as flat-bottom, V, round, deep, dead-rise, etc. Whether it is the best possible design for the particular class, however, can be found only by a study of the line known as the curve of areas.

This is a plotted line and is simply a mechanical device for showing the distribution of the displacement along the water line of the boat. It is the designer's check on his objective, and any change he makes on the hull is reflected in the curve of areas. To keep the design within certain bounds, the curve of areas must fall into certain well-understood shapes. The sketch above gives the shapes (exaggerated slightly) of the curve of areas with the corresponding features of design to be found in the boats from which they have been developed.

The use or discovery in the powerboat of inside trimming ballast is not necessarily an indication of a faulty design. Many boats, in order to bring all the factors making for seaworthiness and balance into proper relationship, are deliberately designed to have ballast installed where needed. Deliberate ballast is usually in the form of pigs, properly cleated and placed, or possibly, even on the straight powerboat, an outside ballast casting. Odds and ends of scrap iron, bricks and rocks, especially if found in lockers or other places into which they wouldn't be designed, might mean an attempt to correct or improve the boat's behavior. Again, this is not necessarily a fault. It is quite apt to represent the difference between fair and good performance.

Good hull design, while most important at and below the water line, should extend to the rail. A certain amount of flare forward is desirable to guard against wetness, that is, every dollop of water thrown becoming wind-blown spray to whip aft. But too much is clumsy looking and indicates a tremendous speed, usually far more than the boat actually has. Flat, square transoms, besides looking like the proverbial barn door, sometimes are unpleasant shipmates in a following sea. Tumble home in the quarters can be beautiful—and it can be very ugly.

Above-the-water-line design in the sailboat takes on more significance than mere eye-pleasing qualities. Here, with the vessel heeled, the topsides become sailing bottoms, lengthening the water lines, affording bearing and stability. Engineering design here is especially important, for as a vessel heels, her water line becomes roughly half-moon shaped and particularly difficult to drive in a straight course.

So much for design. I've talked about it but said little, sincerely believing that good hull design is the greatest single contributing factor to the successful boat—so great in fact, that the tyro, except as noted before, should not jeopardize his entire venture by either designing or passing judgment upon design.

In searching for ideal designs you can trust naval architects, stock boatbuilders, some knockdown hull manufacturers, the custom boatbuilder who has built a reputation, and published plans by names of *recognized authority*.

You should not trust entirely plans by amateurs, even though published in yachting magazines and other books, nor the salt-marsh boatbuilder who assures you that he can and will save you money by designing your hull as part of his building contract. He may do it—more than likely, he won't. If you are interested in some particular design, by all means write to the author, offer to pay for its use, request full specifications and details and—oh, so very important—a photograph. You will be surprised how many of these plans offered are plans only. An actual vessel has never been built from them. Build from them, and you're the trial horse!

Even the technically-trained naval designer discovers limits to his art when he applies the factors of merchant and naval vessel hull design to tiny yachts one one-thousandth the tonnage-size of the type he has been trained to design. The tolerances in large commercial hulls are great. No error could be so large as to seriously jeopardize the design. The tolerances in a small hull of a few tons displacement are nil; the thickness of a pencil line in taking offsets and laying down lines can spell the difference between a good and a poor hull. The naval architect who confines himself to yacht design has seldom been trained solely in pleasure craft design. If he has any professional standing, he has an M.E. degree from a recognized engineering college, and at some time in his career chose to specialize in yacht design. This probably means that he also has, or has acquired, the necessary social contacts to get his start in this perilous field; that somewhere along the line he created one or more highly successful yacht designs, later sailed by the right people in the right places; and that henceforth he has had no need to experiment: He has the secret and needs only to repeat the basics to practice yacht design. Henceforth his variations are innocuous ones of style, accommodation plans, and novel treatments of unessential factors. This is why yacht designers become known for a particular type, why they indelibly leave their mark on their products, and why some of them *never create a truly new design.*

To be sure, there are great yacht designers who have pioneered in basic design and come up with winners. Behind them, usually, was a *carte blanche* commission and a large budget, and, often, the design is the combined efforts of a group of highly successful architects and engineers, assisted by practical technicians in the form of metal extruders, sailmakers, textile fabricators, and chemical engineers.

There is nothing wrong about all this. It is merely to indicate that the art is complex, chancy, even to the trained talent, and should by no means be attempted by the novice.

One last word about design, even at risk of repeating myself unduly. Do NOT change it! Intelligent changes above the rail, in power and in accommodations can be made but NEVER BELOW THE RAIL. Six inches cut off at the transom can utterly ruin a boat; the beam skinnied down even an inch can turn a good boat into a curse.

The doctors will say about the human ear, "Do nothing to it except with your elbow." That's a good piece of advice for the design tinkerer—do nothing to the design which cannot be done with your elbow!

Reading Plans

This is not a dark art. If the reader will visualize an exact half model of a hull, that is, split fore-and-aft, upon which has been drawn fore-and-aft lines above and below and parallel to the water line, he will have the elements of any boat plan. Indeed, until quite recently hull designs were made in exactly this manner —a wooden block shaped to please the eye of the designer, certain markings as reference points indicated, and then with calipers and dividers, this model scaled off and transferred into full-sized measurements to which the vessel was built.

In effect, the designer is dicing this block for us, cutting it into slices by imaginary lines, and using the intersection of these imaginary lines as reference points. No plan is complete without a Table of Offsets which gives us the exact relationship of these points to some common reference point.

The cross-slices (like cuts of a Bologna) are spaced at predetermined distances and so marked on the profile elevation of the plan. They are called stations, and each is given a number. Next, longitudinal lines, called water lines, are drawn parallel to the actual water line and marked W.L. 1, 2, 3, etc. Superimposed on this profile is a cross section of the boat, one side showing the sections (or stations) from amidships to the stern; the other, sections from amidships to the bow. Below the profile a half plan is drawn upon which the developed water lines are indicated. The Table of Offsets is simply a set of directions saying, "To get to spot A, walk along Water Line number 2 until you get to Station number 5. Spot A is exactly 4' 3½" out from the center."

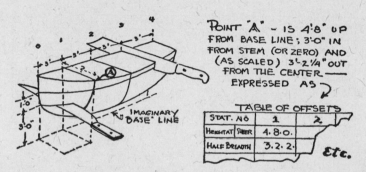

POINT "A" – IS 4'8" UP FROM BASE LINE; 3'-0" IN FROM STEM (OR ZERO) AND (AS SCALED) 3'-2¼" OUT FROM THE CENTER —— EXPRESSED AS

TABLE OF OFFSETS		
STAT. N6	1	2
HEIGHT AT SHEER	4. 8. 0.	
HALF BREADTH	3. 2. 2.	

Etc.

"Slicing" the half boat and using the intersection of the slices as reference points

You will note that 4' 3½" is written 4.3.4. All Tables of Offsets use this system. The first number is always feet, the second inches, and the third eighths of an inch. (Thus, .4 or four ⅛s equals ½ inch.)

It becomes evident that if we "walk" to enough spots, marking each, we will very soon have a pattern or a shape; and that if these are transferred to a paper or floor and a shape is made from them, we will have an actual full-size half section of our boat. If we turn this section over on itself, we have a full-sized whole section. Logically, if we have enough sections and arrange them in

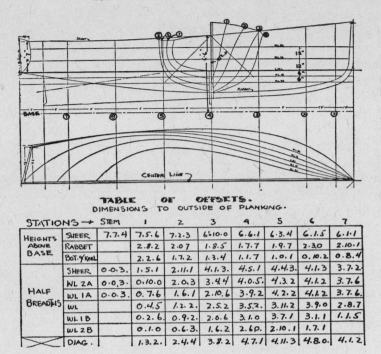

TABLE OF OFFSETS.
DIMENSIONS TO OUTSIDE OF PLANKING.

STATIONS →		STEM	1	2	3	4	5	6	7
HEIGHTS ABOVE BASE	SHEER	7.7.4	7.5.6	7.2.3	6.10.0	6.6.1	6.3.4	6.1.5	6.1.1
	RABBET		2.8.2	2.0.7	1.8.5	1.7.7	1.9.7	2.3.0	2.10.1
	BOT. & KEEL		2.2.6	1.7.2	1.3.4	1.1.7	1.0.1	0.10.2	0.8.4
HALF BREADTHS	SHEER	0.0.3	1.5.1	2.11.1	4.1.3	4.5.1	4.4.3	4.1.3	3.7.2
	WL 2A	0.0.3	0.10.0	2.0.3	3.4.4	4.0.5	4.3.2	4.1.2	3.7.6
	WL 1A	0.0.3	0.7.6	1.6.1	2.10.6	3.9.2	4.2.2	4.1.2	3.7.6
	WL		0.4.5	1.2.2	2.5.2	3.5.2	3.11.2	3.9.0	2.8.7
	WL 1B		0.2.6	0.9.2	2.0.6	3.1.0	3.7.1	3.1.1	1.1.5
	WL 2B		0.1.0	0.6.3	1.6.2	2.6.0	2.10.1	1.7.1	
	DIAG.		1.3.2	2.4.4	3.8.2	4.7.1	4.11.3	4.8.0	4.1.2

Example of plans and table of offsets

proper relation to each other, as indicated by the Table of Offsets and plans, why, presto, there is the complete shape of the boat, seemingly ready for planking! What we are doing, however, is making a full-size plan only, a form or last which has no part in the eventual boat.

Locating these cross forms is simple. Their centers are arranged along a common center line, the keel. Their fore-and-aft locations are exactly the distances apart that are shown by the measurements between the stations on the plan. Their heights are located by measuring up from a base line. This base line is purely imaginary on the plans, an arbitrary point taken by the designer as level and from which to start. It might not coincide at all with what you find most convenient (floor, chalk line, or overhead stringer) as a level starting line. Make the necessary adjustments, adding or subtracting the difference between your own physical base line and the imaginary one shown on the plans.

Many plans, particularly of large vessels, have additional reference points called diagonals; these are almost self-explanatory. The amateur is cautioned here about one matter. These dimensions are always given to the outside of the planking. As the forms to be made from them are to the inside of the planking, the planking thickness must be deducted from the form size which the figures will make. The figures in the table have been scaled from a small drawing. Enlarged many times in laying down lines, small errors often show up. These are not to be taken seriously, but faired up as the various curves and sweeps are sprung from the pliable battens used to connect the series of points given by the laying down.

The keel, stem, and transom dimensions are shown on the plans, and, of course, in practice these members are constructed first and the forms attached to them. A method of transferring the lines as laid down on a wooden floor or paper is shown herewith. After the light batten has been made to fall fair on all the points

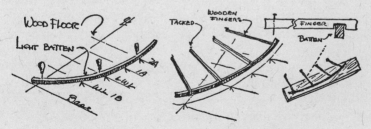

Transferring mold lines from the laying-down floor to the mold stock

for that station, a series of notched wooden fingers is arranged to hold the batten in its final position. This assembly is raised slightly, one side of a form plank slipped under, and the curve of the batten marked on it. Two such shapes, one right and one left, are made. These, tied together with staylaths and the edges bev-

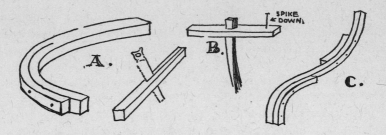

Framing tricks
A. *Saw cutting for the quick bend before steaming.* B. *Frame twister for timber heads at the ends.* C. *Backing the bent frame with a sawn frame at sharp bends*

led to the sweep of the fore-and-aft lines, are the molds (forms).

They are set up on the keel, again tied together with long, strong battens, called ribbands, and the actual frames of the vessel are bent against them. One by one, as the planking is applied and the frame begins to be self-supporting, the ribbands are removed, and later, the molds as well. It is of the utmost importance that accuracy be the watchword of every step in laying down lines. Any change, however slight, will affect *every other dimension in the hull.* There can be no halfway or compromise. The result of changes of any kind is invariably a hull with lumps and hollows—it cannot be otherwise. I know that there are ancient experienced builders who can kick battens, adze here and there, and sock in a shim and come out with a boat—but they never come out with the same boat twice. And they seldom can sail their boats without first fooling about endlessly with ballast, perhaps even putting in a fish well, smack style, whether plans call for one or not!

Hull Woods

There are only two American woods of time-proven value as keel stock: white oak and yellow pine. There is little difference

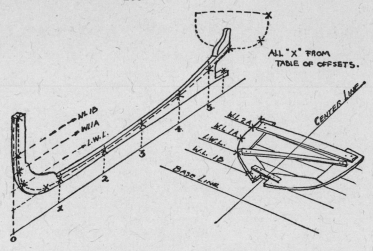

All "X" from
Table of Offsets.

Showing how dimensions are transferred to full size

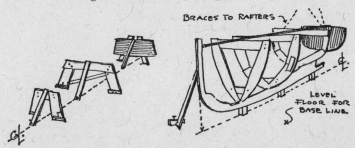

Braces to Rafters

Level Floor for Base Line

Upside-down construction for small boats *Molds set up for a large vessel*

between them either in lasting quality or in strength. Mahogany? Yes, if you can afford to hang mahogany anywhere but where folks can see it! For the amateur, who so often has extreme difficulty in locating white oak, I would most certainly recommend regular lumberyard, air-dried longleaf yellow pine. Contrary to popular opinion, it is not much easier to work than white oak though it often represents less work because it is purchased as sawmill stock, fairly smooth and true, and not as flitch-sawn plank, just off the tree.

DEADWOODS AND SHAFT ALLEYS

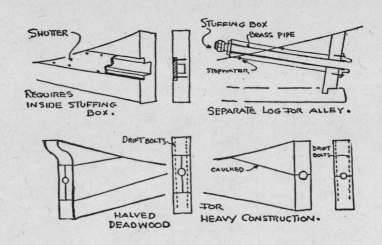

SHUTTER

REQUIRES INSIDE STUFFING BOX.

STUFFING BOX

BRASS PIPE

STOPWATER

SEPARATE LOG FOR ALLEY.

DRIFT BOLTS

HALVED DEADWOOD

CAULKED

DRIFT BOLTS

FOR HEAVY CONSTRUCTION.

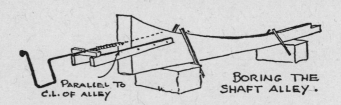

PARALLEL TO C.L. OF ALLEY

BORING THE SHAFT ALLEY.

RULE: ALLEY 25% LARGER DIAMETER THAN SHAFT

SHAFT STRAIGHTENER: WROUGHT IRON PIPE WITH BACK-BEVELLED SAW CUTS OPENED WITH A COLD CHISEL AND SHARPENED: DRAW IN AND OUT ~

WELDED

HANDLE

SHAFT TRIMMING IRON: IRON END TO FIT EASILY INTO ALLEY. HEAT TO "RED HOT" AND BURN OUT HIGH SPOTS AND KNOTS

In either case, the stock must be thoroughly dry. Air drying should extend through the full four seasons. Kiln drying ruins boat wood and is to be avoided except possibly for interior joiner or cabinet work.

There is only one American wood of proven value for frames or ribs: oak. Experiments have been made with other woods—even as in Nova Scotia, and her softwood ships last, with luck, all of twenty years! But oak, especially white oak, still stands as the ideal. There are two schools as to whether or not it should be dry before use. Up along this stretch of seacoast which has been build-

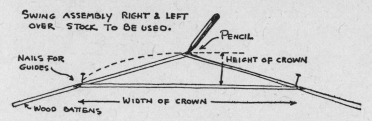

Make triangle out of light wood. With nails, locate the extreme width of the crown proposed, and from a line between these measure up the exact height of the crown you want. Now adjust the legs to these three points, tack the base leg in place, and with a pencil in the notch swing right and left for the true crown. It must be reset for each beam forward or aft or as the height of the crown changes according to plans

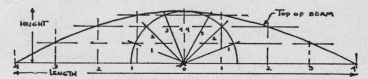

Another method of laying out crown, especially good for crowns of low height. With a radius equal to the height of the crown (usually ½" per foot of length) describe a circle and divide into four parts either left or right of the center line. Now divide the length of the beam into eight parts, extending the lines as shown by the dotted lines. The intersections of the length and height projections are noted and a light batten bent, touching all intersections, and the pattern marked. Note that the sweep will be the TOP *of the beam*

ing ships since 1630, we use wet (as distinguished from air- or kiln-dried) oak, and folks seem to agree that New England hulls are pretty good. Wet oak bends more easily, is not so apt to sliver or snap in bending, and after all, in the small dimensions of frames and ribs, can hardly suffer from later dangerous drying and shrinking. Perhaps the situation is best summarized by remarking that there is so little difference between wet and dry oak for frames that it matters not which is used.

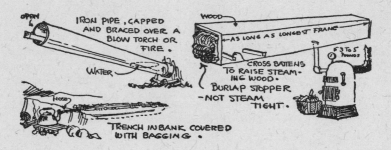

Steam boxes

In using oak, sap pockets and bark should always be cut away. Such defects rot out very quickly, sometimes in only a matter of months. Knots, shakes, and actual splits are, of course, out—usually whether you will it or not, as this is just where the frame will break while bending.

For the round-bottomed boat, steam bending of the frames will be necessary. This is simply a matter of actually softening the wood by increasing its moisture content to the saturation point. In some type of a steam box, the frames, sized and dressed, are "cooked" for about thirty minutes for every inch of thickness. When "done," they are quickly drawn out with gloved hands, rough-bent, stapled with a bending hook, and in the hull, clamped to the ribbands with C-clamps until ready to plank.

If the stock is large enough, say at least 1″ × 1½″, you can fasten the steamed frames into each ribband with an appropriate com-

mon nail, driven from the outside. As the nail is driven, it should
be backed up by a topping maul. In all cases, the frame heel is
nailed or screwed into the boxing at the keel. Before tackling the
framing job, you should mark the ribbands in at least two places
so that you can quickly set the frame to the marks and thus keep
them at the correct plumb or cant line. Do not hesitate to double
frames (called sistering) in the way of the engine or at other
stress points. Organize your work carefully, allow plenty of time,
and tackle it with a full understanding of what you are doing—
and steam bending loses its bug-a-boo.

Old-timers often mix turpentine or kerosene with the steam
water, or paint the frames with it before steaming. This does
much to prevent the oak from running and splintering along the
outside of quick bends. Oakite mixed with the water until it feels
slick to the fingers is said to do the same thing.

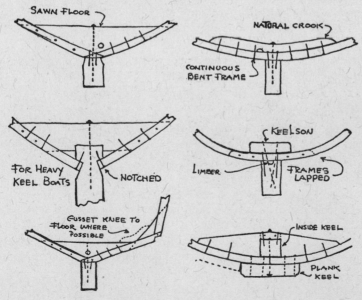

Types of frame construction

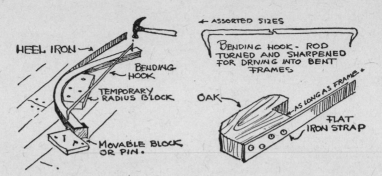

This shows another manner in which to frame and which is especially good for light framing, such as on lapstreak boats, canoes, etc. The frame is bent upon the floor by being jammed between the heel block and radius block, both placed in approximately correct positions. The heel iron is then inserted to prevent the frame from slivering at the sharper turns and the frame slowly hand pushed to more than the required bend. The bending hook is then driven home to hold the shape, the heel iron removed, and the frame placed into the boat and clamped to the ribbands and fastened into the keel

The Navy Department writes that it has been making some experiments with rock elm as a rib material but does not state whether any conclusions have been reached. Rock elm, as well as hackmatack and tough gnarled pasture oak, has its uses as knees and braces throughout the frame. For use at these points, it should be air dried at least, and selected with a natural crook or grain along the lines of greatest strain.

There are several good American woods for planking. For the finest yacht work, there is nothing to compare with mahogany. Today this material can be bought from stock in most centers at fairly economical prices. It is easy to work, takes a fine finish, and, even at quick turns, does not require steam bending. Mahogany, liberally soaked with kerosene and left to stand for thirty minutes, will soften and throw itself into a masthead knot for you.

White pine and cedar are still in popular use, as they have been since Colonial times. Both are softwoods and easily worked. The best cedar today comes from the West; clear, straight-grained lumber, barren of the pinholes and shakes of our remaining northern cedar.

Boat for boat, the native cedar costs as much or more than the clear Port Orford cedar. Not only does it cut very wastefully, but it requires a few days work boring out the knots and pinholes, inserting a sound wood plug in them, with always the chance that one will be forgotten and very shortly rot out, causing a leak.

Caulking correctly

A. *Open seam. Can never be made tight. Cotton can be seen from inside. Swelling tends to pull planking from frames. B. Wooded seam. Cotton ironed into plank edge, possibly plank edge split. C. Correct seam. Cotton firmly driven against wood seam inside, payed with paint and puttied, slightly hollow on surface*

Cypress, yellow pine, oak, teak, and occasionally Oregon pine also are used for planking. Unless required for some special purpose, weight or strength, these, however, are second choices. It is difficult to make paint adhere to them, and actually working the planks is more of a chore than working pine, cedar, or mahogany. They do, however, seem to have just as good lasting qualities under water as the other woods.

In order to be modern, I shall mention one more planking wood: resin-bonded (or waterproof) plywood.

Now, shipmates, I think this waterproof plywood one of the grandest things to hit yachting since stainless steel and quick-dry yacht finishes. But I can't see it as planking, except possibly in a small pram or tiny class sailer which MUST be light. In every case there has been some compromise between perfect design and the plywood boat in order to use the material. Plywood will bend substantially but one way—and very few boats are bent but one

★ FITTING PLANKS ★

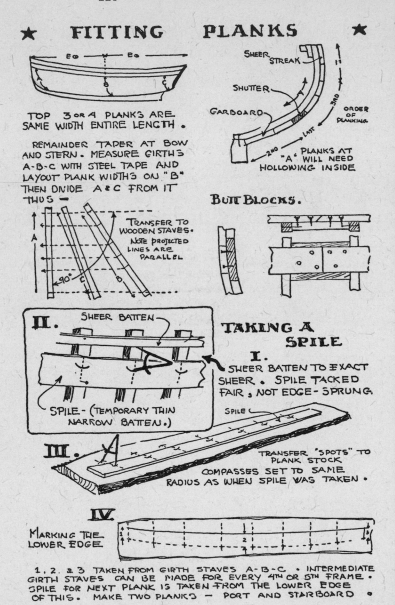

TOP 3 OR 4 PLANKS ARE SAME WIDTH ENTIRE LENGTH.

REMAINDER TAPER AT BOW AND STERN. MEASURE GIRTHS A-B-C WITH STEEL TAPE AND LAYOUT PLANK WIDTHS ON "B" THEN DIVIDE A & C FROM IT THUS —

TRANSFER TO WOODEN STAVES. NOTE PROJECTED LINES ARE PARALLEL

SHEER STREAK
SHUTTER
GARBOARD
ORDER OF PLANKING
3RD
2ND
LAST
"A" PLANKS AT "A" WILL NEED HOLLOWING INSIDE

BUTT BLOCKS.

TAKING A SPILE

I. SHEER BATTEN TO EXACT SHEER. SPILE TACKED FAIR, NOT EDGE-SPRUNG.

II. SHEER BATTEN
SPILE - (TEMPORARY THIN NARROW BATTEN.)

SPILE

III. TRANSFER "SPOTS" TO PLANK STOCK. COMPASSES SET TO SAME RADIUS AS WHEN SPILE WAS TAKEN.

IV. MARKING THE LOWER EDGE

1, 2, & 3 TAKEN FROM GIRTH STAVES A-B-C. INTERMEDIATE GIRTH STAVES CAN BE MADE FOR EVERY 4TH OR 5TH FRAME. SPILE FOR NEXT PLANK IS TAKEN FROM THE LOWER EDGE OF THIS. MAKE TWO PLANKS — PORT AND STARBOARD.

way. I do not quarrel with it as a material. It stands up, does not
check or separate, and does all its makers say it will do. However,
I can see no great advantage in it except the possible saving of
weight, which is important only in certain types of tiny boats. It is
messy to work with, requiring special rabbeted members, chine
caps, glue joints, odd-looking stems, etc., and according to several
designers, is more expensive to use than ordinary construction.
Undoubtedly, for the quantity manufacturer, building over lasts,
plywood has certain advantages, but it seems that any amateur
builder, contemplating a boat larger than the longest length of
stock plywood, had better stick to old Noah's style of boatbuilding. For bulkheads, decks, interior uses, by all means, yes. I shall
have much favorable to say about plywood in later chapters.

Honestly, I'm sorry to be old-fashioned about this. But, you see,
I rode in a plywood cruiser last summer. They told me pridefully
that it weighed only two tons; but, boys, she had ballast in her
bilges that must have weighed another ton! Somehow, that didn't
seem quite sane—build her light and load her with lead pigs to
give her seaworthiness. They also told me she wouldn't sound like
the inside of a drum under weigh but, believe me, she *felt* like it.

Today many hulls are built in composite construction, i.e., of
wood covered with glass. Generally, it is unsatisfactory to cover
wide planking with glass, especially that of an old vessel; and so
strip planking has been developed with considerable success.
"Planking," or strips, are generally almost square in section, say 1″
× ¾″, and are all milled to this size, planed on four sides, and
stored flat. Cut away knots and shakes and discard any length less
than the combined length of three frame spaces—or about three
feet.

Strip planking may be laid exactly as board planking but with
frames spaced two to three times that of board plank construction. For small craft, which have interior supporting members
such as thwarts, bulkheads, or kneed decking, the frames may
often be omitted completely, for strip planking is extremely
strong. Now, if the hull is to be glass covered, there is no need to
taper the strips. *Bevelling* is sufficient, even though the wood ends

of the upper planks may terminate at the sheer line. All will be covered with glass, and the lubberly planking not be seen. It will, fortunately, be quite as strong as *bevelling* and *tapering*, in which case all wood ends will end against the rabbet of the stem, the

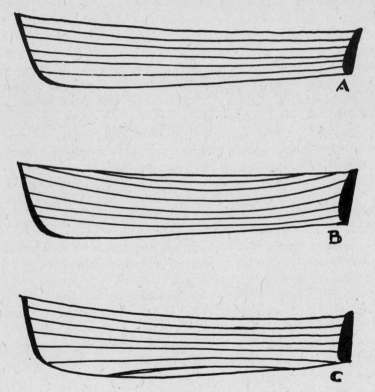

The evil effects of not tapering planks on an average hull. All these planks in B and C have been bevelled but not tapered. A shows the way tapered and bevelled planking should appear when set. B shows untapered planking started at the garboard strake (parallel to the keel). You end up with wood ends exposed to heaven and a lubberly job. C is a truly horrible example, which occurs when planking is started at the shear line. Even though the visible evidence of this sloppy method is below the waterline, it poses impossible problems in butting the wood ends into the rabbet of the keel— which, mates, can't be done

stern, or the transom. If your strip boat is to be natural finished by all means bevel *and* taper.

Whether bevelled only or bevelled and tapered, start at the keel with a full-length strip, carefully fit it (for we will use no caulking or putty later), and apply the sealing agent you have chosen. These are many: rubber base, ordinary waterproof glue, thickened varnish, or one of the epoxies. Set the strip in place and nail from the top into the member immediately below with galvanized finish nails of appropriate size, spacing these nails every three or four inches. Select a nail for which you will not have to bore, which means fine wire. It should penetrate the top strip and go *through* the next one beneath and about one-fourth to three-eighths of an inch into the second strip beneath. If you have frames, screw, *do not nail,* into them; or rivet them. As you reach the upper planks they will take quite a curve, so save some long and sound stock for this.

When the boat is planked, clean off the glue with a scraper or a glue-scraper plane, then with a hand plane, a block plane, and a light disc sander, and smooth and fair the exterior skin. (The inside will be a mess and probably remain so if there are frames.) It is now ready to cover with the glass of your choosing, about which more later.

Such a planking job is extremely difficult to repair, but it will serve a long time and take a great deal of wracking and hard usage. With a glass covering it becomes still stronger, and in my opinion greatly exceeds glass-only as a hull. I do believe that were it not for the cost of labor, we would find many such hulls on the market, for they are truly a superior product.

Fastenings

The strongest fastening for the heavy timbers of the frame is, peculiarly enough, one that has been used since the days of the Ark itself: treenails (or trunnels). Next strongest is what is used today: the driftbolt of steel or galvanized iron. It should be used

The driftbolt

wherever possible, even in preference to the common carriage bolt and certainly in preference to the lag bolt, wood screw, or spike.

There is an art to driving driftbolts, and their holding power is dependent upon correct setting.

The hole for the drift fastening is *always* bored smaller (by one-sixteenth or one-thirty-second of an inch) than the rod itself. The hole is started at the correct angle and direction with an ordinary bit, having a lead screw, and sunk for about one inch. From here on a barefoot bit is used (ship's auger) which has no lead screw, is self-cleaning, and will bore straight, once started straight. The rod is slightly tapered on one end with a hammer, a washer rove, and as driving home proceeds, is headed over by hammer blows about, *not on*, dead center.

Such a fastening, after swelling, rust, and certain chemical processes have taken place, will hold as long as the wood lasts. A series of driftbolts should be toenailed for extra strength. While the carriage bolt must sometimes be used because of physical conditions, the driftbolt, headed over washers on *both* ends will prove even stronger.

Ballast bolts are mentioned only in passing. It is important that only iron or steel be used with the iron keel, and bronze with the lead keel. Some of the bolts, at least, should pass not only through the keel, but through the floors as well, especially in the deep keel which exerts usual side strain on the frame. In either case the bolt

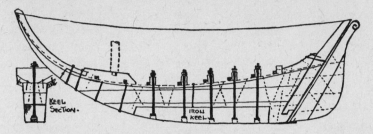

Hull fastenings

Note the keel bolts extending through the floors and the driftbolts staggered and toenailed. Bolts at stem scarf might be carriage bolts, better yet would be driftbolts headed on both ends

holes will have to be spotted and provided for as the keel is cast and should be one-sixteenth of an inch larger in diameter than the bolt. Heads, of course, must be countersunk and plugged with wood or a trowel cement.

TABLE OF KEEL BOLT SIZES

BALLAST WEIGHT	BOLT SIZE	MINIMUM NUMBER
2,000 pounds	¾″	6
3,500 pounds	⅝″	8
5,000 pounds	⅞″	12
10,000 pounds	1⅛″	16
20,000 pounds	1½″	20

Removing the remains of a ballast bolt which must be replaced sometimes presents a stubborn problem. Generally, it is wisest not to try turning off the head nut but merely to shear it off with a cold chisel. A rust solvent will help free the bolt, or try heating outside with a blowtorch on both sides of the keel casting in the way of the bolt. By shearing all bolts at once, the keel weight itself will sometimes help to start them as you drive the bolts out. Replacing should always include a new gasket (canvas soaked in white lead) between the wood and metal keels.

Plank fastenings have provided yachting magazine editors with a controversy since the days of Tom Day, the skipper of *The Rudder* back in the nineties. Nothing, as nearly as I can observe, has ever been proved. Iron is good, copper is good, screws and rivets are good. Take your choice of these, using the one best suited to your type of construction, scantling, size, and taste. However, whichever fastening you use—use the best available.

Galvanized iron boat nails are old stand-bys. I believe that, from experience, nothing holds as well when driven into oak. But be sure that they are hot-dipped galvanized (not merely tinned, processed, or dipped in silver paint!) and that, as you drive with the nail set, you do not chip all the galvanizing off. Sink the heads

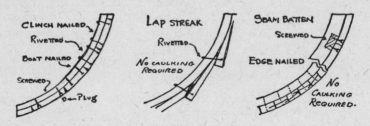

Type of planking and plank fastenings

in a *bored* countersink and bore both plank and frame. Remember that even a slight exposure of the bare iron will result in a rust spot, eating into the nail on the one hand and discoloring your topsides on the other. The practice of using a chisel-pointed boat nail, without first boring, is ruinous and lubberly. Generally, the blunt-pointed boat nail affords more strength than the chisel-point, especially for the underwater fastenings.

Copper and bronze nails have the least strength of any fastening. Clinched or riveted, they become stronger, providing that in the bending and burring the metal has not been ruptured. Far better are the modern screw fastenings of non-rusting alloys of great tensile strength. While these require great care in setting (as

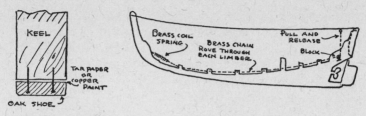

Anti-worm shoe   Limber clearing gear

well as costing "heap wampum") they are, under certain conditions of vibration and construction, the only fastenings to use.

In the following sketches will be found hints and short cuts for
the builder as he proceeds with the frame. While many of them
show not the only method, they do show what the writer considers the simplest method.

We shall close this chapter with a word about that arch enemy
of all hulls—dry rot.

To keep it out of the boat altogether is the ideal, if you can do
it. No man has yet found out the sure-fire trick of doing this. Dry
rot is a fungus, attacking the fibrous walls of the wood cells. The
fungus can feed only under certain moisture conditions, and the
trick seems to be to keep wood reasonably dry. On shipboard, this
is well-nigh impossible. Recommended, then, as the next best
thing, is ample and positive ventilation, on the theory that while
we must have a certain amount of moisture, we can take steps to
immediately disperse it and thus destroy a condition favorable to
dry rot.

Very seldom does salt water encourage dry rot. The old ship-
masters understood this well, going so far as to place salt boxes
between timberheads and, by means of a deck filler-plug, keeping
them filled with rock salt which went into solution with any water
approaching its neighborhood. On salt water, a vessel almost invariably will develop her rotten spots high above the water line,
very likely in the vicinity of the quarters, bow, or her clamps and
covering board—places which are likely to suffer from lack of free
air passage, fresh water deck leaks, and the heat of the sun.

Salting is almost a forgotten art. It might well be revived in the modern yacht, at least at certain suspected points such as quarters, bow, and behind fixed interior features.

The discovery of dry rot should send you to an examination of every piece of wood in the vessel. There is no cure for it save the complete removal and burning of all the affected timber.

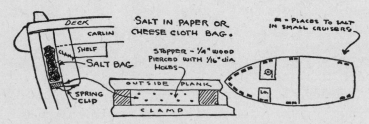

Salting to prevent dry rot in the modern boat. Rock salt, or commercial ship salt, is sewn in cloth bags or secured in a small paper envelope. After inserting between clamp and outside planking, high up and tight between frames, the stopper is clipped in and the bag punctured with an ice pick in several places. Any fresh water reaching the point will be salted, lessening the likelihood of a condition favorable to dry-rot fungi

Prevention of dry rot, however, is possible. Coating or impregnating with *coal tar creosote* is one approved method.

One of the most effective and cheapest is the following:

To 1 gallon of cold soft water, add 6 oz. of commercial *sodium fluoride,* making a 4 per cent solution.

Give all woodwork at least two coats with a brush, running it well into cavities and cracks.

While paint acts as a waterproofing and is an effective barrier to the fungus spores of dry rot, just the reverse is true if painting is done over wet or damp wood. Antiseptics and household disinfectants are useless for the control of dry rot.

A word belongs here about "pickling" bilges. While there are

RUDDERS

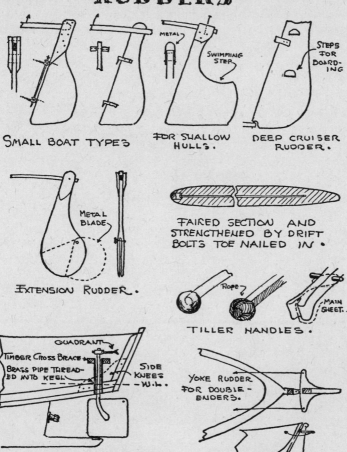

SMALL BOAT TYPES

FOR SHALLOW HULLS.

DEEP CRUISER RUDDER.

METAL

SWIMMING STEP

STEPS FOR BOARDING

METAL BLADE

EXTENSION RUDDER.

FAIRED SECTION AND STRENGTHENED BY DRIFT BOLTS TOE NAILED IN.

ROPE

MAIN SHEET.

TILLER HANDLES.

QUADRANT

Timber Cross Brace

Brass pipe threaded into keel

SIDE KNEES — W.L.

POWER BOAT RUDDER

YOKE RUDDER FOR DOUBLE-ENDERS.

FINDING RUDDER AREAS FOR POWER BOATS
WATERLINE LENGTH X EXTREME DRAFT.

FOR BOATS 20-30 FEET   5% OF RESULT = AREA.
  "   "   30-45   "   4% "   "   =   "
  "   "   OVER 50 "   3% "   "   =   "

several proprietary compounds available through ship chandlers, the whole secret, as far as small boats are concerned, is keeping the bilges clean. There cannot be foul bilges or bilge odors if they are kept clean. This means a tight floor, a drip pan under the engine and possibly under the water closet, and an icebox which does not drain into the bilges.

The best bilge sweetener for small yachts is simply a cleaning. Remove all floor boards and open the bilges as much as possible. Make a strong solution of water and trisodium phosphate (which is simply chain-store Oakite), about six ounces to one gallon of water, and, after saturating the bilges by sloshing, scrub and scrape clean. Rinse with a hose or a bucket and squeegee and let dry. You won't have any more bilge smell.

VII *Above the Rail*

In la mode of the advertising people, we shall, for this chapter, have a slogan and build around it. By all means let it be—

"Above the rail—as strong and as tight as below!"

As I sit here, staring at my typewriter and deciding upon the mechanics of expounding upon that slogan, I feel a marked inclination to sink the thing in six fathoms and reach for my drawing pen. Why not? I have always felt that one illustration is worth a thousand words at least—and there are many thousand words necessary to do justice to the subject of this chapter. So let's set a few standards for these "above the rail" features and then look at the pictures!

The Deck

A ton of water dashed against the hull does not exert nearly as much force as a ton dashed on deck. No single point below the water line ever gets as much strain as does the deck when you jump upon it from a wharf.

So, decks MUST be strong; at least as strong as the hull. Deck beams and carlings should be equal in size and spacing to the frames of the hull. The fastenings at the junction of decks and topsides must be just as strong as at the junction of ribs and keel.

If at all possible, deck planking should be tongued and grooved and secured with boat nails in preference to brads or common nails. If this is impossible, screw-fasten the decking, using two screws, sunk near the plank edge in the way of each carling. If narrow strips are used, blind-nailing from the vertical outboard edge makes a strong and exceptionally neat job.

With the improvement of exterior plywood, it is probably today quite sound good-building practice to use a sheet underdeck. If a laid deck is to go over it, use ¼" genuine exterior grade with one face good (which means free of sap pockets and the inserts applied at the mill in the way of knots), this face providing the finished overhead for the spaces below. Over this a painted or teak deck should always be *bedded down* and the seams caulked or payed exactly as if there were no plywood beneath. At all costs, water must be kept out, or trouble will rapidly ensue. Painted decks should be bevelled to a regular planking seam and caulked with cotton, then payed with paint and puttied. Flow prime coatings liberally into seams. A teak deck should have no cotton, but the usual payed seam edge; then the seam should be filled with one of the rubber or plastic *flexible* seam compounds. The novice needs no longer fear the "hot pitch devil," for modern seam fillers are readily worked with a putty knife or a gun during the usual generous "working life," i.e., time to apply before the compound chemically reacts and sets. It is usual to edge both edges of the seam with common one-half inch masking tape, fill the seam, strip off the tape, and cut the now-hardened compound flush with a sharp knife.

Both glass and canvas may be used as a "deck" over plywood, but in this case the plywood will need to be somewhat heavier; at least one-half inch thick, and certainly three-fourths inch thick for a heavy boat or a sailing craft, for the deck still must be regarded as an integral part of the hull and as such must be strong and solid. Lacking the fastenings supplied by a laid deck above, plywood will have to be well fastened to the beams and, because plywood will run to the hull edge, to the edge of the shear plank as well. Screws and anchor-fast type nails, of bronze, are best. Boat nails may be sufficient for a small craft foredeck. Set fastenings hand deep; then sand the surface, removing all splintered plywood in the way of the countersink area; and putty flush with a seam or hull-surfacing putty. Then apply canvas as suggested in the illustration.

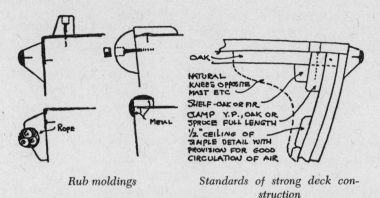

Rub moldings   Standards of strong deck construction

As good as paint these days are the mastics made for such service. Waterproof linoleum cement is acceptable and probably as good as the same thing with a fancy marine name. Avoid the contact types of cement; they stick too well and, once bonded, can never be removed to correct a mistake or work out a wrinkle or bubble. It is a good idea to wet the canvas, thus shrinking it; but allow it to become almost dry before applying. Do not hesitate to work it flat with an iron, kept at medium warm.

With the cement set, proceed with a filler or primer coat and build up the deck paint. Canvas, taken care of, will last a long time. However, unless the undersurface is fastened down tight so there is no movement at seams or joints or deck fittings, the canvas will rupture, rot, and soon vanish.

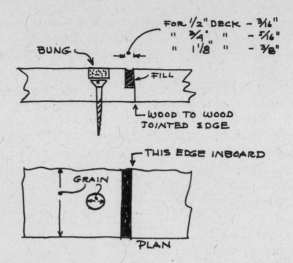

The proper seam for paying, such as on a modern teak deck using one of the rubber or plastic seam fillers. Depth should be about three fifths the thickness of the deck stock. Note how to bung so that bungs stay in: cross the deck grain. Thus deck and bung shrinkage oppose each other and do not dry and shrink in the same direction

It is common today, even on wooden-hulled vessels, to cover horizontals with glass, usually with some roving applied in successive coats to a final, or jell, coat. Proceed exactly as with a canvas deck. Be positive that there is no grease or paint or oil putty exposed, and apply the glass in accordance with the directions of the supplier. There are so many glass-resin applications available today, each with a different setting time and procedural instructions, that this manual cannot be specific. Follow the supplier's instructions. To the letter! Do not hesitate to try the process on a small panel off the boat. Once you know the exact setting time, temperatures, humidity conditions, and mixtures of resin and hardener, you will have a confidence that will go far toward assuring a sound job. But do not take liberties! If the supplier says a 70 degree minimum temperature is required, that is gospel. Sixty-five won't work, and seventy-five will work too fast!

In general, glass work requires temperature- and humidity-controlled working areas and experienced labor, plus some necessary basic equipment. You will want several flat pans, similar to baking pans, for the "mix"; putty knives, scissors to cut and trim the glass roving, and a roller or very cheap but stiff wide brush as well. You will seldom salvage any of these items as the resin will harden, or "kick over," of a sudden, and from there on in, you can do nothing about removal. Before hardening, acetone will remove the resin. Get a box of glassine working mitts for this work. They are inexpensive and arranged so that you can slip a hand into one as needed. At all costs, keep the resin off your hands and fingers, or you will be a vast mess of sticking tools, materials, and people that can spell only ruin.

Newer rovings, under various trade names, provide a stretch quality which permits hauling and bunching and serves in a superior manner when glassing irregular or curved surfaces such as hulls, hull patches, molded rails, forms with taper, tumble home, shear, or crown. Unless the surface you mean to cover is curved only *one* way, buy this type of roving. Do not hesitate to use tacks, or staples (non-rust!) to work the material into your shape; you can later haul some of these out. It is wise never to cut the material to exact size before applying the resin. Always leave two edges for trimming, which is done as the panel is worked onto its bed. Trim on these two edges as the panel falls into place, using a scissors, and, immediately after, apply an acetone wash to them.

When the panel has hardened, sand, not too heavily, *by hand or with a vibrator only,* dust off well, and proceed with further coatings, brushed or rolled on. No roving will be needed unless unusual problems are to be solved. Usually three coats, plus a jell coat, which is glossy and not to be sanded, will do a nice, professional job. If color is to be added, start on the next to the last coat. If special textured panels, such as anti-skid grids, are to be included, lay these over the jellcoat while it is still wet. Most special insets will require manufacturer's instructions. Be very sure all coats are compatible; the best assurance being to buy a "process" from a particular supplier, which includes a set of instructions. It is folly for the novice to assemble his own materials, willy-nilly, from discount or surplus outlets.

On old deck work (indeed with any glass application) you should not look for 100 per cent success. Even though you have removed paint or varnish or canvas cement, the wood will have absorbed considerable invisible amounts of it, and there will be difficulty in bonding glass to that surface. I have never seen a perfect job of glass covering an old deck or old hull; and, sooner or later, there will be a mighty parting of the ways. Glass is not a cure-all and can never replace a base which has failed through age, neglect, or poor build. It is a modern water- and acidproof covering that is just as good as its base, not one bit better.

Canvas and roving comes in all weights up to 120 inches wide, though at extremely high prices per linear yard. Costs can be reduced considerably by planning one or two fore-and-aft seams which appear only between deckhouses, cockpits, etc., and using a narrower-width canvas. The premium on wide single canvas runs the cost for a thirty-footer $25 to $50 above two or three narrow widths.

Like most yachtsmen, I love a clear white-pine or a teak deck— but I'm just like the rest when it comes to maintaining such a deck. I just don't do it and in consequence have a far worse-looking deck than a painted one kept up without much effort.

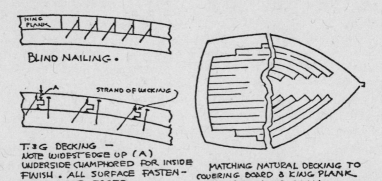

BLIND NAILING.

T. & G. DECKING —
NOTE WIDEST EDGE UP (A)
UNDERSIDE CHAMPHORED FOR INSIDE
FINISH. ALL SURFACE FASTEN-
INGS NEAR EDGES.

STRAND OF WICKING

MATCHING NATURAL DECKING TO
COVERING BOARD & KING PLANK
WITH BUTT JOINTS ONLY.

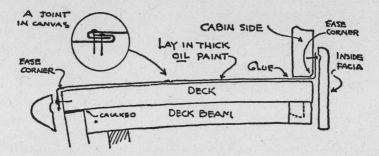

A JOINT IN CANVAS

CABIN SIDE

EASE CORNER

LAY IN THICK OIL PAINT

EASE CORNER

GLUE

INSIDE FACIA

DECK

CAULKED

DECK BEAM

Laying deck canvas

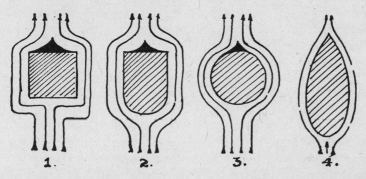

1. 2. 3. 4.

Streamline shapes for cabin and deck furniture of high-speed boats. The black area shows the drag. For practical purposes 2 or some adaptation of 4, the ideal shape, lends itself best to cabin design

Laying such a deck is an almighty chore, the guiding rule being that there shall be no feather edges. Therefore, the butt ends of the deck planking must be carefully housed, not only into a king plank but into the covering boards themselves as well as the framing around houses, hatches, cockpits, and masts.

Extra deck strength is needed in the way of certain deck features. This is usually achieved by doubling or strapping or both. Doubling should always be of hardwood, oak, or larch (hackmatack) and should be natural knees.

Trunks, Houses, and Hatches

Here again we can, with profit, remember our chapter slogan. The trunk, hatch, and companion too often are flimsy afterthoughts, not nearly comparable in strength to the hull itself. One of the reasons that the trunk so frequently leaks is that it is not inherently rugged enough to resist the wrenchings and strains of the hull.

It should be standard practice always to through-bolt trunks, hanging cockpits, etc., into a heavy part of the frame itself. The necessity of quarter rounds or other bed-type moldings should never exist; the wood-to-wood fit of these features, caulked if required, should be sufficient for watertightness and strength. All deck furniture should be set into rabbeted members which are a part of the deck framing and laid in elastic marine glue.

Ordinarily caulking methods here in the sun and air are not always satisfactory nor water-resistant. I once had a small auxiliary with a trunk cabin. Came a heavy rain or boarding seas and the trunk deck-seam never leaked a drop. Yet on 90 per cent of the clear summer nights afloat, the morning dew would seep through and soak my bunk and me. It took a real wetting to swell the seam and make it watertight. (The cure, by the way, was the removal of the trunk and its resetting in marine glue, sans cotton.)

The openings in the trunk or house itself need careful and wise planning. Nothing can be more annoying than a leaky hatch, skylight, or companion slide. In designing these it is not enough to consider only ordinary methods of watertightness, such as might be used on a dwelling roof. The water that hits them is usually under force, either with the pressure of wind or bulk behind it. The sketches following show some details of standard water-tight construction of companions and hatches.

It seems to me that many of our cruisers, especially sailers, have too many and too large glass areas for either safety or comfort. While the wheelhouse or windshield of a straight power-cruiser

Grab rails of wood   Fixed sash for trunks

rightfully has a considerable number of windows, the idea is hardly practical in the trunk cabin where boarding seas or the careless sea-boot can easily stove them in. Port and starboard portholes are of little real use in ventilation (it's the forward ones that do it!), and these might better be fixed lights of wire glass most carefully set and sealed. Square sashes certainly have no place near the deck. The average skylight with its large square panes and protective grille is a dangerous shipmate, almost sure to need reglazing at least once each season because of breakage. The porthole idea, giving equal light with far greater strength, can well be used here.

Ordinary hatches such as used forward have come a long way from their originals, appearing too often as fancy, leaky, and dangerous pieces of cabinetwork. The hatch and its framing should be very strong, designed to take the hard knocks of anchors and ground tackle. Under no circumstances should there be any projecting edges or shelves on which lines or toes might foul. A thoroughly watertight joint is needed, one that, under certain sea conditions, can be caulked or stuffed against solid, green water. Above all, the proper hatch requires a positive inside latch and, in addition, some method of securely clamping it down. There is no excuse for the hatch which jumps with every steep sea; to actually loose one, under certain conditions, is as disastrous as loosing a garboard!

The power-cruiser cabin or deckhouse presents its own problems of windage- and weathertightness. In general these struc-

TRUNK CABINS.

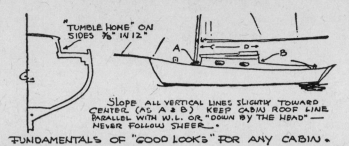

"TUMBLE HOME" ON SIDES 7/8" IN 12"

SLOPE ALL VERTICAL LINES SLIGHTLY TOWARD CENTER (AS A & B) KEEP CABIN ROOF LINE PARALLEL WITH W.L. OR "DOWN BY THE HEAD" — NEVER FOLLOW SHEER .

FUNDAMENTALS OF "GOOD LOOKS" FOR ANY CABIN .

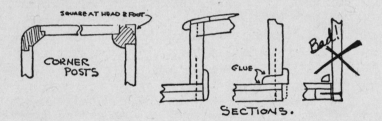

SQUARE AT HEAD & FOOT

CORNER POSTS

GLUE

Bad!

SECTIONS .

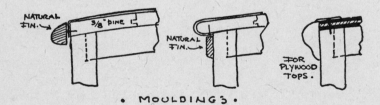

NATURAL FIN.→

3/8" PINE

NATURAL FIN.→

FOR PLYWOOD TOPS.

• MOULDINGS •

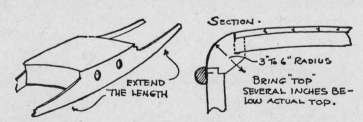

SECTION .

EXTEND THE LENGTH

3" TO 6" RADIUS

BRING "TOP" SEVERAL INCHES BE-LOW ACTUAL TOP.

TWO METHODS OF REDUCING APPARENT HEIGHT

SKYLIGHTS AND HATCHES •

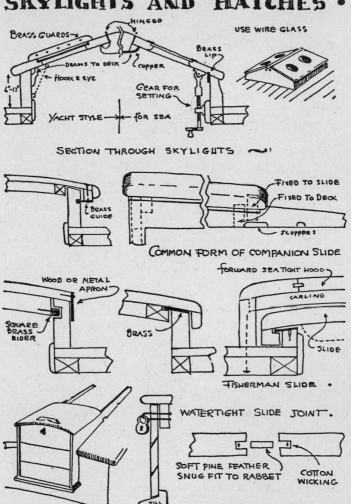

USE WIRE GLASS

Brass Guards
HINGED
DRAINS TO DECK
COPPER
Brass Lip
HOOK & EYE
GEAR FOR SETTING
YACHT STYLE — for sea

SECTION THROUGH SKYLIGHTS

BRASS GUIDE
FIXED TO SLIDE
FIXED TO DECK
SCUPPERS

COMMON FORM OF COMPANION SLIDE

WOOD OR METAL APRON
SQUARE BRASS RIDER
BRASS
FORWARD SEA TIGHT HOOD
CARLING
SLIDE

FISHERMAN SLIDE •

WATERTIGHT SLIDE JOINT.

SOFT PINE FEATHER SNUG FIT TO RABBET
COTTON WICKING

SILL

BOOBY HATCH — A GOOD
SEA·TIGHT AND SIMPLE
TYPE FOR SMALL BOATS.

← PULL TOGETHER WITH DOOR CLAMP →

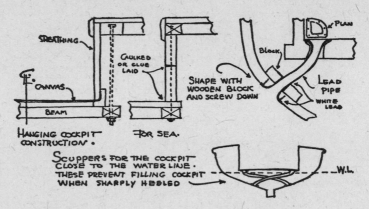

tures should be very strong yet very light. Plywood as a covering serves admirably here. Mahogany for the frame and stanchions not only is light and strong but takes the fine finish which most deckhouses require instead of paint treatment.

Most of these deckhouses suffer from a common ailment—the sashes are the weakest and leakiest points. On the market are excellent devices for adjusting plate-glass frameless sashes—the same as in an auto—but most of us could build a boat for the cost of a dozen or so sets. However, if you want sashes of this type you can get 'em cheap enough. I bought eight complete sets, without glass, for $2.00 at an auto junk yard—then paid a guy by the name

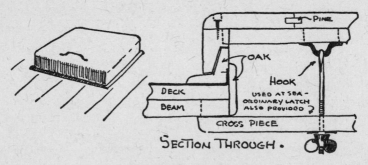

A proper hatch for sea

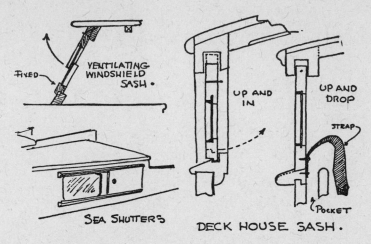

SEA SHUTTERS

DECK HOUSE SASH .

of Henry $1.50 to get them off the wrecks and clean them up. I haven't a 100 per cent marine fitting, but my sashes work, and they are tighter than any wooden-framed sash I ever shipped with. Just a thought, mates.

The mobile home manufacturers now offer many units admirably suited for boat use,—of aluminum extrusions, sometimes available anodized (which does what galvanizing does for steel) and with built-in screens. For fixed sash, rubber formers offer a great variety of wood-to-glass flexible mouldings. For all these, see the mobile-home catalogs.

Deck Hardware

Deck hardware seems to be a necessary evil of yachting—a constant reminder, as we stub a bare toe or foul a line on some cleat, that it's the little things in life which count. However, I think that many of the items could be placed *off the deck* and still serve their purposes just as well.

Cleats can go on trunk sides or top, substituting a removable belaying pin for the cleat occasionally used; filler caps, etc., can be

WHICH IS SIMPLEST ?

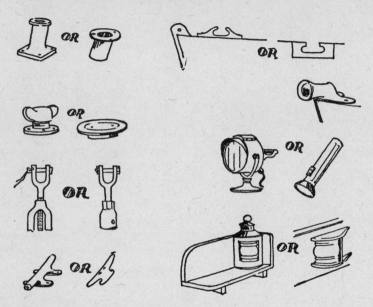

flushed and the deck generally cleaned up. A careful check of deck hardware on the average sailing cruiser will reveal that a big percentage of it is never used. Take a look at a commercial dragger next time you are at Block Island or Stonington or Gloucester. For the work they do at sea, they carry an absolute minimum of deck hardware. They'll tell you it's to keep the nets free of the danger of fouling.

Deck hardware should always be bolted—not screwed—and the fastening put through the deck and into a block fastened between the deck framing. To prevent leaking at these fastenings, a turn of cotton or wicking or a canvas gasket is set up with the fitting. Use bronze in preference to either brass or iron. Most cleats need reboring for larger-diameter fastenings.

Wherever possible, select a fitting that is smooth, chunky, and

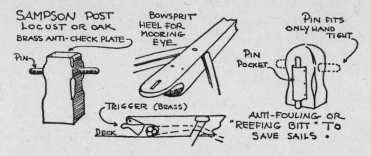

streamlined, avoiding castings which, because of crevices and detail, are difficult to paint around or polish.

In recent years a new type of alleged deck fitting has hit the
nautical scene; it is the pot metal casting, complete with a quick
job of chrome covering. The best of them last a year in fresh
water; a season or less in salt water—and all the while they look
like nothing fit to put on a washing machine! If you care to trust
your vessel or your safety to a truly inferior, however cheap, fitting, get one of these abominations by all means. It is called aluminum, is die-cast, and has several trade names, but its sole value
is to look good in a nautical chandler's and so sell to the novice.

One of these fittings is the extruded aluminum "rub" rail, or
half-oval, supposed to protect rails from chafing. Moreover, it is
used to cheat on certain inexpensive mass-spawned small craft;
that is, to hide seams and joints and to match dissimilar materials
(i.e., linoleum and wood). Avoid it all. You save no money in the
long run and take a chance in placing your trust in this inferior
merchandise, usually offered by some kitchen-utensil manufacturer or his equal with not an iota of marine history or experience.

Chrome over honest bronze—now that's a good combination
for those who want spit and polish, and there's nothing against it
at all. It stands up well, and will stand up even better if waxed or
lightly sponged with fuel oil or if it is hit once a season with a
mild silver-polish. It is, essentially, a work saver and, incorporated
into a plush design with matching features of quality, can contribute much to a fine yachtlike craft.

Deck Layouts

One of the great differences between the professional and the amateur designer lies in his approach to the deck layout. The amateur takes it as a result of the many physical factors already in the design. His actual layout on deck has been determined by interior layout, location of spars, power plant, steering station, etc., and perhaps by appearance. The professional recognizes the deck as the most important working space on the vessel. It must have certain features of safety, roominess, and convenience; and he often first lays out the ideal deck for that boat and lets nothing seriously interfere with its layout as the rest of the design advances.

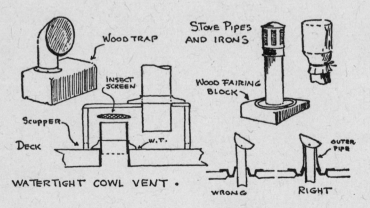

This is absolutely right and correct, particularly in a boat which will go to sea often.

The ideal deck should have at least the following essential features:

1. Room to work under all conditions of weather, angle of keel, and light conditions (at masts, winches, power plant, tiller, wheel, etc.).

2. A minimum of openings, trunks, hatches, skylights, etc.
3. All these features concentrated near the fore-and-aft center line and aft of the foremost mast and forward of the main-sheet and tiller.
4. Smoke pipes, cowl ventilators, and similar fair-weather pro-tuberances removable and their deck openings capable of being sealed sea-tight.
5. A space for the dinghy which will in no way interfere with the working of the ship or docking.
6. Lounging space for the crew which is comfortable, dry, and capable of being covered by an awning or a boom tarp, or which has a permanent roof.
7. A minimum of deck hardware, sheets, fair-leads, etc., which may cause fouling of lines or tripping of the unwary hand.

It has always seemed to me that too many boat designs go to great pains to provide below-deck accommodations amounting to almost luxury, but utterly fail to give more than leg room on deck. I can recall a large cruiser upon which I once sailed. Thirty-seven feet long she was and slept eight in real comfort; but, mates, four crowded her cockpit aft, and with six—why, the gang was always split up, two lounging forward, two at the wheel, and more than likely, two below. After all, shipmates make a cruise. The good cruiser should provide space for a group, each member of it entitled to a place to park his carcass without going solitary.

One of the finest of the new trends in design are these spacious deck living-rooms, so well done on many stock cruisers. The com-fortable Pullman-type berth doubles as a nook; the steering sta-tion is compact and free from gear handles, floor starter buttons, etc.; there is space for movable chairs, a radio, bridge table, a rug, and a tray of drinks; and the space is weathertight, screened, shaded, and decently lighted at night. They are the happiest com-binations of deck and below-decks that I have seen, and are prac-tical and possible even on very small craft. In no way are the more rugged operations of anchoring, docking, fueling, and sail han-dling mixed into the business of living and loafing on board.

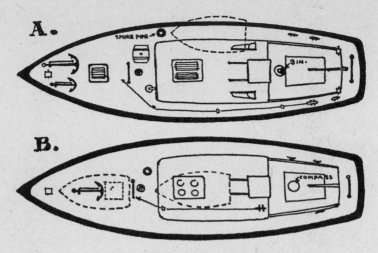

"Cleaning up" a deck

Note in B. how waterways have been cleared. Jib sheet has been rove over trunk top, stove iron moved inward, and dinghy carried forward or on trunk. Light boards have been placed on shrouds and compass placed under a deadlight in the cockpit floor; tiller now projects from below deck level. Cleats have been placed on washboard, one anchor stowed below, as has been the fog bell. Simplicity of deck arrangement is the path to safety at sea

Too many decks suffer from added features. These may be necessary, yet a little forethought might present a method of combining or building in or otherwise constructing the addition so that it does not clutter up the deck. Light boards need not be two separate assemblies, mounted like architectural features on the deckhouse; one anchor on deck is sufficient in most cases; the anchor cable need not lie coiled forever on the foredeck to foul the boat hook; nor do we need on deck Junior's snapper rig and the skipper's drying bathing-suit.

The whole approach to sane deck layout is the careful planning of it beforehand and not merely accepting what other design considerations leave you. Above all, it must be safe; free from hazards to life and limb.

VIII *Painting*

Where, or where, is the paint of yesteryear? You used about 20 per cent of it, mate—the rest used itself up during the long idle months when your fireside was a pleasanter place than the deck of your little hooker. So now, the March winds cold about your city-clad ankles and the pool of rain water above the plugged scupper still frozen solid, you've got to think about replacing it.

Here's the way to start a shipboard painting job:

1. Do all the engine work.
2. Do all the alterations.
3. Take every piece of gear off the boat.
4. Take off the winter cover.
5. Wash down everything in sight.
6. Sand and scrape everything that's to be painted.
7. Wash down again everything in sight.
8. Put back the winter cover.

THEN—*start painting inside!*

145

Inside Painting

Praise be the Captain of Fiddler's Green, the inside doesn't need repainting every season. Elbow grease and a cleaner will do as well as a new coat of paint or varnish. If any paint is needed, be very sure that the woodwork is thoroughly dry and that blisters and scale have been carefully removed. See that adequate ventilation is present to dry the paint or varnish with no chance of condensation spoiling the half-wet coat.

Be very careful yourself while painting inside. The combination of paint fumes and the old "shipmate" throwing out lovely gases along with its welcome heat can knock you out very quickly unless good cross-ventilation is assured. Start painting forward; *do everything* there; then move aft, doing *everything;* and finally close the companion doors on a complete inside job. Store all your paint and tools in a deck alcove, lock the companion, and give the key to your wife until you are ready to move your gear back on board. As sure as you're a yachtsman, you'll ruin that spiffy inside job if you thereafter use it for your paint locker, lunchroom, and general base of operations.

We shall not discuss "inside painting" too deeply because later remarks on exterior painting will also apply to it. However, there is one *must* about all marine painting that should be applied here as well as outside. Use—oh, please use—only MARINE PAINT. Any other kind, no matter who says so, no matter what pretty advertisements claim so—will POSITIVELY NOT DO.

Marine paint is chemically different from land paint. Land paint cannot possibly give the protection and durability of marine paint. Marine paint is more expensive, of course—but that's only because it's better paint and not because yachtsmen are being victimized by the "Paint Trust."

Now for the outside:

1. Take off the winter cover and dust.
2. Start on top.

3. Finish as completely as possible the highest parts first, remembering that paint drops always fall *down*.

For painting tools you will need an assortment of brushes as the backbone. All sizes, of course, not forgetting several size sash tools and a light camel's-hair lettering brush. The new bevel-cut sash tools are much superior to the old type, especially on panel work. The hook-scrapers with inexpensive replaceable blades are by far the best. They come in various widths, small enough for sash and corners and large enough for decks. A dull blade, by the way, can be touched up with a fine file or a rub on the oil stone, and it is not necessary to do as the manufacturer would like you to—to

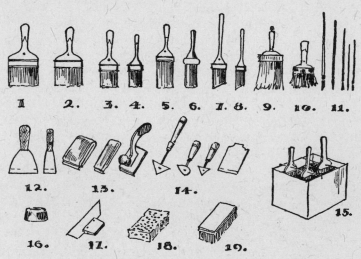

1. *4″ Brush.* 2. *3″ Brush.* 3. *2½″ Brush.* 4. *2″ Brush.* 5. *Long-bristled varnish brush.* 6. *Round or oval varnish brush.* 7–8. *Bevel-point sash tools.* 9. *Dusting brush.* 10. *Old brush for varnish remover.* 11. *Assorted flat and round lettering-brushes.* 12. *Putty knives.* 13. *Hook scrapers.* 14. *Knife scrapers.* 15. *Gallon can trimmed down to hang brushes on cross wires in turpentine.* 16. *Rubber anti-drip cup for painting overhead.* 17. *Sheet metal guard to put against glass when painting sash.* 18. *Cork or sponge-rubber sanding block.* 19. *Fine-wire scrub brush*

reach immediately into the magazine for a new blade. For the contoured molding to be cleaned, a cabinet scraper is necessary. An old saw-blade will do the trick, filed to the needed shape and the edge turned to make a slight hook. Almost as good, is glass. Lay a sheet out flat and tap it in the center with anything handy (except the bare fist)—you'll have practically every shape you'll ever need. Old brittle glass is better than new glass as it breaks with a cleaner edge. Bottles sometime break with nicely bevelled cuts ideal for reaching deep corners.

Sandpaper is commonly used for finish after scraping. Better than this and of much longer life and bite is emery cloth or garnet cloth.

For professional-quality varnish work use wet-and-dry paper, which is used *after* a finish dry paper. Place a small swatch under a sponge, soak both in water, and work over all sanded surfaces. Then dry the surface, and you can varnish within an hour, less if in sunlight.

Ordinary steel wool, even stainless-steel wool, has no place on the briny deep. Nobody can remove the final hairlike strand, and shortly rust will begin, and the job will be ruined. There are many grades of bronze wool available today; some brands are readily available in chain stores, and the same brands, now called by a fancy nautical name and packaged with a picture of a boat with a naked girl on the bow, are available in marine stores at a 300 per cent markup. (The girls are supposed to get your mind off the markup.) On this subject, 'ware iron filings, such as are made when sharpening tools, for the filings will surely cause rust stains.

Brushes will last a long time if properly cared for. Always hang them in a square can of turpentine or mineral spirits, boring a small hole in the brush handle through which a supporting wire, resting on the can edges, can be passed. Old, hard brushes can be brought back to life by immersing them in a paint remover, the formulae for which will be given later. After a certain age, brushes can be given a "haircut," i.e., can be trimmed with a scissors and "side-whiskers" removed or the blade squared up. Usually this trimming amounts to merely cutting off the short bristles which have become worn. After the season's use, brushes should be thoroughly cleaned, dried, and stored away with a few chips of camphor.

Preparation of Painting Surfaces

New work is always better if a coat of priming shellac is used to close pores and stop suction. Cheap orange shellac for painted work, white shellac for brightwork. After shellacking, a light sanding is necessary before proceeding. Build-up coats may then be applied, the first thinned (as recommended by the manufacture), with a sanding and dusting after each.

However, in the case of a repaint job, all loose, dead, or scaly paint must be removed by scraping. Let nothing convince you that covering over the checked or lifeless paint spot is treating the little ship right. If the surface is very far gone, a complete removal of paint is indicated. This may be done by burning off, using a blowtorch and a three-cornered scraper. Be careful not to apply heat to the extent of burning out the putty in topside seams or charring the small bungs over the fastenings. Woodwork adjacent to the surfaces to be burned may be protected by holding a sheet of metal (to which is riveted a wooden handle) over them. Burning off is usually confined to topsides or other smooth surfaces of great expanse. For the bulkhead, house, or brightwork, a paint or varnish remover is generally more satisfactory.

It is utterly important that sufficient time be allowed for the remover to penetrate. As ordinarily applied, it seldom "eats" into more than one coat per application. The professional lays it on as a jelly with a quivering motion of the brush, allowing as much as an hour for it to soften the paint. Drying can be prevented by covering with an old sail or erecting a screen to windward.

At the risk of being hated by the paint people, I am including here some paint and varnish removal formulae which ought to save some real money for the reader.

A solvent type (which is the same as commercial remover at $8 per gallon) is made as follows: Take two quarts of benzol and shave into it one to two pounds of ordinary household paraffin. When dissolved add one quart of denatured alcohol and one quart of acetone.

You will have slightly more than one gallon of the finest varnish or paint remover you can buy, and it will have cost you, if you have gone to a chemical supply-house and not the corner drugstore for the materials, less than $1. You will also have an explosive mixture—so keep it clear of flame and provide good ventilation of the space in which you use it.

The softened surface is easily removed by a handful of excelsior, scraping only after the last application has touched wood. A careful washing is then given with gasoline, alcohol, or diluted vinegar, and the raw wood built up as if it were new work.

Sometimes paint will flake off a certain spot year after year. Look for a wet condition behind or around it and cure it before painting again. Certain woods such as fir, yellow or sap pine, and cypress do not always offer a bond to paint and will peel constantly. The only way in which to overcome this is to burn the surface slightly with a torch, removing the flame as the wood commences to char. Sand over and build up with a heavy shellac coat.

It is very important in marine painting to paint all surfaces, even though they are not seen. Not only does this prevent warping by closing both sides of a board or plank to the dampness but also, and especially in the care of oak, it prevents the staining of surrounding paint work. The purple and gray streaks so often seen festooned from the rail are usually due to the back side of the rail being set unpainted or uncoated.

Finishing Coats

First coats of paint should always be flat, as flat paint has a base of oil and turpentine and will cause the pigment to penetrate and adhere in cracks and crevices better than a glossy paint with a varnish base. Remember, too, to sand lightly and dust well between each coat. A good painter can always be recognized because he has two brushes, one his paint brush and the other a dusting brush. During the build-up coats it will be necessary to putty cracks, nail holes, and defects. The best putty for marine use is made of half white-lead and half whiting. For large spots or spots in which you would ordinarily use one of the commercial compounds of the plastic-wood types, add litharge to white lead in oil. Such a putty will dry quickly, become very hard, and can be sanded nicely. For puttying brightwork, color should be added to either of these putties, of course. It is of the utmost importance that all crevices and cracks to be puttied be thoroughly dry. If there is any doubt about this, due possibly to a recent storm, touch the spot lightly with a blowtorch. Putty should be applied only after the hole or crack has been payed, that is, painted, so that the raw wood will not soon draw the oil from the putty and cause drying and resultant crumbling.

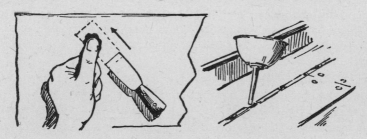

Professional puttying

Use the palm of the left hand as a magazine for a "sausage" of putty, feeding it between thumb and forefinger and pressing it firmly in the crack. Cut off with a quick motion of the knife. If the hands are first powdered with whiting the putty will not stick to them

Filling open deck seams with linseed oil to permanently swell them

The resins have made possible some very fine putties and fillers. All are two-part mixes; the easiest, because they require no actual weighing, are those known loosely as "fifty-fifty," meaning equal parts of resin and hardener by bulk and sight. Any epoxy, which is the general name of the type, can be made into a putty by adding bulk. For large seams, or deep gouges, use fine sawdust. Teak, mahogany, and fruitwood sawdusts are best and will not stain as oak or sap-pine sawdust might. For finer fillings, use talc; a cheap bath talc is as good as any.

Sometimes wood will "bleed" through paint, showing stains around sap pockets and heartwood. Common or "punkin" pine is a usual offender. Shellac or any alcohol-base pigment will serve as treatment, and a thin epoxy wash is even better. These areas should be treated *before* sealing or painting if possible.

The question of flat or gloss paint is one which the boatowner must decide for himself. A hard or gloss paint will give much more wear than a flat paint, and there can be no question about its use on decks and floors. However, gloss paint will build up very quickly with each seasonal painting and soon begin to crazy-check, and nothing short of a burning off will reduce it to a proper surface for further painting. Gloss paint looks good, washes nicely, but is not a most practical finish for the boatman doing his own work.

Flat paint is softened during the summer washing down of a boat. Much of the actual paint will chalk off, and it takes a great many years for it to build up into a thickness that will necessitate removal. It has the further advantage of being very easy to touch up in case of the accidental bump by the dinghy or a piece of floating driftwood. On the other hand, it is a dead, flat, uninteresting surface, unrelieved by the "depth" of the gloss paint. The situation resolves itself down into the question of, look swell—and burn off frequently; or, look flat—and wash off.

There are semi-gloss paints on the market which are probably the sensible answer to the question for the average man. If, in the spring, the paint is washed off thoroughly with a strong solution of washing powder (Gold Dust is best) and the surface sanded immediately, much of the paint will have been removed and a good surface prepared for the new coats.

When painting topsides, cabin trunks, and the like, a neater and even a quicker job can be obtained by removing all the hardware and fittings rather than by cutting around them. Not only is this the professional way of doing it, but also it affords the opportunity of examining for rot or weakened fastenings.

The deck, as has been stated, should be given a hard varnish-base paint. If it is canvassed and has cracked in a few spots, prime it over with a flat paint, as the base of this is oil which will flow into and fill the small cracks rather than bridge them as a varnish paint will. The deck which is really badly checked should be treated with paint remover. However, do not attempt to remove *all* of the paint from it. This will be next to impossible to do without tearing the canvas, and the paint remover will loosen the bonding of the canvas to the wooden deck beneath.

Some boatmen attempt to give their decks anti-slip qualities. I have seen decks painted with a mixture of paint and powdered pumice. This seems to me to dull the paint considerably, and I like better the practice of painting as usual and then sprinkling with fine sand from a large-size salt shaker.

Now to the brightwork. Wood which is to be varnished, and depends for its attractiveness upon the natural grain and color, generally needs a certain amount of toning. This is best done by using an oil stain directly on the raw wood. The staining necessary on a natural-finish job would consist of merely evening the various tones found. Mahogany can be so evened by applying mixtures of varying strengths made up of small quantities of water into which ordinary household lye (chloride of lime) has been dissolved. Dark spots in both mahogany and oak can be lightened by bleaching with oxalic acid, ten cents' worth in water being sufficient for the twenty-five footer. A tablespoonful to a pint of water makes about the right strength. Bleaching is best accomplished, not by strong acid solutions, but by several applications.

Only after the woodwork looks even and uniform in the "raw" should varnish be applied. The modern quick-drying or four-hour varnishes are entirely satisfactory providing they are a marine spar varnish. Varnish should not be thinned, but applied as found in the can. The success of the work is dependent upon brushing the varnish out well. When dry, sand and brush and brush and brush before the next coat. At least four coats will be needed to make a presentable job of the new work.

A good stain for mahogany is made of dry burnt sienna in turpentine, to which is added a dash of oil and dryers. This is liberally painted on, allowed to set for thirty minutes, and then rubbed off with a coarse material—burlap, old canvas, or carpet swatches. Philippine mahogany needs a penetrating stain as this wood is inclined to bleach very rapidly. A stain of pure aniline dye penetrates better than oil stain. Better yet is to mix the color (a shade darker than you wish it to finally be) with the filler. In this way the open pores are both filled and colored, and a very uniform color is possible. Use color ground in oil for this (or mix an oil color from dry powder yourself); do not add dry color directly to the filler. Allow to set for about fifteen minutes (depending upon the drying character of the wind and sun on that particular day) and rub off with coarse cloth, *across the grain.*

A revarnish job will take at least two coats of unthinned varnish. Before applying it, wash the old work thoroughly with a strong washing-powder solution and sand while wet. This will take a lot of the old surface off and leave almost a hand-rubbed base to build on.

If you are one of the fortunate owners who finds his boat equipped with teak decks, for goodness sakes, don't varnish them. Teak has enough natural oil to outlast your fastenings. In these days when holystoning is unpopular, pine decks are often varnished and should be treated exactly like other bright wood. If the decks are leaky they will, of course, need reputtying. A good stunt for curing leaky decks is to squirt into the cracks with an oilcan quantities of linseed oil. This causes swelling and consequent tightness and is not apt to dry out if varnish is immediately applied.

Teak should appear white and bleached in most cases. This is achieved by elbow application of a "sogee" made of Clorox, a powerful abrasive cleanser (such as "Comet," "Dutch," etc.), and water and worked with a pad of bronze wool. If you later want dark teak, treat with one of the penetrants, "Woodlife" being one of the very best. Under no circumstances apply an oil or a wax.

Don't forget while the varnish mood is on you, the spars, binnacle box, flagpole, and all the small gear which is too often left until the moment of launching.

This leaves very little unpainted other than the bottom of our ship. Do here the nastiest jobs first, the centerboard and trunk, if you have one, all around the rudder even if it means unshipping it, and the metal keel. Most keels become pitted, offering a very rough surface that materially reduces speed. This can be faired up by applying a trowel cement to the rough surface or, in extreme cases, by chipping with a chipping hammer. After the metal surface has been built up, sand it smooth and apply several coats of heavy red lead. If the keel is iron, under no circumstances apply copper paint directly to it, as this causes electrolysis, which is one of the reasons your iron keel is pitted in the first place.

A trowel cement, by the way, can be made as follows: Dry mix one ounce of powdered sal ammoniac and sixteen ounces of cast iron filings or borings. Mix with water to a thick paste and let stand several hours. Old recipes quaintly suggest that you can also add one-half-ounce of flower of brimstone and some sludge from a grindstone trough. However, the first three elements mentioned are sufficient in these grindstoneless days.

Proper preparation of the underwater surfaces should have commenced upon hauling out. At that time an old broom and a stream of fresh water would have taken off the accumulation of grass, barnacles, mussels, and other flora and fauna which you have neglected to do. Thus, your first bottom-job will consist of a pleasant half day of scraping, sanding, and coughing. The coughing, and possibly a mild case of poisoning, can be prevented by attacking the copper paint with a dampened handkerchief tied over your mouth and nose.

Racing or cruising, the bottom should be prepared just as carefully as any other part of the boat. Sand very smooth and brush off well. We are drawing close to two great and perennial arguments of the rocking-chair fleet. I'll not attempt to answer them but merely present the facts of both sides.

Number 1: Should the bottom be coated first with a lead paint? I personally believe "No." The little teredos, previously mentioned, wax fat and woolly on the linseed oil contained in lead paint. I personally see no reason to go out of my way to make the bottom of my boat more attractive to them. On the other hand, boatmen will point out that a good coat of lead paint will form a smooth surface for the copper paint. This may be so, though it is entirely possible to prepare the raw wood itself so as to present a smooth under surface even in the 100 per cent racing craft. Being essentially a cruising man, my own boats will never be painted underwater with anything but copper paint. I would use it even in fresh water. A river or lake boat, while hardly a desirable meal for frogs, salamanders, and crawdads, will gather a certain amount of vegetable growth on any but the copper bottom.

I have always made it a practice to paint everything below the water line, even the lovely, shining propeller, which seems to lure barnacles especially.

Number 2: What color copper paint is best? This is another of the great unanswered questions of the rocking-chair fleet. From personal experience I believe that the fisherman brown as first choice, or one of the reds as second, gives the fullest and longest protection to the bottom. I must immediately qualify this by saying that my sailing waters are 75 per cent on the coast of Maine with occasional runs farther eastward or up a brackish river. Fisherman brown may not be the best for St. Petersburg, Florida; Santa Barbara, California; or Newark Bay. But once again, I would use as my gauge the color and type of copper paint used by the local fishermen and commercial boats. You may be sure that the nature of their businesses have long ago sent them to the best bottom-paint for that particular locality.

There is only one green bottom-paint I know of which gives absolutely positive protection against barnacles and grass, and that is the paint into which has been mixed mercury. It costs up to $60 a gallon but covers very well and will positively (at least where I sail) last a full season. Considering the cost of a midseason hauling-out and a scrape and repaint job on the bottom, it is probably worth the high price charged.

Most boats look better for the addition of a boot top. Good combinations are red above green or green above red, or black above either. A black boot top should be narrower than a colored one, and it looks especially good if it is separated from the bottom color by a narrow white stripe. Boot tops should be painted with engine enamel, as this type of paint best resists the gasoline and oil films too often found upon our cruising waters.

The racing-bottom paint is different from the cruising-bottom paint. Here anti-fouling qualities are less important, and the racing skipper strives for a smooth, hard bottom. Such a bottom must be built up very carefully and painstakingly. Anywhere from two

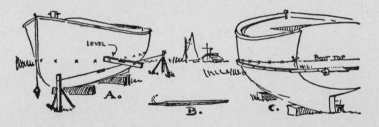

Springing water lines

A. Set up a line parallel to the boat, its ends level with the extreme marks of the water line desired. Now, with a carpenter's level, aided at bow and stern by a straight edge, transfer the levels of the line to the hull, marking the spots with a pencil. Tack a light batten along the marks, fairing up as you tack. Then score deeply with a backsaw or a hooked file (B.) along the top edge of the batten. The boat must be first plumbed, of course, using a plumb bob dropped from the stem head. A boot top with a sweep averaging between water line and sheer is made by letting a heavy string fall naturally into a fair unbroken sweep from the bow and stern boot-top marks. It is then spotted very carefully with a pencil and the batten laid to the marks. Score in as above to five coats will be required, with a week's drying between each, as well as a thorough sanding and glassing down. The final coat should leave the hull slippery, hard, and unbroken; just as fine to the touch and the eye as a piece of hand-rubbed period furniture. The racing boat must be frequently hauled up during the season, its bottom washed off and groomed.

A word about when to paint bottoms. The ideal plan is to put one coat on in the fall after careful preparation of the bottom and the last coat a few hours before the spring launching. The vehicle in copper will thus not set up hard and will afford longer protection. Do not paint and immediately launch as an oil scum will rise from the almost liquid paint and most certainly will discolor your topsides.

Most boats have some metal parts which need paint. The secret in painting metal is twofold. Number 1 is to use an enamel made especially for the purpose. Number 2 is to be absolutely sure that the metal to be painted is free of grease or oil of any kind. Engine enamels, so called, are best applied with a camel's-hair brush.

Any paint required to stick to metal, even bare metal, should have a base of fish oil rather than of mineral oil. It is available under various trade names, often comes in spray cans, usually is colorless, and is claimed to inhibit rust—which it does. But do not confuse this with removing rust. That must be done by mechanical means using wire brushes, bronze wool, files, sanding papers, etc.

Almost all professional yacht-painters use seal or dado brown on yacht fittings. Aluminum paint is the mark of the amateur, and with the possible exception of the anchors, has no place on the trim yacht. Touches of color are permissible and desirable, but they should not be allowed to approach the color schemes of the Greek sponge boats. A dash of red inside a cowl ventilator or a porthole or on the port light-board enlivens the color scheme.

I am aware that color is extensively used on the modern yacht. Unfortunately not all colors are equally successful. The reason that most yachts are combinations of white, buff, and varnish is because these colors have been found by years of experience to stand up the best. Any dark color, and most certainly black, absorbs a great amount of sun heat instead of deflecting it as the light colors do and thereby causes excessive drying of the wood beneath. Black-hulled boats are often seen which show every seam, plank, and fastening because of this. If you must have a black-hulled boat, be certain that every coat from the prime coat on is black and that the seam putty is black, and remember that you will need frequent midseason touching up.

Colors running into the blues, such as the ultramarine of topsides or the blue-green of decks, bleach very quickly and do not weather well. This is an inherent fault of the blues, and not even the automobile manufacturers have been able to manufacture a completely satisfactory blue or green.

Small boats should take the color scheme from the mother ship, the only exception being the varnished skiff. A varnished small-boat appears much smaller than the same size boat which has been painted. The varnished small-boat when carried on davits or on deck seems to take its place as an accessory and to blend with other above-the-rail features better than the painted tender.

Trimmings

Along with Dewey's confection fleet of the Spanish-American War, gold leaf, scrollwork, and gingerbread have fortunately disappeared from our yachts. About the only gilded features of present-day boats are the occasionally seen nameboards with incised gilded letters or the long sheer arrow on de luxe models. Maintenance of such "fancy work" is a tiring chore. Real gold leaf, after being applied, should be protected by thin coats of Egyptian lacquer. Radiator bronze or gold powders will not serve on shipboard. Indeed, from a few yards off there is very little discernible difference between gold and a good yellow-orange enamel, and most boatmen so treat their gilt work.

However, if you must gold leaf, purchase the modern type which is attached to tissue. Handling it with a dry brush, even indoors, is a job for the master craftsman only. Before applying the gold leaf size (which is slow-drying Venetian varnish) the neighboring surfaces should be coated with whiting, or better yet, a cheap talcum powder. This will prevent the leaf from sticking to adjacent surfaces. Professionals use a color in the size to give the gold various casts. Bright yellow is best for yacht work. Green will tint the gold to a thin brassy color, red to a bronze color, and brown or blue to "antique" colors. For very fine gold leaf work a burnishing pencil, made of smooth rounded onyx, is used to flow the leaf together after laying. This is hardly necessary for yacht work except possibly on the nameboard or some interior feature.

Many a fine-appearing ship has been spoiled by careless lettering. If you can hand letter, by all means do so. However, if you're one of the thousands who cannot, purchase ready-cut metal letters. These are very expensive in bronze, and real money can be saved by purchasing house number letters of aluminum at about one tenth of the cost. These should be roughened with sandpaper and painted with two or three coats of engine enamel before being applied to the transom, bows, or nameboards. Don't forget, while painting, to do the screwheads.

The annual cutting around and repainting of letters can be saved by mounting them on a varnished or painted backboard which is removed from the boat during the winter months.

Any painting job depends a great deal upon painting weather and painting mood.

Before starting any painting job, get a weather prediction for the next forty-eight hours. Unless a temperature of 50 degrees or above with clear skies is promised, it would be folly to tackle any exterior painting. Varnishing, especially, needs clear skies and fairly warm temperatures. One of the best temperature indicators is the paint or varnish itself. If it flows freely and spreads without pull, it may be applied. The practice of warming paint by setting the can in a container of hot water does very little good as it is chilled immediately upon touching the cold surface to be painted. Thinning down may help somewhat; remember to use linseed oils for enamels and turpentine for flat paints and varnishes.

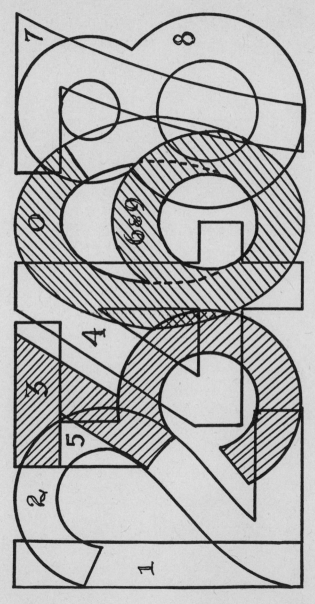

Figures are the required three-inch height

Watch the sun as you paint, following it around the boat. It will do much to warm the surface even on a cold day. Nightfall often brings a heavy dew, ruinous to newly applied paint, so it is unwise to paint or varnish much after 3 P.M. Decks, roofs, or cockpit floors should certainly be done in the morning.

There is probably no job around a boat requiring more time or patience than painting. It is probably a mistake to tackle an extensive paint job too early in the season. The old hooker looks good after a winter away from her, and it is natural that you will want to see something done. A day spent at painting will seem almost discouraging when measured in terms of accomplishment. Let, rather, these first week ends be for lusty bouts with real jobs of work: sandpapering, scrubbing, things that get you tired and show immediate, satisfying results. The painting mood will come upon you later when some of the early energy has been worked off. And this is the time to paint! No matter how fine the surface or how excellent the paint—it's the painter alone, who by his care and patience, turns out the professional-looking job.

IX *Interior Accommodations*

In another chapter I condemn the rubber boat. For the purposes of this one, I wish I had it back. In no boat but a rubber one can designer or builder fit in all he wants in the way of interior accommodations. Sleep, eat, lounge, wash, keep cool, keep warm, have guests, cruise offshore—there never was a vessel into which the physical requisites of human demands afloat fitted with space left over. Every interior design has been a complex—and usually very clever—compromise between what we want and what we can get within the limitations of that particular hull-size.

Key factors limiting us, in addition to length, width, and height, are mast locations, power plant locations, tank sizes and locations, deck arrangement, and this thing which amateurs are prone to utterly ignore: trim. In the space left we can fit all we want to in the way of furniture. And somehow, we do it. No man familiar with small boats can fail to marvel at the ingenuity displayed in interior layouts of yachts. But there is one great difference between the interior layout of the professional and the lay designer or builder. The professional accepts the limitations of mast locations, tanks, trim, headroom, etc., as inherent in that design. These things are located where they are as a result of careful calculations and no consideration is great enough to materially change their locations without a complete re-design.

We amateurs may snort, "Huh! A thirty-two footer and not even full headroom!" The reason for that particular vessel's not having full headroom is not because the designer can't do it (he's put full headroom in eighteen-footers!), but because to do so in that particular boat he would have to sacrifice speed, usefulness, safety, or some other factor more vital to the design than headroom. It is the amateur who raises topsides, trunks, loads on ballast, moves masts, and whatnot to achieve his pet idea of below-decks arrangements.

So, in planning the interior layout, the approach must be sane. It will always be a compromise, with the interior designer yielding much more than the hull designer. Naturally, complete design can be a happy compromise. Headroom can be achieved in even the very small boat, providing that headroom has been ever present in the mind of the designer—long, in fact, before he has put a line on paper. To some extent, all designers, regardless of their professional status, attack the bare interior as a space with utterly fixed dimensions and features. Into this, striving to maintain certain standards of interior comfort and usefulness, they fit the necessary furniture, much as a jigsaw puzzle is assembled.

This furniture has certain minimum standards of size and usefulness which must be present for it to be useful at all. Lacking these standards it might be, in many cases, better to omit the feature altogether and thus raise the usefulness of other features by alloting them more room, weight allowance, etc. The icebox which will not hold ice for twenty-four hours at least is a *waste of space;* it is not something which justifies crowding some other bunk, locker, or galley dresser.

So, in this chapter, let us concern ourselves with these standards. From the layout angle, we are most concerned with standards of size: How much of our small space is this feature going to occupy. A berth takes up exactly so much space; we cannot change the size without sacrificing comfort, usefulness, or both. However, we can—and here is where so many interior layouts

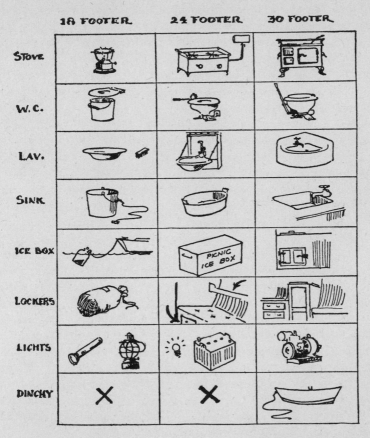

	18 FOOTER	24 FOOTER	30 FOOTER
STOVE			
W.C.			
LAV.			
SINK			
ICE BOX		PICNIC ICE BOX	
LOCKERS			
LIGHTS			
DINGHY	X	X	

become amazingly ingenious—double; that is, by careful designing and building, give the berth other uses in addition to its primary use as a sleeping bed. Thus, it is common, on smaller vessels, to consider the berth as a daytime settee, a locker, a working space, and possibly a life-preserver cushion as well!

In practice, the plan and a few cross sections of the boat are drawn to a scale, one-half inch being convenient. Then the furniture required is cut out of stiff paper, also to the same scale. The designer now simply plays house, arranging and rearranging the cutouts to his choice but NEVER reducing them in governing dimensions merely to fit into some nook or cranny. He will soon find that his interior layout essentially resembles all other layouts for an equal water-line length and that his own pet ideas are confined to this doubling, to decoration, and to special treatment of some individual feature, and not to the treatment of the interior as a whole.

To go haywire here, to disregard this tendency for your boat to lay itself out like all others of her size, is to court disaster. Layout is a result of trial and error and much experience; you may be sure that thousands have tried to be different before, but you will notice that the concerns who make their profits designing and building boats stick pretty close to standard time-and-sea-tried layouts. Only occasionally does some new feature become popular and permit basic interior layout changes. Recently, we have had the doghouse on small auxiliaries and the Pullman-type berth on both sail and power vessels; and even more lately, that abomination: the deckhouse galley. Just why, on a sixty-thousand-dollar boat, you have to sit in the kitchen while you wine or dine, surrounded by dirty dishes, used pots, and a sinkful of tomato rinds, I don't know. I suppose it does conserve space of a kind—but unless you wash dishes and pick up the galley before I sit down to your meal, please don't invite me aboard.

None are new in the sense that they are inventions. It is merely that ideas have caught on and become popular; or at least the advertising which introduced them has been successful to the point of making us want these features.

To seriously diverge from these standards of layout and treatment is to steal from yourself. I have never heard of one of these personally designed interiors bringing a premium on the used boat market. I have heard of their materially contributing to low resale prices; the new owner counting it as a negative, not a positive, feature. The only possible excuse for serious divergence is the case of the man who requires some very special purpose of his ship. Thus, the world-girdlers, or even the North Atlantic cruisers, must arrange interiors in such a manner that sufficient stores and

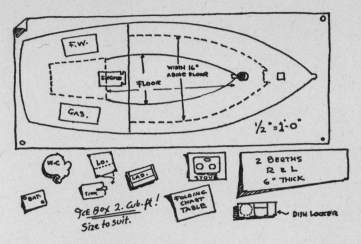

Cardboard cutouts of interior features for arrangement on bare plan

fuel can be carried, and this arrangement may be at the expense of orthodox layout, perhaps even of personal comfort.

Headroom, Leg Room and Elbowroom

"Has she got full headroom?"

"You bet," the seller states proudly.

"Ouch! My head!"

"Hey, not there! Come aft, under the companion slide."

Mates, that's not full headroom. That's full headroom under the companion slide, and you can have it. You can get that kind of headroom on a fourteen-footer by merely opening the slide.

Full headroom is six feet; not a millimeter less, and more if you don't want to be a liar to a tall man. It is six feet under the deck beams and carlings in any part of the ship in which you might have to stand up. Nothing can change this. Full headroom gives comfort, freedom, and safety. There is no dimension under six feet which will provide these until that dimension is such that it forces a man definitely to sit and thereafter move about the cabin by

Headroom

sliding on his fanny. I deplore, I hate, I loathe these cabins with 5′6″ headroom or thereabouts. A week end spent in one of them always leaves me with bumps on my head, a hollow chest from hanging my arms apelike, and a general all-gone feeling. Not a few skippers—this is the truth—with such headroom wear hard hats and derbies to protect the head. I was once on a boat which had her deck beam, immediately forward of the slide, padded with sponge rubber. No alleged headroom should make such measures necessary.

The minimum headroom practical is 3′ 9″. Anything under this becomes cruel. The ideal height for the boat with less than six feet headroom is about 4′ 9″. This height is definitely a sit-down height, and there is no inclination to want to attempt a normal walk or step. In the final analysis, these low headrooms are fixed not by walking-height requirements but by sitting-height requirements, and this in turn is determined by the height of settees and bunks. A normal person needs about thirty-nine inches in which to sit straight. While this is seldom possible under the main deck, usually berths are wide enough to afford such a sitting space over their inboard edges. When lounging or slouching, even less room is required; and a man can be quite comfortable under the waterways when sprawled. However, when sprawling, leg room becomes more important; the old feet have got to extend into some space. The secret of giving leg room, curiously enough, is correct design of the seats or settees. The low seat should be wide and the high seat less wide, and the legs will fall into natural comfortable positions. Quite often it is possible to overhang the berth several inches, making the floor space wider than the space between berth edges. This gives footroom both while sitting and while moving about.

The average person requires about twenty-four inches in width when sitting straight, more at table when arms must be used. Sprawled, this requirement increases to thirty-six inches or even more. For walking erect, openings should be a minimum of twenty-two inches wide; twenty-eight inches sliding through, as is necessary in the low-headroom cabin.

Tables, dressers, stove work-tops need special attention in the "sitting room" interior. Generally their height should be figured by actually taking a position which you would normally use in working at that piece of furniture and without regard to height of the top from the floor. Actually, it will work out to be about the distance from the chin if one were working at the same table while standing.

These are seemingly small items, yet they are exactly what makes a small boat comfortable or uncomfortable. The movements involved in the various below-decks activities in all weathers, with slides and hatches closed, should be carefully studied. Without too much hitching everything should be at arms reach. Perhaps the keynote of success is the same as for everything on shipboard—keep the layout utterly simple.

Too many small-boat layouts suffer from attempts to ape shore standards. There is no real need for dividing the interior into small spaces, alleged staterooms, etc., by bulkheads and partitions. Privacy, such as provided by the plaster walls of your home, simply cannot be gained on even a large vessel. Indeed, this privacy, save in the matter of the W.C. (Larry, Billy, or John), isn't even required until it's time to turn in. Yet, for all the waking hours, the ship's company must govern its movements by the limitations set by night arrangements. How silly to design a cruiser to sleep eight when four will crowd her dining table! But it has been done—plenty.

Study the published interior layouts of William Hand. Here is a past master at handling interiors. You will be instantly impressed by the simplicity of arrangement in all his designs. Analyzing them, you will find an amazing amount of sensible design, possible only for a designer who has himself cruised extensively. There is one other feature in good interior designs to bring to note. That is the effort the professional designer makes to give the *feeling* of room without actually having it in so many inches. He does this mainly by eliminating bulkheads, by retaining a large free ceiling area (for example by stopping his lockers *short* of actual framing to the ceiling), and by providing as much natural light as possible. But more of this later.

Sleeping

No matter what the shape or width of the berth, it should not be less than 6′ 2″ long. You yourself may be but 5′ 6″ and fit it quite comfortably, but you must not forget that the next buyer may be a six-footer. He would have to turn your boat down if he couldn't sleep in her berths.

No permanent berth should be less than twenty-six inches at the head, nor should it taper to less than eighteen inches at the foot. Thirty inches wide the full length makes a comfortable single berth, allow forty-six to fifty inches for the double berth. The pipe berth perforce must often be narrower. However, the curse can be taken from it by overlaying it with a sleeping pad and arranging its hinges so that the outboard edge comes several or more inches from the topside ceiling. This makes it unnecessary to snuggle between the hard cold pipe frame and gives a trifle more of welcome shoulder and hip room.

Distance between upper and lower berths and between upper berths and the roof should never be less than twenty-four inches. Tradition, or possibly Pullman car practice, has taken such a firm grip upon our standards of boat design that the berth which sleeps the occupant with his head aft is almost taboo. There is no

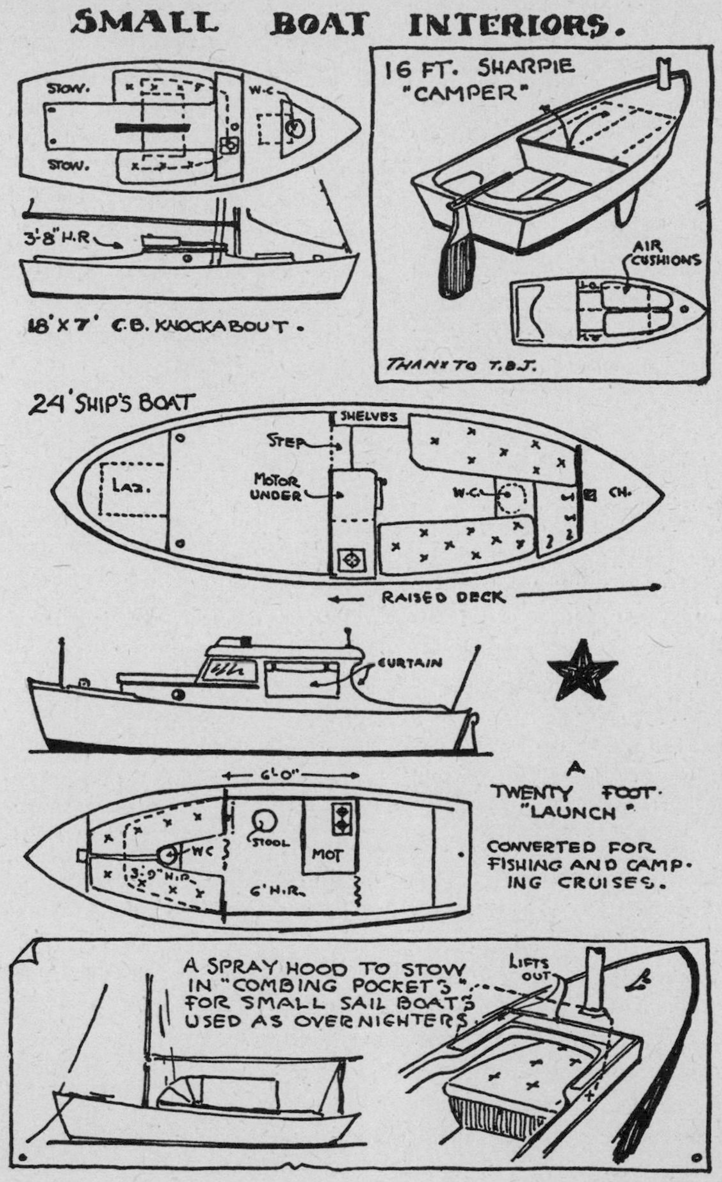

SMALL BOAT INTERIORS.

STOW.   W-C   STOW.

3'-8" H.R.

18' X 7' C.B. KNOCKABOUT.

16 FT. SHARPIE "CAMPER"

AIR CUSHIONS

THANX TO T.B.J.

24' SHIP'S BOAT

LAZ.   MOTOR UNDER   STEP   SHELVES   W-C   CH.

← RAISED DECK →

CURTAIN

A
TWENTY FOOT.
"LAUNCH"

CONVERTED FOR
FISHING AND CAMP-
ING CRUISES.

← 6'-0" →

WC   STOOL   MOT
3'-9" H.R.   6' H.R.

A SPRAY HOOD TO STOW
IN "COMBING POCKETS"
FOR SMALL SAIL BOATS
USED AS OVERNIGHTERS.

LIFTS OUT

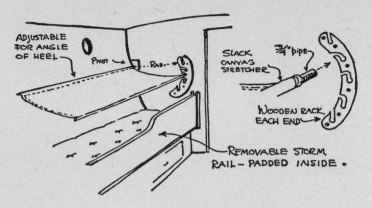

Deep-water bunks

real reason for this since the forward motion of most boats is
never felt by the sleeper. The average small-boat layout permits
bunks with wide stern ends, and one ought to take advantage of
this. Examples are the forward staterooms and the transoms in
little week-enders. However, great care should be taken to have
such berths level, or better yet, slightly high on the after end. We
have a similar taboo on the thwartship berth, with some reason in
this case. Certainly for the sea cruiser such a berth is not practical,
for the motion is felt distinctly when running in a choppy sea or
ground swell. But for ordinary use—most of us anchor at night—
there is nothing seriously wrong with it. Actually, however, there
is no space saving to the thwartship berth arrangement, and a
little ingenuity will usually place fore-and-aft berths in the same
space.

Generally, the transom berth does not make a comfortable seat.
It is too wide, affording no back support. Remedial steps are these
clever arrangements of upper berth which serves as a back and
forms a useful bedding bin behind it (see sketch). If there is
space for it, the best arrangement is certainly a separate folding
berth, built to comfortable dimensions and specifications. The
transom can then be designed as a comfortable seat without com-

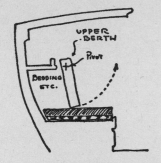 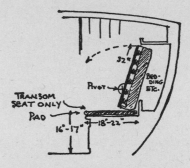

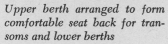

Upper berth arranged to form comfortable seat back for transoms and lower berths	*A "luxury" berth. Can be made up and covers strapped down for instant use*

promise. To be comfortable as a seat the following proportions should be maintained:

SEAT TO FLOOR	DEPTH OF SEAT
18″	18″
16″	19″
14″	21″
12″	24″
10″	27″

The depth of the seat varies somewhat according to the rake of the back, becoming less if the back slants excessively. All seats become more comfortable if they are an inch or so lower in the back than in the front, making for snugness. A fine solution of converting a comfortable seat into a comfortable berth is to arrange an extension slide the same width as the seat bottom. Over this lay the seat cushion which rests doubled on the seat during daytime use.

One of the most uncomfortable nights I ever spent afloat was in a hammock. Undoubtedly British sailors, who regularly sleep in hammocks, would find a conventional bed just as uncomfortable. There is nothing against the hammock; it certainly is a space saver

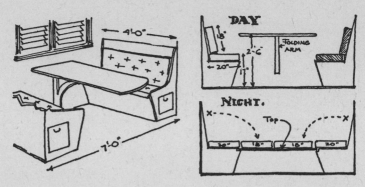

The Pullman Berth

and possibly a self-trimming bunk at sea, but it demands too radical an upset of normal sleeping habits for use by yachtsmen. Indeed, the whole key to comfortable and healthful sleep aboard our small boats is just this—keep shipboard sleeping arrangements as nearly as possible similar to those you consider best on land.

Cooking

Fifteen years ago, I would have placed cooking before sleeping on this list of interior accommodations because then it would have been more important. So, if you do not creak from mildew, rust, and dry rot as I do, switch 'em around. They are both important and essential to shipboard life and deserve the very best of careful thought.

Cooking, as a subject, is divided into two parts: keeping things cold and making things hot. And the means to achieve this is related to the basic subject of "power." What power is available on your ship? It sould be silly to have an alcohol stove, a gas hot-water heater, an electric refrigerator, and an a.c. generator to charge the batteries. Far better would be to have and use a single power source for all power demands. Thus the correct stove for your vessel, even though you or your first mate *like* L.P. gas for cooking, may be electric since you may also have a generator. But before we get into the interesting possibilities, let us discuss the relative merits of the several types used on small craft.

Standards for stoves start at safety. Electricity is safest, bottled gas follows, kerosene is next, then alcohol, and last is gasoline. Most stove accidents are not caused by failure of the stove but by carelessness in filling or in locating the fuel tank. By all means study carefully the procedure necessary to refuel, and locate tanks accordingly—in the next compartment or on deck, if at all possible!

The next most important consideration is that the stove be equipped with pot rails. This is necessary, even at anchor, as the wake of passing boats is often violent enough to send pots adrift. At sea, the pot rails must be fitted with clamps to hold the utensil securely on the stove. Naturally, the stove itself must be securely bolted down, preferably with through bolts and into a framing member rather than into a shelf or top. Iron stoves, such as the "Shipmate," are secured with turnbuckles from the end rings to the *frame* of the vessel as well as with screw fastenings in the legs.

Every stove space should be guarded by a handy fire extinguisher, hung between the *stove and the nearest exit.* The space itself should be lined with sheet metal or sheet asbestos, or in the case of a coal or wood stove, with both. Nearby should be a ventilator to carry off fumes and heat, and it might well be one of the power exhaust type.

The galley, of which the stove is the center, must be very carefully laid out. Unfortunately, most are not. Their biggest lack is adequate working space. After all, covering the stove and the sink with a pretty mahogany board does not make working space. Both these fixtures are in constant use during the preparation of a meal, and with boards removed, can hardly be counted as useful space.

The preparation of a decent meal, served decently (on plates, sailor, and we drink from cups, not cans or bottles, and still figure

GALLEY GEAR

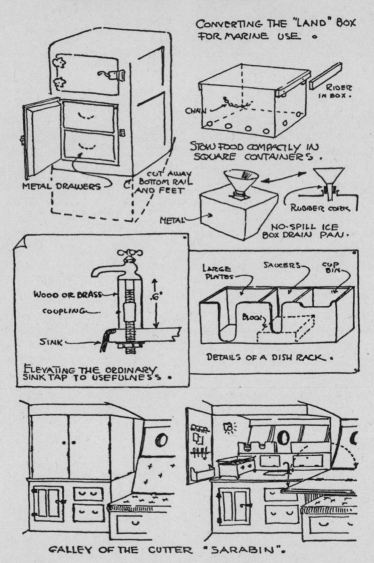

CONVERTING THE "LAND" BOX FOR MARINE USE.

CHAIN

RIDER IN BOX.

STOW FOOD COMPACTLY IN SQUARE CONTAINERS.

RUBBER CORK

METAL

NO-SPILL ICE BOX DRAIN PAN.

METAL DRAWERS

CUT AWAY BOTTOM RAIL AND FEET

WOOD OR BRASS COUPLING

SINK

ELEVATING THE ORDINARY SINK TAP TO USEFULNESS.

LARGE PLATES   SAUCERS   CUP BIN

BLOCK

DETAILS OF A DISH RACK.

GALLEY OF THE CUTTER "SARABIN".

GALLEY GEAR.

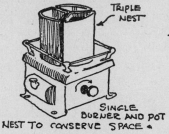

TRIPLE NEST

SINGLE BURNER AND POT

NEST TO CONSERVE SPACE.

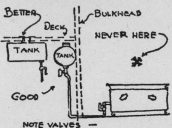

BETTER

DECK

BULKHEAD

NEVER HERE

TANK

TANK

GOOD

NOTE VALVES —

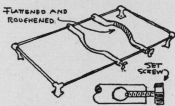

FLATTENED AND ROUGHENED

SET SCREW

POT DOGS FOR THE COMMON MARINE STOVE.

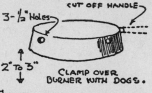

CUT OFF HANDLE

3-½" HOLES

2" TO 3"

CLAMP OVER BURNER WITH DOGS.

SMALL CABIN HEATER FROM A CAST IRON SKILLET.

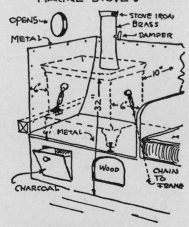

OPENS

METAL

STOVE IRON

BRASS

DAMPER

10"

32

6"

METAL

WOOD

CHARCOAL

CHAIN TO FRAME

THE WOOD STOVE
NOTE FASTENINGS BY THROUGH BOLTS AND TURNBUCKLES TO FRAME MEMBERS.

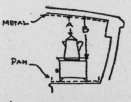

METAL

A

B

PAN

"A" AT LEAST 9"
"B" AT LEAST 18"

ALC.

RIGHT

WRONG

CARRYING FUEL.

we're pretty rugged!) requires, exclusive of stove and sink space, about four square feet. If a drop board can be arranged, adding to this area, so much the better. The sink is useless until it reaches dimensions large enough to accommodate dishes for washing and has enough depth to permit the filling of ordinary vessels from its spout. As a minimum, say 12″ × 16″ × 6″ deep, a stock size.

The icebox, as a built-in unit, becomes useful only when of large enough capacity to hold ice and preserve food for the longest hop between ports you are likely to make. This will be found to be, if the box is well insulated, one which holds about 150 pounds of ice, chopped into small chunks and solidly packed. The small boat can do with one of the inexpensive picnic boxes. Be sure that it is deep enough to hold a milk or other tall bottle. Unless an icebox has been especially built for marine use, the top opener is the most satisfactory. Otherwise, come a long tack well heeled over, and the contents will next be seen *couchant* on the cabin floor.

Ice will not last very long if the box is constantly opened between meals—if you know what I mean. Many cruisers carry a smaller auxiliary container which holds ice only, or possibly only ice and the ginger ale. Thus, every time it becomes necessary to lift one, the main box is not opened and its stored cold allowed to escape.

If water temperatures are low, say in the fifties, you can keep food in a watertight container hung over the side, probably weighted or sent under the surface via a small gun-tackle. Water will keep fresh and cool by the use of a "desert bag" hung from the boom. Fabricated of flax, the bag permits just enough evaporation to reduce water temperature to pleasure.

From these primitive refrigeration methods, we jump to the mechanical "icebox." It has marked advantages (such as instant ice cubes, holding frozen foods) IF you have the power. You have little choice. Electricity requires a complex system of supply. The other choice is L.P. gas—and I hope you won't select this one. So does your insurance company. And the United States Coast

Guard. It is dangerous, not only because of possible gas leaks but because it utilizes an open-flame evaporator which becomes a real danger when heeling or jumping at sea.

Both these types are available in combinations, i.e., L.P. and 12-volt d.c. and 110-volt a.c. and 12-volt d.c. Both require large and limitless supply of 12-volt direct current power from your battery or batteries. The demand is great and without a generator almost impossible to provide. To be sure, the vessel with a generator has less problems, but your anchorage or marina mates will frown upon a popping generator and may even stuff a potato into your exhaust. Or you may have diesel main engines and a gasoline generator. This is common, due to the prohibitive cost of diesel generators (a gas generator costs about one-fourth as much as a diesel generator for some strange reason) and the natural reluctance to surrender the safety advantages of non-flash fuel. Engine-room space on a small cruiser simply cannot support a generator—since it will logically also supply cooking electricity, it must be of at least 3 kw. rating, which is quite a large piece of iron.

An excellent dodge for those with shore-side 110-volt power available *most of the time* is to fit a holding plate into the electric refrigerator. The cost is about $75 to $100 for a small under-the-counter box, and it will freeze into a solid block the equivalent of about one hundred pounds of ice in half a day. With care in door openings and placed out of the sun or engine-room heat, such a box will make ice cubes for a day, hold them for two days, and hold the box safely cool for as many as four days. Small holding cans, about one quart in size, can be bought at picnic-supply and sporting-goods stores at about fifty cents each. A bank of eight will hold the contents of a four-cubic-foot electric refrigerator or icebox for a week end. They may be frozen at home and carried to the boat thus obviating an on-board freezing period before departure. Most of these are rustable cans. Their lives may be extended somewhat by painting them with a latex coating once a year.

So here are some practical stove-refrigerator combinations that tend to simplify the complex little boxes that our small boats have become.

A. A generator of at least 3 kw. output (110-volt a.c.) and not more than 6 kw. unless you also want to run air conditioning, food freezing (as for game fish), and area heating. To this you hook an electric stove which has two burners, totalling about 2,400 kilowatts, fitted with an interlock so that you cannot draw more than 2,000 kilowatts at one time; and which has an oven-broiler, and, possibly (as found on at least two marine electric stoves), a rotary barbecue spit as well. You also hook to this a refrigerator using only 110-volt a.c. current but fitted with a holding plate good for three to four days at sea without an electrical boost. You now have a good deal of flexibility. Because you can charge batteries at sea (even the generator's starting battery, in such case starting the generator by hand), you can fire an adequate lighting system; pump bilge and domestic water; play TV, hi-fi, or a tape deck; freely use the radiotelephone; and have main engine starting power at all times. You can even refrigerate by refreezing the holding plate.

You will note that not recommended is a demand generator, i.e., one which starts every time current is called for—even a tiny amount such as required for a trickle charge through the automatic charger, or a refrigerator lamp. These are a nuisance and wake you up at night with mighty snorts because a faucet leaks or a lazy battery wants a jolt. As a cruising practice, we wind up the diesel generator every second or third day for a few hours in the A.M., build up all needed electrical and other reserves, and forget it. Of course, under weigh the alternator (which is a 60 amp. affair) keeps batteries up and systems working.

B. L.P. gas for cooking is clean and quick and, in careful and wise hands, safe to use provided the gas lead from the tank(s) is short and a valve is fitted above the deck and is used faithfully. A sniffer in the galley area is highly recommended. However, when we now must refrigerate, gas is, as before stated, utterly dangerous and unsafe, and we are back to an icebox. Do not be tempted by this seemingly easy way out; you are creating a certain hazard. L.P. gas, as power, has no other uses on shipboard, and I think that excellent as it may appear for cooking, it should be discarded.

C. The marine liquid fuel stove, while not as convenient as L.P. gas or electricity, is quite adequate if—a very large IF—it is burned without pressure. Alcohol and kerosene both can be burned in patent elements which build their own small nozzle pressures. Gasoline must be vaporized, by a hand pressurized supply tank, before igniting and is therefore quite dangerous and subject to explosion. DO NOT TOLERATE A GASOLINE COOK- OR HEATING STOVE ABOARD YOUR SHIP! The power for any of these stoves is useless for other tasks aboard; and you will need other means, and other systems, to perform work of the automatics on board.

D. There are available (for the larger ships) fuel-oil burning apparatuses to be used in iron, sheet steel, and similar stoves. These generally are blower types and require electric-motor fans and sometimes fuel injectors. If you sail with one of these, be very sure you have a sealed marine-unit. The shoregoing variety, with a gravity pan, exposing open fuel, will not serve aboard and are extremely dangerous. Quite often the stove manufacturer will offer such a burner, and it is by all means preferable over an adapted unit. Stamford Foundry, which builds the time-honored line of Shipmate stoves, offers such a unit, even for the small Model 211 and 215 stoves.

However, this type of equipment belongs really to winter fishermen or ocean sailors or the chap who sails into the ice caps and is, actually, gear for the ship which needs space heating as well as concentrated cooking heat most of the time.

Hot water on tap is a handy blessing, but a little difficult to come by. The generator can readily keep up 6- to 12-gallon domestic heaters. Several manufacturers offer heat exchangers whereby the engine-exhaust gases heat and circulate fresh water into a storage tank. These are expensive, take a little power, and form just another bit of gear to service and maintain. Do not— Oh, do not—be tempted by the L.P. gas hot-water heater. It has the same faults as the gas refrigerator. Incidentally, the big mail-order houses carry excellent electric domestic hot-water heaters which have limit controls and are Underwriter Approved. These are likely the same numbers that are put out as marine items at much-increased prices.

A novel source of shipboard hot water is shown in one of the nearby sketches. The trick is to form a fairly flat container with a large solar surface and to paint it *flat* black. In northern summer weather, and all year in the tropics, this gadget will supply you with limited hot water. I have burned myself under a shower supplied by this novelty. Mount one immediately above the galley and another over the head, for a short pipe lead is essential.

Space heating on shipboard is not a great problem. Usually what is wanted is only a bit of fog dispelled or a chill eased. Dockside, of course, the electric heater is standard. It should have a fan and an automatic control. I believe all are now equipped with automatic shut-off switches in the event of capsizing. For a day-long bit of heat, you can obtain in sporting-goods stores and at mobile-home suppliers several makes and shapes of kerosene heaters. None of these require pressure, and most are odorless and quite foolproof. Tanks supply fuel for up to thirty-six hours of continuous use. Positively, even dockside or at moorings, arrange to bolt or otherwise secure such a unit to the deck or to a bulkhead.

I have a small Franklin stove on my vessel (Portland Foundry, Portland, Maine, Franklin No. 1) which is sometimes why I go cruising. It is a lovely thing to fire it up with briquettes (which I bag beforehand in chain-store food-storage bags) and have my ship become home to me. Imported from England these many years, are the tile-faced shipboard solid-fuel heaters; they are admirably suited to marine use, having nonferrous parts and being only ten inches wide, fitting almost any handy space. Yes, there is a coziness to open-flame fireplace heaters which is charming and heart-warming—if you have a diesel boat or a straight wind-boat. If you have gasoline aboard, forget it—you are asking for trouble.

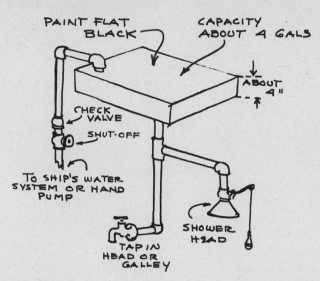

A solar deck heater for shower and domestic warm water. One or two of these on a thirty-footer will supply a surprising amount of fairly hot water on a sunny day. To fill, open the lowest tap so that air is not trapped in the heater tank. The tank and all exposed piping must be painted flat black to absorb the heat rays. Tank can be any metal, although copper is best

If you want heat under weigh, you can't much improve on a heavy-duty truck heater, hooked into the main engine. These units have a powerful fan (6-, 12-, or 32-volt d.c.) and, via sheet-metal ducts, can drive heat a long way. Be sure to provide a shut-off in each duct and, in the outlet area, a relieving grille to the outdoors.

Cooking stoves can be utilized as space heaters by inverting a frying pan or stew pot (especially an iron one) over a burner. The idea is to provide an area which can interrupt the flame, causing heat, and in turn radiate it. In the sketch is a simple one- or two-burner homemade stove-top radiator that works in a small cabin. In use, turn the flame way down and always provide an inlet for exterior fresh air.

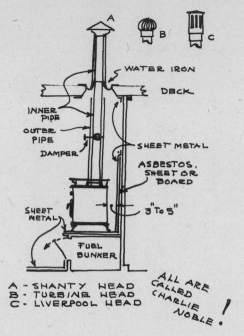

Safety standards for solid-fuel heaters and stoves. The double flue piping is necessary. The outer one can well be partly decorative, such as sheet brass or copper (kept polished). Some of the common smoke heads shown are: A Shanty Head, B Turbine Head (which actually creates its own strong draft), and C Liverpool Head, the all-time favorite, mostly because it is almost leakproof when water begins flying

A hot engine, after a day's run, will provide a lot of evening heat. Jim Emmett, master of the *Chinook* and a talented writer on the nautical scene, has a double hatch over the engine room; the lower one being a teak grille. Many a chilly evening we have sat in snug warmth with no more heat than this bonus from the engine.

And so to the galley itself, worthy of any skipper's best abilities and—rightfully—the specifications of his wife, for she *really*

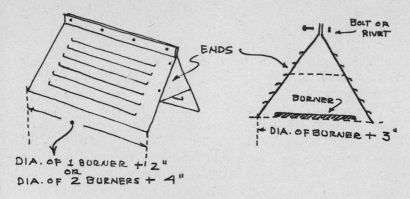

A homemade stove-top space heater

Any builder's supply outlet can furnish the inexpensive aluminum louvered panels in various sizes. Get them unpainted, heaviest gauge possible, and rivet or bolt them together as shown. Can be used on any type of stove

knows about such things. Use the mock-up system, full-size, with cardboard panels in a small home-closet. It's worth it.

All drawers in the galley need some sort of reliable fastener to prevent their unshipping in a seaway. Likewise, china and glassware need a bin especially fitted with nests and cradles to suit the crockery you are using.

There can be no question but that the galley is best located about amidships. Not only is there the least sea motion here at the center of balance of the hull, but the adjacent hatch provides headroom and ventilation. On any vessel under forty feet, there seems no earthly reason for enclosing it; converting it into a steam room, a hotbed for dry-rot spores and a real danger to the cook. Design it in harmony with the general cabin furnishings, keep it clean and picked up, and there can be no question of the galley's detracting from the cabin layout. If it must be forward, it is essential that an escape hatch be placed over or near it and that some provision for seating the cook be made. A drop stool, screwed to a bulkhead, or a drawer with a seat on it, will serve.

Eating

Eating arrangements can seldom reach home standards on shipboard. The smaller the vessel, the truer this becomes. Nevertheless, some thought must be given to the question.

Perhaps the greatest fault is that the diner, because of cramped quarters, must sit, kneel, or slouch in such a position that digestion becomes almost impossible. Usually, on the small boat on which this is true, the basic trouble is in making an effort to sit at a shoregoing table of sorts. Such a table, too low or too high, and its edges not in the proper comfortable relationship to seats, will

One-arm mess tables for the small boat   Laptray instead of center table

cause hideous contortions during a meal. On any vessel which cannot accommodate table and seats of the approximate comfort of land furniture, it seems to me that some other arrangement can be made. One-arm arrangements are simple; so is an adaptation of the bed-table idea. Both have the advantage of not occupying floor space. Most small cabins, with the mess table rigged, become crowded and dangerous, hampering free movement about the ship. Another good arrangement which has not yet received the attention it should, is the Pullman berth-nook idea discussed elsewhere in this chapter. It is entirely possible to design this feature below decks. In the boat up to thirty feet, it will fall about amidships where the turn of the bilge reaches its greatest draft. While a step is often required, the reduced headroom is of no consequence, for the space is occupied only when either sitting at table or sleeping.

All shipboard tables should be fitted with storm rails *without* scuppers. If possible, a drawer or Lazy Susan feature for condiments, napkins, silver, etc., should be built in. Normally, the comfortable table, used with the normal chair with a height of eighteen inches, is thirty inches from the floor. On shipboard, when we must resort to other than standard arrangements it is well to preserve the distance of twelve inches between seat and table top and to hold the edge of the table about plumb with the edge of the seat.

This chapter might go on forever, but before beating toward its end, I want to put in a good word for those grand shipmates of the "eatin'" yachtsman: paper plates, cups, etc. Nothing contributes more than these to the enjoyment of a cruise. No dishwash-

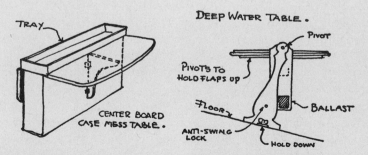

ing, no fresh-water shortage, no breakage. And, if you go to a paper wholesaler for them, practically no expense. Good stiff 8-inch paper plates start at $1.20 for 500; partitioned club-plates, at 90¢ per gross—who wants to ship with china dishes at these prices?

Sanitation

The modern marine water closet is almost foolproof and needs no discussion in this work. The smallest one manufactured requires a space 17" × 17" including the pump. It should be set on blocks to raise it to about 18" to 20" above the floor. Standard practice should always see a sea cock fitted on both intake and discharge connections, lead pipe instead of rubber hose connections, and a spare washer- and gasket-kit on board. The intake must always be a foot or more forward of the discharge, or better yet, they should be on opposite sides of the keel.

Its care should include frequent greasing (before it needs it!); the cleaning of the outboard strainer in which mussels, barnacles, and weeds love to set up house; also instructions posted in the neighborhood for its operation. Too many W.C.'s are ruined by exasperated landlubbers, and a quick course of instructions from the bridge is not always practical. Porcelain, by the way, will clean with brass polish and any gritty powder (such as Dutch Cleanser).

Dry rot is all too frequently found in toilet rooms. These are naturally damp, dark spaces, and care should be taken to provide exceptionally good ventilation and light. If a hatch cannot be provided, deadlights in the deck will not invade privacy. A cowl ventilator or a porthole scoop is good and their action is greatly improved by providing a grille in the compartment door which will give a free draft.

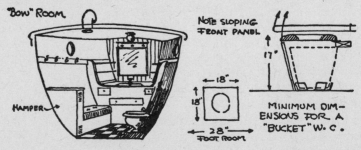

The bow is undoubtedly the most economical location for the W.C. Its natural shape lends itself ideally for toilet room uses. Most such spaces, only slightly enlarged, would be much more useful, serving as dressing room, linen storage, and lavatory as well. Every boat needs some such private space; indeed, having it, there becomes less reason for a stateroom, thus permitting consequent opening up of the interior that makes for a happy, airy, and roomy below-decks.

In recent years, the electric toilet has become fashionable. Nothing wrong with it—save that I have yet to discover one that does not have its own electrolysis problem built into it. Since a marine W.C. uses salt water (save on the lakes and rivers, of course) and direct current is present, we have, in fact, a small battery; and sooner or later internal parts will be affected by a breakdown of the metals. Pot metal, even without electric action, will break down in or even near salt water, and some marine toilets are made of pot metal parts. Avoid these at all costs.

One electric head is simply a motor-and-piston-drive adapted to a hand-pump mechanism. This type doesn't quite fill the bill of quality machinery; just an after-thought. The genuine article has a macerater mechanism, which pulverizes all waste matter and expels it. It is less troublesome and much recommended over the first type. It costs much moola, but is worth it—if you go in for electric toilets.

As part of the modern sanitation system, the waste-treatment unit should today be included without argument. All states have anti-pollution laws. Only a few have laws *and* police. But it is only a question of time. The national program suffers very much because the states cannot get together on what is a proper and adequate system, and the supplier and the boatman are at a loss as to how to comply with general law. A cruising boat usually numbers several states within its normal range and must have uniform law, for it cannot meet the law of *all* the states. A few states have approved the "holding tank," which is a container holding and storing all waste for a period of time (usually a short period of time). The law states that the vessel must then proceed twelve or more miles to sea and discharge its storage tanks; or it may proceed to a shore facility, such as a marina, and there have the tank contents pumped out. Such is the practice, by law, at mobile-home camps. But, sad to say, few marinas have this facility, and there seems to be no great rush to provide it. Wisconsin and Canada have such laws and make them stick. New York, on the other hand, approves only the "chlorinator" type tank; which is a tank into which waste is discharged and, by manual operation of a switch, then macerated and chlorine (common Clorox) introduced and all immediately discharged, supposedly now harmless and free of bacteria. New York makes the requirement stick in lakes (such as Champlain, Indian, Finger Lakes, etc.) but can do little in New York City harbor where liners from the world over hourly flaunt the law—and little motorboats happily follow suit. Which system is best I do not know, but those salty souls who sailed with New York-approved equipment to Expo '67 and into Montreal marinas soon found that it was not approved there and had their heads sealed by police.

By and large, it would seem that the amount of pollution caused by the pleasure boatman is infinitesimal when compared with that of industry and commercial shipping, oil refineries, and wood and pulp processors. But do-gooders have long been aiming at pleasure boating—partly because it has so far been a free sport, enjoyed by people who enjoy and value freedom, and here is a good place to start. As far as you are concerned, obey your state law—and fight it if it needs fighting. I suggest that you do NOT invest in a holding-tank type, for I believe that voluntary shore pumping stations will not spring up in great numbers. Actually, the chlorinator type makes sense and is much needed in some crowded marinas and basins on an esthetic basis, if not a sanitary one. Meanwhile, urge your state senator and representative to press for a uniform, national law, or a symposium to finally unify the state laws. As it is, it is a hardship on the individual boatman —and is doing exactly zero in controlling pollution of our waters.

Lighting

Most boats have good lights but not enough of them. A light to be useful must light what you want without shadow. Almost automatically this relegates the center fixture or dome light to the lambrequins and horsehair settees of the yachts of 1900.

Shore lighting in the last decades has taken on new usefulness and beauty. The reasons, when analyzed, are applicable to boat lighting, and almost the same equipment may be used. Wall and dresser lamps, the efficient reading lamp, and the shaded wall bracket light, well supplemented by portable lights and a goodly sprinkling of outlets, make up the lighting system of the modern cruiser. Low voltages are safest afloat, but the fixtures should be standard sizes for the sake of economy. Lead cable makes the best conduit and is neither subject to the rust of BX nor the chafing of rubber cable.

A central switchboard, from which the various circuits depart, is desirable near the battery. Generally an inside circuit, bridge circuit, ignition circuit, and controls for running, anchor, and searchlights are sufficient on the small cruiser. Each circuit should be protected by a fuse and all connections soldered.

The small boat will usually find a full season's juice in one of the unit 6-volt dry cells. I have used one for a full season. There can be no real reason for kerosene lighting today—save possibly the romance of it. The lamp, chimney, smoke bell, funnel, and reserve fuel can will be found to take up far more space than a battery, wire, and lights, and, penny for penny, cost even more—what with broken chimneys, blackened paint-work, fuel, and wicks.

It seems to me that the small auxiliary would do far better to regard her out-of-doors lights as portable, right from the electric outlet to the lamp itself. These installations of cables creeping up a mast or seized to the shrouds must stand the weather and the sea 100 per cent of the season afloat and ashore even though they are actually in use only 5 per cent or less of that time. Somehow, through corrosion, rupture, and dampness, they always fail at the wrong time.

Once again, simplicity is the keynote of the successful electric system. Surface wires, soldered connections, a minimum of through-the-deck connections, sane location of fixtures, and no wires near the bilge make for simplicity. Keep wires as far away as possible from the compass, lest you get yourself some deviation trouble.

So much boating is presently based at marinas, which provides 110 a.c. power as part of the rent package, that a family cruiser should take full advantage of such electrical service. This calls for a system somewhat different from the simple direct-current battery circuit, though navigation, compass, chart and search lights. should all still remain on a ship's battery circuit.

It is usual to provide a 30 amp. entrance cord of about #8 H.D. stranded wire with a shore terminal allowing the following plug-in combinations:

A. A 3-prong watertight lock connection.
B. A 3-prong receptacle adapter between A. above and a 3-wire (grounded) outlet box.
C. A 2-prong receptacle adapter between B. above and a 2-wire (ungrounded) outlet box. This adapter will not polarize the boat circuit, and you must insert a telltale light or buzzer between the hot side of the circuit and the boat's ground in order to obtain the correct polarity, or you will risk not only shock but electrolysis as well. (See sketch)

The boat end of this entrance cord is usually a lock connection into a permanently-fixed receptacle let into a trunk side or bulkhead about amidships on the boat (Do not set such a receptacle into the topsides; you will soon have corrosion at work.) Inside, often in the engine room, this leads to a fuse and distribution panel from which required circuits depart. It is common to run one circuit to an automatic battery-charger, which keeps batteries at full charge at all times while connected to shore power, and

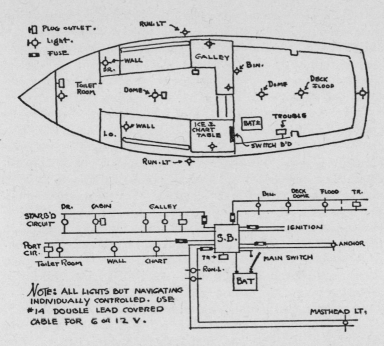

Wiring diagram for a 28-foot cruiser

then operate all electric lighting circuits at ship's standard current, usually 12-volt d.c. Another d.c. circuit operates bilge pump, shower sump pump, fresh-water pressure pump, etc.

For dockside use, a few utility outlets distributed within the vessel are useful for vacuum cleaners, lamps, radio and TV, and power tools. Both stoves and refrigerator are connected directly to the a.c. power supply; also, any heating, air conditioning, etc. If the power demand is heavy, you will need two entrance cords totalling 60 amp. capacity or a circuit designed for 220 volts a.c. (which is available at extra cost in most modern marinas).

Before entering the distribution panel, a double-pole double-throw sealed-unit switch may be introduced to cut off shore supply and introduce the ship generator's 110 a.c. supply. Thus, with a generator, you have the same system in use whether you are tied-up or steaming. With a small generator, say 2 to 4 kw. output, it is wise to wire in a separate stove circuit, supplying only the cooking stove and a few nearby galley lights. Such a circuit will protect the system from an overload caused by automatic demand accessories such as hot-water heater, battery charger, and refrigerator starting surge. To be sure, the cookie has to somewhat plan the attack and switch over to general service as soon and as often as possible.

Should you support heavy-drain utilities such as one or more air-conditioning units or space heaters, you should have the system professionally designed and balanced. After *any* system is installed, you should make a systematic test for electrolysis; which is escaping electricity leaking into salt water via metal fittings. In time (for we have a slow battery here) the tin and zinc from your costly bronze fittings will disappear and only pure copper remain —and copper has no strength or life of itself. Every metal fitting below the water line, even though not electrically connected to any other part (ie., a rubber exhaust line into a bronze through-hull fitting), should be grounded with a #12 wire to other parts and all to a common ground such as shaft, engine, tanks, etc. The professional marine electrical-systems designer will do this as a matter of course. In marine ports, you can often find a "bonding" expert, owning the proper test instruments and experience to protect your vessel.

Even on the craft without shore-side power, bonding should take place for direct current (the kind in your battery) does more damage than alternating current (the kind in shore power lines). It does not require a metallic connection to cause electrical energy leakage in either a wooden hull or a glass hull, because water soakage, the contents of rubber hoses and bilge pools all make mild conductors of even non-metallic materials.

A warning is in order about cheap-john marine fittings, of which there are more and more on the market. Toilets, raw water strainers, seacocks, radio ground-plates, and certain foreign-made hull fastenings are offered in bi-metal construction, or have otherwise not been thought out in terms of salt water use, and electrolysis and metal destruction proceeds merrily on its expensive way. I know of at least four vessels which sank because of defects in raw-water strainer design—a vital part surrendered to electrolysis, and the sea poured in. So check carefully on an old vessel; know the reputation of the supplier of a new vessel.

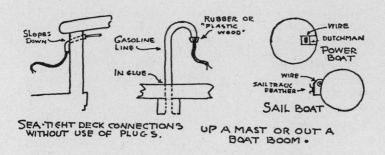

SEA-TIGHT DECK CONNECTIONS WITHOUT USE OF PLUGS.

UP A MAST OR OUT A BOAT BOOM.

Ventilation

In its ordinary sense, boat ventilation conveys merely a picture of cowl ventilators, wind sails, scoop hatches, and motor-driven fans. Such ventilation is necessary for human comfort and health, of course; but there is a much deeper sense to boat ventilation, too often disregarded in interior design and building.

There must be ventilation in the form of a positive and frequent change of air to the most remote parts of the ship. No interior feature, cockpit, house, or deck should completely seal surrounding spaces. Good ventilation of the hull must be provided for in the framing of the hull and nothing be added in the form of bulkheads, lockers, berths, etc., which will hamper the free passage of air to all parts of the vessel. Failure to pay attention to this will not only cause sour, musty interiors but will invite dry rot before your topside paint has set.

Lockers and doors should always be fitted with grilles or some perforation both at top and bottom. Bulkheads should be pierced,

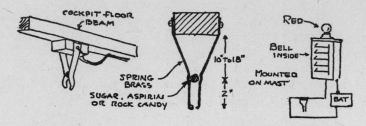

The Quambogue leak alarm. Developed by fishermen, this gadget is attached to a beam in such a manner that its business end is at a point above which rising bilge water would be dangerous. Upon water reaching it, the sugar, aspirin, rock candy, or other soluble matter dissolves, the contacts touch, ring the bell, light the red light, and, as the fishermen say, "Seems somebody ought to ketch on an' bring me the news!"

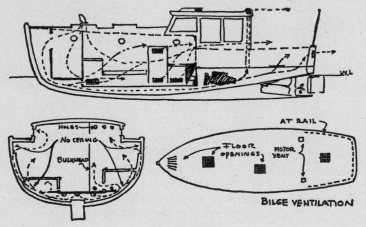

Ventilation

permitting the passage of air between the spaces they enclose. It is a mistake, sometimes costly, to lay a tight floor from side to side. Air limbers should be left between frame bays in the form of notches in the floors, and space should be provided in the way of the turn of the bilge for circulation. A grating aft, at the foot of the companion ladder, and another forward will assure positive

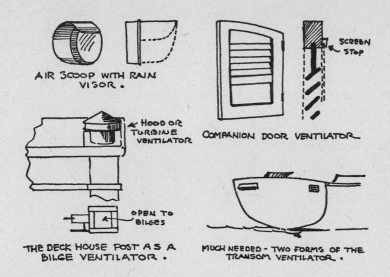

AIR SCOOP WITH RAIN
VISOR .

SCREEN
STOP

HOOD OR
TURBINE
VENTILATOR

COMPANION DOOR VENTILATOR

OPEN TO
BILGES

THE DECK HOUSE POST AS A
BILGE VENTILATOR .

MUCH NEEDED - TWO FORMS OF THE
TRANSOM VENTILATOR .

draft. The motor space, damp-warm as it usually is, needs special attention. Air should be forced to this space through a ventilator of some sort, for it is the source of explosive gasoline fumes, the greatest single fire danger on board.

The average vessel is fairly well ventilated when in use and in motion. However, remembering that most of us hang our boats up at moorings about 80 per cent of the season afloat, tightly locked and all hatches battened, it is small wonder that so many of them become prey to the evils of non-ventilation. Some form of air change must be provided during this time. The difficulty, of course, is in assuring this without laying the boat open to prowlers, soakings in summer squalls, and thieves. Perhaps the cowl ventilator—nasty shipmate that it is on deck—is the best solution. One is of no use; it will function only when air moves because of temperature differences. A draft of wind can only occur with two or more outlets, and common sense indicates one forward and one aft—with a free sweep below decks.

Lacking deck ventilators, a properly designed porthole scoop, rigged port and starboard on the forward portholes, will serve very well. Ventilation aft is simpler because it requires less thought about the question of accidental wetting by rain and because details of construction give many opportunities for building in air limbers of various kinds. Boats fitted with coal stoves can be kept sweet by opening the stack damper upon leaving. There is much to be said for the louvered doors sometimes seen—and a great deal to be said for the practice of trusting your neighbor and leaving the companion doors wide open. Since living in New England I have never had a lock for any of my boats, and they generally remain about as open as when I'm actually on board. The only evidence of anybody's boarding which I ever found was a pair of swell anti-glare sunglasses on the counter—left by some swimmer! The point is—to put it in the form of a question—aren't we perhaps a bit too suspicious of the intentions of the other guy? Personally, I think I'd as lief risk a robbery as a prime case of dry rot!

B-z-z-z-z! Have you ever snugged down in some quiet cove, lights out, and all hands turned in after a last ceremony with the ice pick, and then suddenly realized that you were in for a night of blitzkrieging by assorted insects from the adjacent salt marsh?

A wind sail. For a real circulation of air, such as needed after an off-shore hitch in sloppy weather, rig as shown, open all lockers, drawers, floor openings, etc. CLOSE *hatches and portholes and let 'er blow. Given a chance, this device will positively freshen the most remote corner. It creates a tremendous draft below decks and is hardly to be recommended for ordinary ventilating purposes*

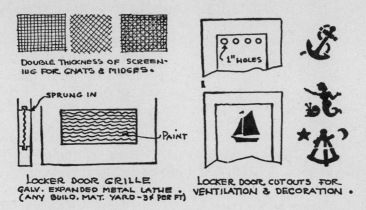

DOUBLE THICKNESS OF SCREEN-
ING FOR GNATS & MIDGES.

SPRUNG IN

PAINT

1" HOLES

LOCKER DOOR GRILLE
GALV. EXPANDED METAL LATHE .
(ANY BUILD. MAT. YARD - 3¢ PER FT)

LOCKER DOOR CUTOUTS FOR
VENTILATION & DECORATION .

You bet you have, sailor! Screens are the answer—and a screen for
every opening on board; screens with a mesh just one millimeter
smaller than the smallest gnat. Hardware cloth is the official name
of this stuff, of bronze for shipboard use and with tropical mesh.
If it's hard to get or too expensive, double up on regular screening, and you'll have the same effect. If you can't screen—Lallacopop! Lallacopop is the only mosquito and fly fender I've ever
been able to be shipmates with. They use it in the deer and black-
fly country; it smells like pinewoods, does not need to be rubbed
on the body, and has always performed for me—in fact, it usually
keeps even the game away. Rub a bit around the hatch or the
portlight frame on the small or open boat which cannot support
insect screens.

As I sit here typing, the smell of Lallacopop comes back to me
—and I shudder a little; and, well, perhaps I shouldn't do that to
my reader. We are not all that rugged. Down in the Virgin Islands
they use a native "punk," called Moogoo, which keeps everything
and everybody away. However, some manufacturer has brought
out the product under the name of PIC, and you can get it at chain-
stores in the U.S. south and from outdoor- and camping-suppliers.
PIC is a spiral of moulded sweet-smelling punk, a little piney and
quite pleasant, which you place in a saucer and light with a
match. It burns for ten or more hours. If you place it low, in a

natural but not strong draft, it will keep *all* insects far away all night long.

The Shell Oil Company has also marketed an insecticide called VAPONA which discourages flying insects for up to three months. Just hang one in each cabin or space and it will be effective, in still air, for a radius of about twenty-five feet, killing 'em dead. This has no odor at all and offends nobody.

Stowing

I have never been aboard an ordinary-size cruiser—or open boat either—which had enough stowing space. There seemed always to be something left over after stowing in preparation for a cruise, and no place to put it. I do not believe that the trouble is always lack of lockers and drawers—I believe that, rather, it is that these so-called bins, drawers, alcove lockers, dressers, hanging lockers, and what-have-you are in themselves not large enough.

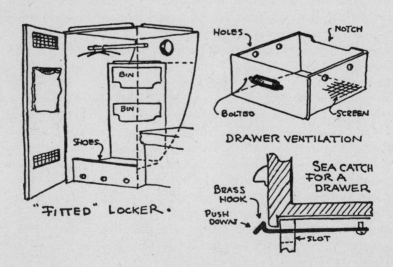

A hanging locker, to be of any use at all, must be wide or deep enough to accommodate clothes on the usual clothes hanger. This takes twenty-two inches exactly. The tall narrow compartment is too narrow to stow clothes in this manner and is actually a waste of space—all we can do is drape our clothes over hooks (usually rusty) around the outside walls, and utterly waste the center space. It must be at least 3′ 6″ long, and if there's any space left over, a drawer or shelf for shoes will be found more than welcome.

There is little need of a small drawer on board ship except in the galley or under the chart table. We need deep, wide drawers —large enough for games, cameras, and supplies, Junior's model speedboat, hats—all these items we lug along. These drawers should be carefully fitted and then, in some manner—paint, filler, shellac—coated to resist dampness and swelling. Each drawer should have some means of having air reach its interior when closed. A series of holes in the sides or a square-meshed screening for the bottom or a front grille are some of the methods used.

The galley should always have a large, clear space left for the stowing of supplies in boxes and crates. Beer, soft drinks, bread in tin boxes, cereals, a watermelon—these are items which few galleys will accommodate without considerable ingenuity. A great many cruisers carry this space about with them, but unused. To port and starboard of the motor there is quite apt to be bin-size spaces which can be bulkheaded off and access provided by doors under companion steps or by means of flush deck-hatches. There should always be a well-planned space—more than a drawer or a locker—for bedding, quilts, and pillows. Sketches in the early part of this chapter suggest bins behind the upper berths, a scheme which many cruising men use. Such spaces should be especially well ventilated and have their bottom limits end where there is no possibility of slopping bilge water reaching the contents.

Deck gear belongs on deck—always. It should not be necessary to enter the living cabin for any item required in connection with the navigation of the vessel. Keep your boat hook in the galley if you'd keep your frying pan on deck skids! Deck gear stowed below won't do too much damage—but, when you're in a hurry, probably wet and maybe sore—you yourself will do the damage. Come off deck just once in a wet oiler to rummage for the sounding lead in a dresser drawer—you'll sleep on a wet, clammy bunk that night, sure as whales spout!

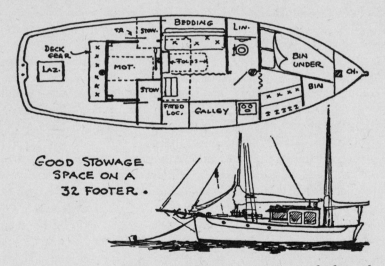

GOOD STOWAGE
SPACE ON A
32 FOOTER.

I am rather proud of the stowage space on my own little packet and will therefore include her plans as an example of the proportion of living to stowing space necessary for comfortable shipboard life. Even at that, I wish I had more! Last year we purchased a ship model while cruising Down East and finally, after trying everything short of dismantling the thing, we covered it with a tarp and towed it in the dinghy. You may not buy ship models, skipper—but I'll lay my last yen that someday one of your guests will board you with a slab-sided suitcase. And then you'll be worse off than I and my ship model!

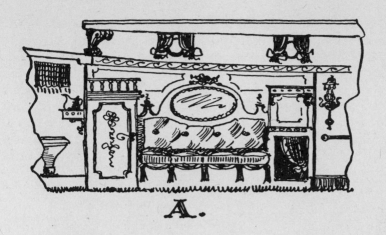

A.

B.

Decorative Treatment

Sketch *A* shows an interior view of Mr. Murgatroyd Van Rock-bilt's yacht *Dashing Wave* of Newport about 1902. Sketch *B* shows what a 1968 professional designer would do to the same interior. Mates, I contend that we've made progress!

There seems to be no particular period to yacht interior treatment (though there could be). But at least we have learned to handle our detail simply, and that's a grand step forward.

The plainer the surfaces are, the simpler the moldings are, the more easily the interior can be kept trim and clean. Flush doors, drawer fronts, bulkheads, and built-in features are the watchword today. And for being able to so handle our interiors we must give a big bow to resin-bonded (waterproof) plywood. It is a strong, time-tested material, simple for the amateur to handle and not as expensive as ordinary construction, say of a bulkhead.

A few design wrinkles, and we shall close this chapter.

1. Painted (in white or tints) interior surfaces make for the feeling of space. Keep ceiling even lighter, or it will seem to crowd you down.
2. Natural finish is fine—if confined to light moldings. Spots of it (drawer fronts, door rails, panels, etc.) are best confined to spaces below ordinary dresser-top heights (say not above 2' 9").
3. The large cabin or deckhouse, having daylight in goodly amounts, will stand for light, natural wood finishes such as honey-colored pine or oiled British-oak.
4. Mirrors (if not too tiny) will make the interior appear spacious.
5. Floors not too dark. Kept fairly light (varnish only on a fir floor, for example), they reflect light to ceiling and walls.
6. Fabrics gay and "summery"—nothing like heavy brocades, solid reps, or tapestry designs.
7. Let books, pleasant lamp shades, spots of color, and refined appointments form the decorative note—not carvings, decalcomanias, gaudy curtains or floor coverings.
8. Longitudinal lines of architecture or color make an interior appear longer; vertical lines, shorter.
9. Architectural balance of bulk (along the fore-and-aft center line) makes for unity of the entire interior.

10. Concealed or "cove" lighting and shaded light makes for larger interiors; open lights draw the walls in.

Once again, keep EVERYTHING simple: detail, color, and workmanship. It's the only road to the interior which will please you and continue to please you in the years to come.

X *Shipboard Upholstery*

Somehow, in our annual fitting-out sprees, we he-men seem to utterly neglect the good ship's upholstery, carpets, cushions, curtains, mattresses, and other of her more feminine appointments. Yet many an otherwise nifty cruiser or runabout looks decidedly shabby when judged by her stuffin's.

It may be argued with some truth that, after all, this is the mate's job—though the mate will probably argue right back at you. Be that as it may on your own ship, the care and upkeep of the fabrics is not difficult or expensive.

Analyzed, most of the trouble will be found to be dirt, grease from engine and galley, salt water, smears and smudges—and perhaps some honest-to-goodness wear.

Mattresses

The first requisite of a ship's mattress is that it be a seagoin' mattress and not one of the land varieties. The cotton-filled mattress or cushion positively will not do on shipboard. Nothing soaks up fog, gin, gas fumes, bilge odors, or water more readily—or releases it more stubbornly.

There can be little doubt that the best mattress today is one of the "foam" type, of rubber or plastic, or plastic-covered "hair." Blanks are available from any mail-order house, or at local bedding-manufacturers, and are readily cut on a band saw or with a long galley-knife. Cut the blank about two inches less all around than the berth dimension so that bed covers may be tucked under. The blank is covered directly with whatever you decide upon, with a piped seam and a zipper down the middle of the end. To get a good workmanlike fit, bevel the outboard edges if they meet the skin of the ship, but do not make a snug fit or the mattress will incline to pop up.

It seems to me that the ordinary small cruiser ought to have innerspring mattresses in staterooms. In her general living saloon, where berths do double duty as daytime settees, I should prefer a separate web spring on which a mattress pad about three inches thick is placed. Same for upper berths. Deckhouse cushions, used only occasionally as berths and subject to more dampness than inetrior mattresses, could well be of sponge rubber covered with a more water-resistant material.

That grand old pipe-berth or other canvas-type berth which deepwater men prefer to any other type while under sail at sea because you have a reasonable chance of staying in it, should have a kapok-filled mattress. This should be stuffed somewhat lightly, more like the old feather beds, and tufted to keep the filling from shifting and bunching. I have seen boats equipped with inflation type mattresses but cannot conceive of their being comfortable or even safe except at anchor in a still cove. They do, of course, have the great advantage of saving room when deflated, and perhaps belong more to the open boat which is occasionally used for an overnighter.

Mattresses may be (and have been, mates!) covered with every conceivable kind of material, depending upon the swankiness of the yacht and her owner. For interior covering in the straight stateroom there is nothing like regular canvas ticking or waterproof duck. Saloon cushions should have a strong *woven* material such as rep, heavy denim, or a linen; plush and mohair, only if you are extra fussy and not at all practical. An allover figured pattern in brown, rust, or green stands up best. The blues fade very quickly, and the yellows and tints soil very quickly. Cover both sides of the cushion or, as many do, cover one side with a "dress" material and the other with something more rugged for use when the gang goes fishing or week-ending.

Mattress covers are made just as slip covers are, i.e., the material pinned *in reverse* to the form, boxed, the flaps pinned on, and then taken ashore for machine sewing. A cover will last longer if it is piped with leather or whipcord, say in a contrasting darker color. Sea-hair and sponge rubber can be very neatly covered by the amateur as these types are as square cut as a piece of lumber. Leave a short end open, insert the mattress, and either sew or close with a zipper.

The kapok- or hair-filled mattress will probably require tufting to make it look good. This is not difficult to do (see sketch), but care should be taken that only a composition button is used. Those which match the fabric and have tin backs which rust in a summer fog are not worth the effort of splicing in. They will soon destroy the surrounding material as well as themselves. Composition buttons, in many colors, are obtainable in most department stores, mail-order houses and, of course, at the upholstery supply-houses.

Most landlubber upholstery shops will make mattresses for you at very much under the cost of the marine supply stores. There is nothing against this, of course. It might be well to remember, however, that the shore upholsterer seldom understands all the extra hazards which descend upon the shipboard mattress. Caution him to follow the pattern exactly, bevelling and shaping most carefully. He should use no iron whatsoever on buttons or fastenings; innersprings should be first sprayed with an enamel; and Italian marling should be substituted for the ordinary jute string. Canvas carrying- and lashing-straps should always be provided and a few screened breathing-grommets let into the edges.

One of the worst enemies of mattresses, indeed, all shipboard upholstery, is dampness. The wet bathing suit, an open port, or

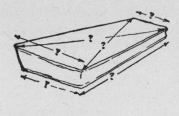

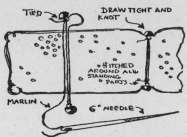

The dimensions needed by the manufacturer to make a mattress. Odd shapes and curves should be marked out on a paper pattern with bevels indicated

How to splice in buttons. Use only marling, not jute string, and composition buttons

excess moisture from condensation all contribute. Worst of all is that a wetting with salt water will leave a salt deposit when dry and from then on will draw moisture, keeping the mattress more or less clammy until the salt itself has been removed. By all means, wash the salt-water stain with fresh water, even if it means a real soaking. This will not only remove the salt but usually the white stain of salt water as well. A little vinegar in the fresh water will help. Many mattresses become decorated on the underside with a series of rust lines from the springs. The springs should be kept carefully painted, using an engine enamel and, in addition, a rubberized sheet should be laid between spring and mattress.

Stains, even mild rust stains, are best removed by a commercial cleaner of the solvent type. This, by the way, can be bought by the quart or gallon at large auto service-stations at tremendous savings over the household-sized can or bottle. You can give any piece of fabric a commercial dry-cleaning after stains have been removed by going over the whole piece several times with cleaner. Sometimes, old paint, varnish, or grease spots are stubborn. Soften these with a spot of paint remover or a paste of Gold Dust and water or with the touch of a hot knife; then clean in the regular way.

The worst stains are made from acids such as those contained in fire extinguishers of certain types or in storage batteries. Left alone, the fabric will soon be eaten away. Immediately neutralize the effects by applications of ordinary household ammonia, and you will have no more than a discoloration. It can, at any time, be dyed by ordinary fabric dyes, applied in boiling water. Should you have the misfortune of an acid hole, dab the edges with glue to prevent its spreading and then darn it (a job for the mate!) or swipe a swatch from the underside, or an edge which rests against a bulkhead, and patch it in.

Life Preserver and Exterior Cushions

Most exterior cushions are made incorrectly. For one thing they should never be tufted. Each depression at a tuft is an invitation for a pool of rain water or spray and most of them show a high-water mark about the tuft. This water usually soaks into the cushion causing rot and a general hardening of the filling—to say nothing of the effect on the buttons themselves. For another, they are too often covered with the worst possible shipboard material: imitation leather. I have yet to find one of these materials which will actually stand up for even a reasonably long time. Once it starts cracking nothing can be done. I have tried several valueless preparations which blistered in the sun and remained tacky for an entire season afloat. By far the best solution of the outside cushion is to have them flush and covered with an ordinary waterproofed, UNCOATED fabric such as brown duck.

Further care of these would be to have them rest, not on a flat seat or locker top, but on a slat panel so that they can never become soaked from actually standing in water.

On certain classes of motorboats, the kapok-filled cushion is accepted as a life preserver. To pass, it must be soft and fluffy, untorn, with both loop handles securely fastened. Such a cushion must be springless and kept ready for use. The ordinary berth cushion will hardly serve.

A leatherette cushion which has become wet or hard should be opened at one end and taken for a sail, that is, hung aloft in sun and wind until it becomes light and buoyant before being sewed up again. Unless it is opened the filling will never become really dry. If it has been in salt water, a good rinsing in fresh water is first necessary before drying.

Floor Coverings

The finest floor-covering for any boat is a good, tight wooden floor—but, oh skipper, how cold on a brisk duck-shooting dawn! So if you want to keep your tootsies warm, use carpet. There is no real reason that it should not be used on a boat; it is only necessary to get the right kind of carpeting. This emphatically does not include the wool carpets or, to be elegant, rugs. The twin enemies of floor coverings, sand and dampness, seem to attack the pile carpet with particular glee, and you'll soon have bare spots, discoloration, raggedness, and a foul odor.

Boat carpet—and this means for the interior only—should be of the pileless, woven type, similar to the rug in the back of your car. It should be bound, easily removable, and should have some positive means of assuring its staying on the floor. This can be done by snap buttons or by sprinkling sand into the last coat of floor paint. Coating the back with wall-paper size will assure its lying flat and adhering to the floor. Carpet edges in the way of uncarpeted floor should be held down by a removable metal binding strip or small roundhead screws and a brass washer.

Of late, we have seen the development of synthetic carpeting; not wool, not pile, not woven—just a durable, soft, and pleasant mass of fibers smashed together into a thickish pad that will resist pressure, rot, water, acid, weather, ice, and sun-fading. It is fine stuff; much needed—for interior decks and floors! Unfortunately, it is such marvelous material that it has been too often used on exterior decks, in cockpits, and in open wheelhouses. One ketch in Florida has it pasted over trunks, including the sides, over hatches, and around the base of the spars for three feet in height! It is a fine tribute to the lasting qualities of the material (for it appears sound after some years), but I shudder to think of what is going on *below* the carpet. I would guess that a prime case of dry rot is rapidly developing in the deck beneath.

Yes: Use this freely—but inside. It can be neatly cut with a scissors and laid down; or it can be cemented with linoleum cement or equal, or tacked. It does not tend to curl, and creeping can be controlled by painting the deck underneath with anti-skid finish. There are many colors available (some quite garish, and look out for them) and two thicknesses, ¼″ and ⅜″. The kind I have used is called Ozite.

Linoleum has become very popular as a boat floor-covering and certainly has its place in galley, toilet rooms, and on the enclosed bridge. It should always be cemented down with commercial linoleum mastic and the edges covered with brass binding-strips. (Be certain that these are genuine brass, not merely coated steel.) Linoleum can be protected and made to last for a long time by using linoleum lacquer, which is colorless and non-slip. A pale spar-varnish will stand up equally well, but repeated applications will muddy the color. Under no circumstances use wax on shipboard linoleum. To do so is a sure ticket to Davy Jones's or the bonesetter's.

The common oilcloth type of linoleum is not suitable. For the boat, linoleum should be at least the best kitchen quality. A plain color, in the confined space of a small cabin, looks better than a patterned covering. Tile effects, to me at least, encourage seasickness and probably cause compass deviation.

Its care should include frequent washes with *fresh water* and renewal of the surface. Catch cigarette burns and heel gouges at once, puttying with colored white-lead and dryers and varnishing over. Remove linoleum if for some reason the underside has become wet, otherwise rot and mildew will surely break down the jute backing. Handle linoleum only in warm weather when it is soft, pliable, and not apt to crack or chip.

Often rubber mats are used at various points on the vessel, at the steering station or on companion ladder treads. Keep away from the rubber covering which is ribbed in only one direction— that's the direction in which you'll slide! Rubber needs no surfacing but, for your life, keep it away from oil or you will have no rubber in a startlingly short time. To remove stains from it, rub with steel wool or an abrasive and water. In stubborn cases, a spot of acetone or gasoline will loosen the spot and the rubber, too. So will carbon tetrachloride (fire-extinguisher liquid to you). Wash off immediately, and the rubber will again harden with no harm done. The torn rubber mat can be repaired by cementing it together and backing it up with a piece of inner tube, using one of the so-called self-vulcanizing liquids.

Perhaps in the long run it is best to hold fabrics of any kind on shipboard to a minimum compatible with decent and homey shipboard life. The experienced deepwater cruiser seldom goes in for Park Avenue drapes, carpets, and fixin's. He has even learned to cut down on linen carried, using paper towelling in its many present-day forms. You won't find oilcloth dresser tops on his boat, or fancy hanging curtains between staterooms, or lovely chintzes slung over his air ports.

Curtains are present only if a MUST, such as to afford privacy of sleeping arrangements, and these will be of heavy, lined, and weighted material such as used in Pullmans. Nothing arty for him. The problem of deckhouse curtains has been admirably solved by modern designers by using Venetian blinds.

Canvas

Canvas is used in so many places on even the power cruiser that a volume could be written about it. Boat covers, dodger cloths, binnacle and wheel jackets, wind screens and whatnot. Its care is simply a matter of keeping it dry and clean. There are no magic formulae for cleaning canvas. Take it off the boat, spread it on a flat surface, and get out soap, hot water, and a scrubbing brush. Oh yes—and elbow grease! To this, if necessary, may be added a

*Cockpit and other storm cur-
tains hung with sail slides and
track so as to be entirely removable*

*A porthole "shade" that does
not keep air out. Make of metal
or plywood, 2″ larger than glass
diameter*

bleaching agent such as carried by any chain store. Beyond this,
the sun alone can take charge. Spots are removed by solvents,
holes patched or sail-stitched, and crushed grommets replaced.

The appearance of areas of dark spots, varying from the size of
a dime to a pinhead, means that mildew is present and that unless
steps are taken to kill it, you soon won't have a very serviceable
piece of canvas left. To some extent, these spots can be bleached
out. But the cause should be removed as well, that is, the opportunity for the canvas to become first wet, and then dry, under a condition of heat, dampness, and lack of ventilation.

Cotton duck which has been dyed a khaki color with mineral
dye (not organic) is fairly mildew-proof. The U.S. standard Army
duck alone is absolutely safe to use; the double and single filled
ducks are of but short life afloat. A test for mildew-proofing can
be made by burning two equal size swatches of material. The one
with mineral dyes will leave an appreciable amount of ash, dark
colored, while the untreated material will leave a small white or
gray ash only.

Mildew is caused by moisture. The only way to prevent or retard it is to apply waterproofing to the canvas. There are numerous commercial waterproofing compounds for this purpose, a quart covering about twenty-five square feet on one side. For the small area of canvas, it will pay to purchase a small can. However, if a large amount of water- and mildew-proofing is to be done, it will be more economical to make your own liquid. This is the best formula of the U. S. Department of Agriculture.

CANVAS WATERPROOFING

Petroleum asphalt	8½ pounds
Vaseline (amber)	1½ pounds
Dry earth pigment (ocher or umber)	5 pounds
Gasoline	3 gallons
Kerosene	2 gallons

Melt slowly, over fire, stirring the while, the first two items. Remove from flame and pour in the mixed gasoline and kerosene. (The earth pigment should have been first dissolved by stirring in a *very small* amount of the liquid and then strained into the mixture.) When the waterproofing material settles to the bottom or thickens, it will be necessary to warm the mixture just before applying. This is done by immersing the container in a tub of hot water, never by heating over a flame.

This quantity will waterproof about 400 to 450 square feet of canvas on one side. It is applied with a wide brush or by spraying, and it is usually possible, by being generous in the spreading, to treat both sides by soaking just one side.

If a white treatment is desired, use dry zinc oxide in place of the khaki-colored earth pigment. For smaller amount, reduce the material listed in proportion. This preparation will leave the canvas soft and pliable, capable of being handled and folded. For the permanent or standing canvas, such as a dodger cloth or wind cloth, use the formula below:

Boiled linseed oil	2 quarts
Aluminum "bronzing powder"	½ pound
Japan drier	¼ pint

The powder should be dissolved in a small quantity of the oil, making it into a smooth paste, before adding it to the mixture. No heating is necessary, and it can be used at once. The formula will cover fifty to seventy-five square feet, one side. After treatment, the canvas should be left to air dry for a week or more. If stored before thoroughly dry, spontaneous combustion is liable to take place.

Use the first formula for sail covers, skylight and other jackets, cockpit awnings, and canvas that is to be used or wind-blown much; the second formula for tarpaulins, boat covers, dodger cloths, and more or less standing or fixed canvas panels.

Along with canvas preservation comes a thought for oilers and other storm clothing. If this is of the fisherman yellow type (not rubber) and is sound, it can be re-waterproofed very simply. Clean thoroughly with gasoline (in the open, please) and then soak with this mixture:

Beeswax, refined	½ pound
Turpentine	1 gallon

No heating; merely dissolve the beeswax and apply with a brush. Allow to dry for a week or more. There are other formulae, but I think this the most satisfactory as it adds but 10 per cent to the weight while others add from 50 to 80 per cent—and storm clothing is heavy and clumsy enough as it is.

We've pretty well "fancied up" our little craft, even to the lady jobs. Here are a few random ideas along the general lines of fabrics used afloat:

1. Isinglass, as found in storm curtains, can be cleaned with ordinary household vinegar. Then wax it—and watch the water roll off.
2. Instead of the common two pennants left for lashing (such as on boat and sail covers), splice an eye in one side and a wooden toggle in the other. Much time will be saved over the average knot which jams when frozen or wet.

3. Leave a glass port in the binnacle jacket so that the compass can be seen even with the jacket on. When salt spray flies, this may save a polishing job.

4. Make canvas strops or gaskets for furling sail instead of rope ends and keep your canvas looking clean. Make inside-out, just like a necktie, using a machine or hand stitching; then pull through itself and sew the ends closed.

5. A rubber sheet thrown over the cushions while people are sitting on them in wet bathing suits will prolong their life and looks—the cushions', that is.

6. Patch holes in carpet by stealing a triangular piece from a corner and gluing it to canvas. When set, carefully enlarge the hole to fit and cement the canvas backing to the carpet.

7. Squeaking berth springs can be cured by brushing the twisted wire joints and springs with kerosene and drying them off with a piece of waste.

8. The canvas hammock of a pipe berth will be less apt to sag and hollow out if laced with rawhide instead of the common cotton line.

XI Sails

Most of us, lacking relationship to Professor Einstein or familiarity with higher mathematics, must attack our complicated problems of balancing sail rigs, figuring areas, centers and moments, as did the old clipper builders—take a squint at the rig and chew a pine sliver and "allow she'll set right an' if she don't, why, blast it, mates, we'll skinny the foot an' have Stitches sew another cloth on her leech!"

This is most unscientific, 'tis true, but look what our American clippers did in the way of sailing! However, the small-boat man today, faced with the problem of designing, altering, or building a new sail rig for his little ship, unless he be an engineer by training, has little more to help him than did these hardy trial-and-error artists of another age. This chapter will attempt to place some helps at his service, concerning itself more with the *how* than the *why* of sail designing.

The sail cannot be placed just anywhere in the boat. It must be placed in such a relationship to other factors of the boat that balance is achieved. The center of area or center of driving force must be within certain well-established relationships to the center of lateral resistance of the hull itself. What makes the entire problem an inexact science (at least for the man who has not had experience with the sail balance of *many* boats) is the fact that every type of hull requires a different relationship of these forces in order to achieve the ideal perfect balance.

What this relationship is for your boat, no man can say with absolute accuracy; but we shall, later, present a table in which boat types are listed, one of which will probably be quite near your own.

Know at the outset that perfect balance is rare, if not unknown. Perfect balance would mean that the hull and sails are in such perfect relationship that a rudder would be unnecessary except to change the course of the boat. While it is quite possible to design a boat of perfect balance on paper, the moment this boat goes to sea and becomes subject to wave action which alters the hull resistance factors or is subject to winds of varying forces and directions, shifting of ballast and live weight, tides, currents, and many other factors, the balance is destroyed, and a rudder must be used as a corrective force. The object of balance, then, is to reduce the use of the rudder to a minimum, for any alteration of its surface away from a straight fore-and-aft line results in resistance and consequent loss of speed.

In all cases, accurate scale-drawings must be made, say three-fourths of an inch to the foot, as the very first step. We shall take the complete designing of a sail for a small eighteen-foot catrigger as an illustrative problem. The elements of it hold good for all rigs, even unto a seven-masted schooner, with certain additional data which will be given later.

Sail design begins, not with the sail, but with the underwater hull areas of the boat. The forward motion of a vessel with the wind directly aft is as simple as the motion of a drifting dinghy— the wind just blows it, and the boat moves without the need of any special equipment save a surface on which the wind can exert its force.

The only resistance offered is that of the underwater parts of the drifting dinghy to the water itself. Were it not for this, the dinghy would go exactly as fast as the wind. But most of the time we wish to take our vessel against or across the wind to make an objective to windward, so we must convert the wind into a forward-driving force. We must therefore equip the boat with an underwater surface of sufficient area to resist the force which drives it in the direction of the wind; a mechanical device, such as a centerboard or deep keel, to prevent this skidding. Now the wind force exerted against the sails meets resistance from the lateral area of hull, keel, and centerboard, and a forward motion is the result. The vessel is pinched between the two forces and takes the line of least resistance, that is, forward. This forward motion is a middle course, neither directly into the wind nor directly on a course parallel to the center of the boat.

So, as these forces must be in certain defined relationships, we must find a common point in each from which to make the adjustment. This is done by considering the forces concentrated at a single point on the sails and on the underwater areas and keeping these points in their correct relationships for the particular type of hull being considered.

For practical purposes, the center of lateral resistance, (always denoted on plans by the symbol C.L.R.) is the center, by weight, of the underwater plane. Note, that the rudder is not considered in this calculation and that the centerboard (if the boat is provided with one instead of with a fixed keel of considerable area) is about 75 per cent unsheathed.

An exact scale cutout, of cardboard, light plywood, or sheet metal is made of this underwater area. By trial and error, using a pin as a pivot, this cutout is made to hang perfectly level. The point at which the pin permits this is the fore-and-aft center of balance as well as the C.L.R. With a pair of dividers, this point is transferred to the scale drawing and a vertical line from it is drawn upward in the way of the sail plan which you are now ready to draw in.

The simple sail on the boat which we are canvassing is considered at this stage of the design, as a perfect fore-and-aft plane, that is, sheeted home and directly on the center line of the boat.

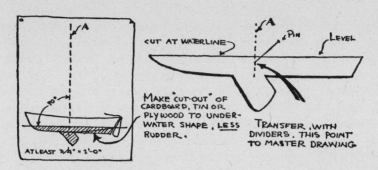

CUT AT WATERLINE — — — PIN — LEVEL

MAKE "CUT-OUT" OF CARDBOARD, TIN OR PLYWOOD TO UNDER-WATER SHAPE, **LESS** RUDDER.

TRANSFER, WITH DIVIDERS, THIS POINT TO MASTER DRAWING

AT LEAST 3/4" = 1'-0"

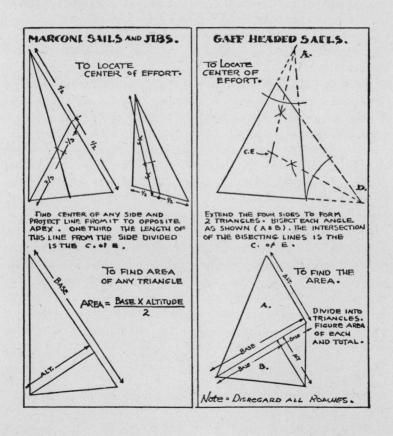

MARCONI SAILS AND JIBS.

TO LOCATE CENTER OF EFFORT.

FIND CENTER OF ANY SIDE AND PROJECT LINE FROM IT TO OPPOSITE APEX. ONE THIRD THE LENGTH OF THIS LINE FROM THE SIDE DIVIDED IS THE C. OF E.

TO FIND AREA OF ANY TRIANGLE

$$\text{AREA} = \frac{\text{BASE} \times \text{ALTITUDE}}{2}$$

BASE

ALT.

GAFF HEADED SAILS.

TO LOCATE CENTER OF EFFORT.

A.

C.E

D.

EXTEND THE FOUR SIDES TO FORM 2 TRIANGLES. BISECT EACH ANGLE AS SHOWN (A & B). THE INTERSECTION OF THE BISECTING LINES IS THE C. OF E.

TO FIND THE AREA.

A.

ALT.

DIVIDE INTO TRIANGLES. FIGURE AREA OF EACH AND TOTAL.

BASE

BASE

BASE

B.

Note = DISREGARD ALL ROACHES.

With spar dimensions and sail area in mind, it is drawn upon tracing paper in the same scale as the general elevation of the boat. Here are the methods of finding both area and centers of effort (C. of E.) as the sail centers are called.

A vertical line is dropped from this center, in this case parallel to the mast, as the mast has no rake. The tracing is then adjusted over the drawing until the two lines representing the C.L.R. and the C. of E. are in the correct relationship, the sail plan is transferred to the drawing, and the correct measurements are scaled off and indicated. Thus will the mast be located and the size of the sail, hoist, foot, and leech be determined. While most sails are roached, that is, have the leech a rounded line, the roach is not considered in these calculations, and the sail is regarded as a simple triangle.

There are no exact rules for determining this relationship of centers. It varies with every boat; it varies with every wave; and at best, it can be but an average, the difference to be adjusted, when sailing, by the rudder. However, when sailing, these planes which have been so far considered as flat and parallel to the keel actually are not so. Their centers move forward an unknown amount. Experience indicates that the C.L.R. moves forward farther than the C. of E., probably reaching the ideal relationship of coincidence some place in the complex picture resultant from heeling, sheeting, trimming, and the action of the waves. For this reason, these two centers of forces are kept separated on the flat drawing, the C. of E. leading the C.L.R., with the foreknowledge that under sailing conditions they will reach a more ideal balance. The amount of this separation is always expressed as a percentage of the water-line length. The designer uses the following table, to which he adds his own experience, gained from the performance of other vessels.

Small centerboard boats,
    Marconi-rigged   Lead   6–7% of W.L. length.
Small keel boats,
    Marconi-rigged   Lead   5% of W.L. length.

Small centerboard boats,				
gaff-rigged	Lead	4–5%	of W.L.	length.
Small keel boats,				
gaff-rigged	Lead	3–4%	of W.L.	length.
Cruising boats,				
Marconi-rigged	Lead	6–8%	of W.L.	length.
Cruising boats, gaff-rigged	Lead	4%	of W.L.	length.
Exceptionally shallow				
boats	Lead	12–14%	of W.L.	length.
Bilgeboard scows	Lead	15–18%	of W.L.	length.

Our boat falls into the class of small centerboarder, Marconi-rigged; and the tables show that the C. of E. should lead the C.L.R. by about 6 per cent. Now, as our water-line length is 15 feet, or 180 inches, we find that this lead or separation is exactly 10 ¾ inches. We may now at last fix the sail and mast location and be pretty certain of a boat of good, safe habits. Further adjustments can be made when afloat by giving the mast more or less rake by adjusting the shrouds, partners, and step; or by fussing with the centerboard or location of ballast, live and fixed, until perfect balance has been achieved. However, these minute refinements won't be necessary in anything but the really fast-class racers. All the gadgets for changing mast locations, giving bow to spars and tautening halyards bar tight are simply efforts to utterly refine the balance between C.L.R. and C. of E.

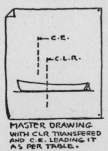

MASTER DRAWING WITH C.L.R. TRANSFERED AND C.E. LEADING IT AS PER TABLE.

TRACING OF SAIL WITH C.E. LOCATED.

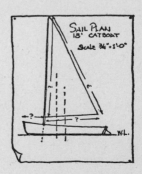

SAIL PLAN 18' CATBOAT
Scale ¾"=1'-0"

It is not meant that the designer take the balance of these centers lightly. Any grave variance from the percentages might result in serious consequences for the handling of the boat; that is, it might suffer from what is called "lee" or "weather" helm.

The boat with lee helm has a tendency to swing her head away from the wind, which must be compensated by keeping the tiller generally toward the leeward side of the boat. Such a boat is dangerous and slow. Unless constantly watched she will fall off into a close-hauled reach; and if left for any length of time to her own devices, she will turn completely about and jibe, with disastrous results to rigging, spars, and heads. Usually, such a boat is found to have the C. of E. too far forward of the C.L.R. It sometimes can be cured by raking the mast aft, or by dropping the centerboard its entire depth, or both. Shifting ballast will also help, and many racers use this trick of distributing live weight about the boat under certain sailing conditions.

In the multiple-sailed boat, the reduction of head canvas will help to cure lee helm, as will the substitution of a regular cut jib for the overlapping or Genoa jib. Naturally, this will also result in a loss of speed and is at best only a temporary measure.

Weather helm is just the opposite of lee helm. The boat here wants to spring up into the eye of the wind, to luff. Most boats have this characteristic designed into them. Thus, if for some reason the helm is abandoned for a moment, the vessel will, by herself, round up to a safe position. She can be felt, and can be steered by rudder pressure alone. A hard squall will send her into the wind, gaining footage to windward and in no way endangering her. Excessive weather helm is an annoyance and a slowing factor, usually due to the C. of E. and C.L.R. being too close together or to the C. of E. being aft of the C.L.R. It can be cured by lessening the rake of the mast or partly sheathing the centerboard, or both. Ballast judiciously placed will help, as will setting an overlapping jib in place of the regular-cut one. Dagger boards which have the forefoot cut away, when reversed, sometimes contribute to a better helm. If at all in doubt about the correct relationships of these two centers, it would be safest, by far, to have too little rather than too much separation between them.

The boat with a multiple- or divided-sail rig presents some additional problems when it comes to balancing. The center of the underwater parts are found in exactly the same way as described, and of course, even though we are now dealing with several sail centers, we still have but one Center of Lateral Resistance.

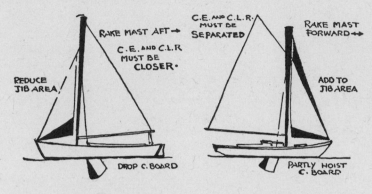

To cure mild lee helm   *To cure mild weather helm*

In finding the common centers of two or more sails, we consider them as weights perched on a seesaw and with a fulcrum, or point at which one balances the other. This fulcrum is called the Total Center of Effort (Tot. C. of E.) and it must bear the standard relationship to the C.L.R. as indicated by the table and by experience.

By simple mechanics the two sail-centers are connected by a drawn line which represents the total sail area of both sails. This is scaled off accurately in inches, and a simple equation is set up. Thus: Total sail area *is* to the length of the line *as* the area of jib is to what? Or: Tot. S.A.:? inches (scale off):: jib area in square feet:?

The "what" is the distance of the center of total sail area from the center of area of the mainsail. This distance is scaled off, along the line connecting the jib and mainsail centers, and a double circle placed around the dot. This dot must have the proper lead over the C.L.R., just as it did when we dealt with one sail only.

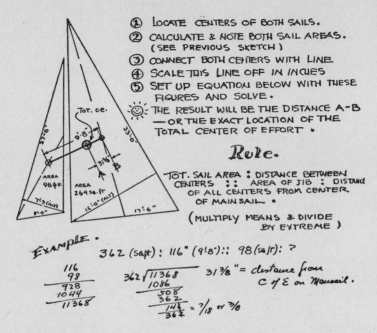

① LOCATE CENTERS OF BOTH SAILS.
② CALCULATE & NOTE BOTH SAIL AREAS.
   (SEE PREVIOUS SKETCH)
③ CONNECT BOTH CENTERS WITH LINE.
④ SCALE THIS LINE OFF IN INCHES
⑤ SET UP EQUATION BELOW WITH THESE
   FIGURES AND SOLVE.
☀ THE RESULT WILL BE THE DISTANCE A-B
   — OR THE EXACT LOCATION OF THE
   TOTAL CENTER OF EFFORT •

Rule.

TOT. SAIL AREA : DISTANCE BETWEEN
CENTERS :: AREA OF JIB : DISTANCE
OF ALL CENTERS FROM CENTER
OF MAINSAIL •

(MULTIPLY MEANS & DIVIDE
   BY EXTREME)

EXAMPLE.

$$362 \,(sq/t) : 116" \,(9'8") :: 98 \,(sq/t) : \,?$$

116
98
928
1044
11368

$$362 \overline{)11368}$$
1086
508
362
148/362 = 7/18 or 3/8

31 3/8 "= distance from
C of E on Mainsail.

The relationship of the two sails to each other cannot be changed now as it would move this point. The clews, tacks, peaks, mast step, partner, etc., must be kept exactly where the transfer from the tracing paper shows them to be on the master drawing. Naturally, there will be some amount of shifting and trials before the ideal sail-plan will be formed. However, this process must be gone through for every change made in the sail plan, as it is adjusted to fit the areas, rigs, spars, and deck plan of your boat. And, incidentally, it's not the long way—every naval architect does exactly this as he designs.

The balancing of schooners, ketches, or other multiple-masted vessels presents a slightly more complicated problem. The endsails (that is mizzen and headsails) are first considered and their common center found, using the same rule as for the sloop or two-sailed vessel. In the case of multiple headsails (such as staysail

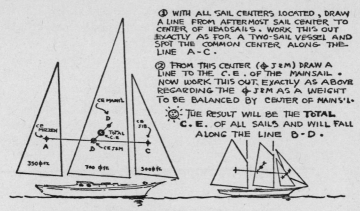

① WITH ALL SAIL CENTERS LOCATED, DRAW A LINE FROM AFTERMOST SAIL CENTER TO CENTER OF HEADSAILS. WORK THIS OUT EXACTLY AS FOR A TWO-SAIL VESSEL AND SPOT THE COMMON CENTER ALONG THE LINE A-C.

② FROM THIS CENTER (⊕ J & M) DRAW A LINE TO THE C.E. OF THE MAINSAIL. NOW WORK THIS OUT. EXACTLY AS ABOVE REGARDING THE ⊕ J & M AS A WEIGHT TO BE BALANCED BY CENTER OF MAINS'L.

☺ THE RESULT WILL BE THE **TOTAL C.E.** OF ALL SAILS AND WILL FALL ALONG THE LINE B-D.

Finding C. of E. of two-masted vessels

and jib or jib topsail or the conventional cutter rig) the common center of these are found, and only then are they balanced with the mizzen, or, in the case of the schooner, the mainsail. This Center of Jib and Mizzen, as it would be labelled on the sail plan of a ketch or yawl, is then balanced with the remaining middle sail and the common centers of all sails—that is, the true C. of E. of the sail plan—placed in its proper relationship to the C.L.R.

Designing such a rig takes much trial and error. Not only must perfect balance be achieved, but the areas must be so distributed by finding the correct dimensions of hoist, foot, and head as to assure the rig's balancing under various combinations of sails. Thus, the ketch should be able to sail safely under mainsail alone or under jib and jigger alone. The C.E. of the mainsail will therefore be in fairly correct relationship to the C.L.R., as will the C.E. of the headsails and mizzen alone.

Further, the addition of light airs (except the spinnaker which is used before the wind when balance becomes less important) must not radically upset this balance. Reduction of canvas should not affect it either. Reef points must be so located, when tied down, as to spread the correct amount of canvas to preserve balance. In the sloop, for example, tying in the first reef should not seriously affect the balance, and therefore should not be too deep. The second reef may be quite deep, and a smaller storm jib designed to be used at the same time. The third reef might be designed to balance the mainsail without the use of any jib. Or the jib itself may be fitted with reef points so that a reef in each sail will keep them in balance and not shift the total C.E.

The foundation of the sail plan is the working rig, that is, ordinary sailing canvas. Light air and storm canvas is designed around it. Remember that roaches are not calculated into the areas and that the overlap of Genoas, etc., is deducted from such sails when their areas are figured. Any good sailmaker, if given the plans of your boat with the rough sail-plan worked out, will balance the rig accurately for you. I have seen sailmakers, after years of experience in building yacht sails, look at a bare spar-plan, and by eye alone, check in the centers. Later calculations showed them to be seldom more than 3 per cent in error. To be able to do this, establishing approximate centers before a sail is drawn, reduces the designing to a very simple process. Adjustments necessary will be but minor and the sail plan completed with but one trial.

There is no accurate manner for the amateur to calculate the exact sail area required for any given hull. Experienced designers do this "by guess and by gosh" and usually succeed. For the tyro (and, boys, the professionals do it too!) the best procedure is to study plans and areas as used on boats similar to your own. Length is not important—twenty-footers carry anywhere from 100 square feet to 300 square feet. The important element is the underwater design and the beam. Select several boats similar to the one you are considering, matching them in general specifications of keel, type of ballast, weight of construction, draft, sailing lines, and character.

In designing, sail areas are usually "shot at" in round figures. All factors weighed, it becomes apparent that about 650 square feet would drive a certain thirty-footer with speed and safety. However, as the sail plan is adjusted to get correct balance, a foot falls off here, and a foot is added there. The result is perhaps 638 square feet or 671 square feet. These odd figures need afford no concern to the amateur designer; they are pure accidents. A 5 per cent overage won't put your Charlie Noble under, nor a 4 per cent underestimate cause you to sail with the stateliness of a brick meeting house. Tolerance, up to 5 or 7 per cent either way (except in racing classes) is permissible for the cruiser of thirty feet or so. However, in the small boat the tolerance decreases with perhaps 3 per cent for the twenty-five-footer and 1 per cent for the fifteen-footer.

The amount of plain sail suitable is a pure estimate, depending upon design, average weather, number of crew, and other factors. It is best to design the normal, safe-and-sane sail plan; then provide a real locker full of light air combinations and several jibs to meet all kinds of weather and sea. Personally, I'd much rather switch jibs than reef!

Every yachtsman needs to know something about the bending, care, and repair of his canvas. Books have been written about the sails, but the subject is still not exhausted. We shall touch here only the highlights, selecting the most practical and simple procedure to overcome the problems, in the firm belief that most folks, anxious for blue water and the feel of wind, want to know *how* and not *why*.

A properly made sail is a thing as beautiful as a fine painting. For the purposes of this chapter, we will analyze a mainsail made

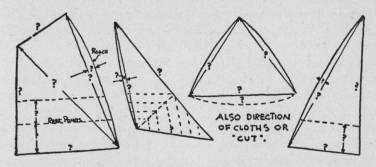

The measurement needed by the sailmaker

by one of America's foremost sailmakers, diagramming each part of it as an example of perfection. But beyond and above all the best of workmanship, the perfect sail must fit perfectly.

Perfect fit can be achieved only by most careful measurement, a sufficient allowance for later stretching and setting, and by the use of only the best material available. It is utterly essential that spars be straight and true, and, certainly in the racing boat, that the irregularly tapered spar has one flat side, or flat track feather, so that the sail, which is straight-cut on foot and hoist, need not adjust itself even to the slight taper of an inch or less.

American-made canvas of Sea Island cotton which is long stapled, is the best. Ordinary duck, canvas, or sheeting is not for sails of beauty or durability, any more than is the labor of the ordinary awning maker or upholsterer. The inland sailor, contemplating the purchase of a suit of sails, should make special effort to have the work done by a seacoast sailmaker whose experience will assure a good suit of sails. There are undoubtedly good sailmakers in a few key cities of the lakes, but too often the western boat has been canvassed by "Ye Awning and Upholstery Shoppe." For long-distance sail building, indeed for any kind, I believe it preferable to send the maker the size, taken directly from the spars, rather than send the old sail and have all its faults built into the new.

Incidentally, the term canvas as used here, refers to the synthetics as well, namely, nylon and dacron. Actually, nylon is disappearing as a sail material, as it should; for while it has excellent qualities, it stretches too readily and does not long remain a fitted and efficient sail. Dacron, its sister material, is almost perfect. The synthetics all obviate mildew and rot (within reason) and generally are used today by most sailmakers. A dacron sail will always be sewn with dacron thread and, to retain like coefficients, the bolt ropes will often be made of doubled and stitched-down folds of the same material.

The awning builder seldom understands dacron and its behavior as a sail, and so we have another valid reason to stick with a bona fide sailmaker. Many of these carry in stock standard class sails, made to class tolerances; and it is possible to obtain a set of sails almost by return mail if you sail a well known and stock class. Such are Snipes, Javelins, Comets, Internationals, the Star Boats, and about two hundred others.

For the man contemplating canvas work, a kit is necessary. This should include the following tools:

Assortment of triangular-sectioned sail needles.
Assortment of roping and marling needles (large eyes).
A palm, fitted to your own hand.
Sail hook (a lanyard and blunt hook on a swivel).
Pricker (for opening small holes).
Beeswax.
Sewing and roping twine.
Brass grommet rings.
Knife, seam creaser and rubber, scissors, tape, wooden fid.

For ordinary sailmaking, the flat and herringbone stitches are sufficient. These are diagrammed below. The round seam, also shown, is for joining the parts of sailcovers, jackets, sea bags, and similar types of canvas work.

Naturally, in these days, the machine stitch is commonly used, and the amateur, contemplating the yards of hand seaming, will look with favor upon the sewing machine in the off-parlor. Okay —but be sure to use a good quality *linen* sail thread or dacron thread. By all means, with machine sewing, use middle stitching; that is, run an additional thread along the seam midway between the two edge stitchings. Machine sewing will be made very much easier if a large table is placed beyond the machine table. I once sewed a sail by machine on the front porch. The machine was a small portable one, and by placing it at the porch edge, near the steps, I got not only leg room, but also a fine, flat surface beyond the machine for handling the canvas.

Some notes in support of the sketches showing the details of the mainsail we are analyzing:

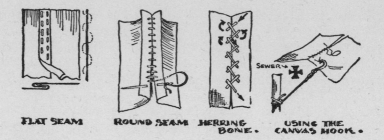

FLAT SEAM   ROUND SEAM   HERRING BONE.   USING THE CANVAS HOOK.

1. Note that the tabling, or material reinforcing, extends only along the foot and hoist, not along the leech.
2. Note that batten pockets are several inches longer than the battens. This, so as not to pinch and cause wrinkles. Battens, by the way, are made of a strong, "whippy" wood which will not stain. Oak, mahogany, and fir are out; ash, spruce, elm, and certain pines are in. One of the plastics (which can be bought as dimension stock), hand smoothed, makes good permanent, non-stain battens.
3. Grommets. Brass machine-inserted ones are cheap, quick, and common. They stain, pull out very easily, and are hard to replace. Hand-sewn ones are cheap, take time and patience to make, and are found on all good sails. They hold, will not pull out, and do not stain. Take your choice.
4. Roping is essential to any sail which is to set well. Use, not common manila, but only a bolt rope especially manufactured for this use. The best of all is a linen-thread balloon rope. It will not shrink or stretch and is free from splinters. Taper the bolt rope off neatly, cutting away part of each strand after unlaying for several feet. Relay, cut some more, relay and rat-tail for a few feet along the leech at head and clew. Use double sail-twine for sewing on the bolt rope, stretching both canvas and rope hand-taut as you sew.
5. Cloths generally run approximately parallel to the foot, usually at an angle of about 15 degrees from the water line. Thus the sail is streamlined, and the wind blows along the seams and not against them as in the old-fashioned running

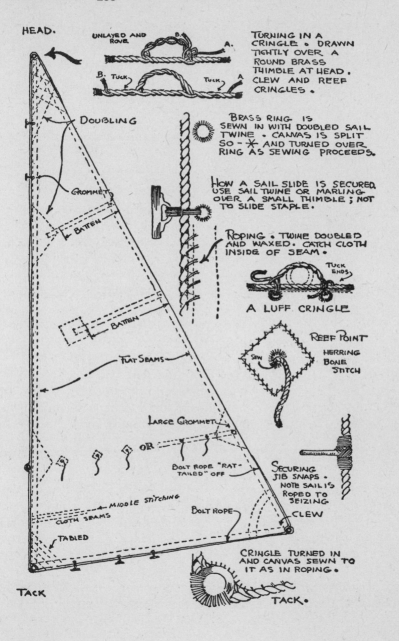

HEAD.

UNLAYED AND ROVE. B.A.

A.

B. TUCK   TUCK   A.

TURNING IN A CRINGLE • DRAWN TIGHTLY OVER A ROUND BRASS THIMBLE AT HEAD • CLEW AND REEF CRINGLES •

DOUBLING

GROMMET

BATTEN

BRASS RING IS SEWN IN WITH DOUBLED SAIL TWINE • CANVAS IS SPLIT SO — ✳ AND TURNED OVER RING AS SEWING PROCEEDS •

HOW A SAIL SLIDE IS SECURED. USE SAIL TWINE OR MARLING OVER A SMALL THIMBLE ; NOT TO SLIDE STAPLE •

ROPING • TWINE DOUBLED AND WAXED • CATCH CLOTH INSIDE OF SEAM •

TUCK ENDS

A LUFF CRINGLE

BATTEN

FLAT SEAMS

REEF POINT

SEW

HERRING BONE STITCH

LARGE GROMMET

OR

BOLT ROPE "RAT-TAILED" OFF

SECURING JIB SNAPS • NOTE SAIL IS ROPED TO SEIZING

MIDDLE STITCHING

CLOTH SEAMS

BOLT ROPE

CLEW

TABLED

CRINGLE TURNED IN AND CANVAS SEWN TO IT AS IN ROPING •

TACK

TACK •

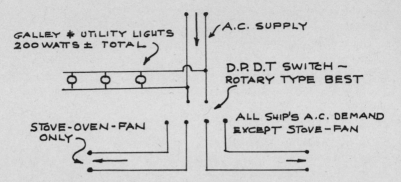

The use of a main line switch to isolate stove from demand circuits and retain full available power for stove use only. This system will save fuse failures and permit the use of low-output generators

of cloths parallel to the leech. Large jibs, however, usually run cloths two ways. The clew angle is bisected, and those above it run parallel with the mainsail cloths; those below it run at approximately right angles to those above. This gives a strong construction, helps the jib to set well, and assures its true shape for a reasonably long period.

6. Reef points are always of cotton line, and reef grommets are backed up by a swatch or strip of material sewn about it. The points are end-whipped, then sewn, through the lay, to the grommet edge, not merely stopper-knotted on each side.

7. Mast hoops, sail slides, and jib snaps are always secured to the sail by marling or doubled sail-twine, not sewn on. A single grommet in the way of the seizing is sufficient for the smaller sizes; two grommets or an elongated single grommet, for the larger sizes. All these items should be of brass—iron, even though galvanized, has no place next to canvas or dacron.

The care of sails can be expressed in few words: Keep clean and dry. I believe that sails suffer far more ashore or bagged than they do while performing. Naturally, there are sane and reasonable ways in which to treat sails while in use, and the books on sailing will give these.

The great enemy of canvas is mildew, the forerunner of rot. Mildew can occur only if the canvas is stored wet or damp. Mildew cannot be prevented by direct attack. Making the canvas water-resistant and water-repellant, thus minimizing moisture saturation, is the only attack on mildew possible. While the discoloring waterproofing-formulae are satisfactory for ordinary canvas, few yachtsmen care to sail with anything but the traditional white canvas.

Therefore, care of sails resolves itself down to just that—*care*. Most certainly, every suit of sails should have its own bag, labelled, and be kept clean and dry. There seems no valid reason for permitting modern Marconi sails, with their slides and simple head, tack and clew shackles, to remain bent during the off days. It is just as simple to remove them as to reeve a sail cover over

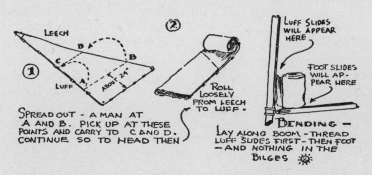

How to fold sails

them. In removing them, battens should be pulled, reefs shaken out (if turned in), and the sail properly dried and folded ready for easy bending. Only after a thorough sunning should this be done—never after the evening dew has settled. If wet, cast off the clew outhaul and brail loosely, allowing a free circulation of air until the sails can be dried by hoisting or unbending and spread over a rail or on dry ground ashore.

Perhaps the man with the gaff-rigger and mast hoops has an excuse for leaving his canvas bent. Sail covers, however, are then necessary as well as frequent midweek dryings after heavy rains or fogs. The covers should be water-proofed and fitted most carefully, especially in the way of masts and stays.

Because of their bulk, dirty sails are best cleaned by commercial cleaners or laundries. There are rust solvents—though I've never found one 100 per cent satisfactory—and grease removers with which to go over the sail first: a job for the owner and not the laundry. Watch the numerals or devices—often these are not of fast colors and, under hot water, will run and stain.

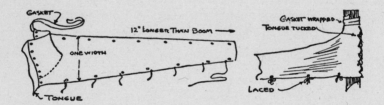

Requisites of a proper sail cover

For the man home-washing a small sail, it is best to use a commercial water softener (such as Oakite) rather than a soap which makes suds and later, rinse as you might, runs down over your decks. The secret is a thorough soaking overnight in tepid, softened water and a bleach; then, many sousings and rinsings in hot water—*no wringing*—and a long drying in wind and sun under no strain or unnatural pull. A brush and strong cleaner should be used on stubborn spots, rubbed in a circular motion, on both sides; loose threads should be snipped, repairs made at once—and you'll have a presentable suit of sails for the coming season afloat.

Winter care should include loose folding with anti-moth and rodent preparations liberally sprinkled between folds. Storage should be in the sail bag; or sails should be completely wrapped in heavy paper and kept in a dry place which will not get too warm or, possibly, moist. If there is any question of your providing a winter home for some of Mickey Mouse's relatives, hang the bagged or wrapped sails from a beam and put a rat guard similar to those used on hawsers of docked ships over the drawstring.

Sails, as near as I can determine from observation and experience, last about three seasons. Actually, their life is many times this when used only as sails—not as boom tents, door mats, lazybacks, deck cushions, and bunk pads!

XII *Masts and Spars*

Wooden masts and spars are either of solid straight-grained and light woods or hollow, that is, built up in order to obtain the needed lightness, flexibility, and strength.

For the solid mast, pine, spruce, and fir are used, with clear spruce the best and most popular. However, it is very difficult for the lone buyer to procure the close-grained northern-grown or Sitka spruce which is the only kind suitable for spars. Certain sources in large cities (which must be found) carry spar spruce in stock, and the amateur is lucky if he can draw his material from such a place. The ordinary pin-knotted spruce which is stocked by many lumber yards is not suitable and is perhaps one of the poorest woods because of the sap pockets, knots, and defects in it.

Fir is the wood most easily obtainable in the long lengths generally required, but it has the great disadvantage of being excessively heavy and often contains long flakes of wood not bonded to the core except by sap. Fir is far from ideal, yet in many cases, must be used or the boat go sparless. Stock cut away from the heart but close to the center of the tree is best, and the particular piece you buy should be selected only after examining all the stock available. If there are any defects which absolutely cannot be overcome, see that they occur between deck and step rather than farther aloft.

1. *T-boom for small boats. Light, strong, easily made. Note holes for lacing.* 2. *Streamlined boom with riding groove for bolt rope of the sail. Made in matched halves and glued together.* 3–4. *Conventional solid booms, each with a feather under the track to permit bridles to pass under track.* 5–6. *Solid masts. Note raised track to allow stays to pass under.* 7. *Slotted mast for bolt rope. Slot is in two matched pieces being glued to spar with "Casco" type glue*

While clear white pine is not always easy to find in the average lumber yard, most local building-material concerns have wholesale sources from which they can order it. If at all possible, make arrangements to visit the wholesaler, and you, yourself, select the stick. If pine is found to have a knot, it is usually so large that it seriously weakens a spar. Small, pinhole knots, about the size of a pencil, if secure and not adrift, won't necessarily weaken the spar to a dangerous extent, though they present a mean piece of wood to work upon. White pine is, in weight, midway between spruce and fir, and is perhaps the one to be used, if lacking real spar timber in the spruces.

The working of a spar is a tedious job, demanding care and patience. No matter what the tree, it should be thoroughly dried. Get it several feet longer than required so that the weather-checks so often found at the ends can be cut away. In making the round spar, the stock is first squared with the required taper; then 8-squared; and finally rounded by plane, scraper, and sandpaper. The taper generally starts about one-third of the length above the step, becoming quicker above the highest band or block.

After 8-squaring, work the ridges off with long strokes of a

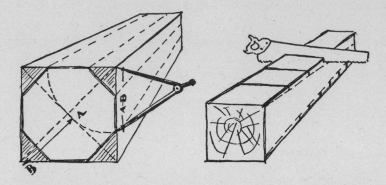

To 8-square a spar. Take half the end diagonal (A-B) and, with a divider, swing a circle from each corner. Where the four quarter circles meet the edge drive a brad. Now do the same thing on the opposite end after tapering. Stretch a chalk line between and snap and work to these marks using a bevel square set 135°.

To taper a spar first carefully square. Then snap a line with its greatest width the greatest diameter and its least width the least diameter. Saw down to these marks on a square cut, chisel out, and plane smooth. Then proceed with 8-squaring.

(Note that these spars have a regular taper the entire length.)

smoothing plane set fairly heavy. Fair up with a jack plane, then work out all traces of the knife with a cabinet scraper or heavy sandpaper. The motion of the sandpaper, which is held in a block made from an old life-preserver cork, is spiral. In a twenty-four

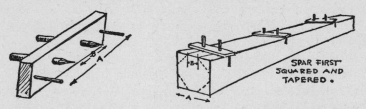

Homemade 8-square gauge for marking irregular tapers. An ordinary block of wood with two nails as guides and pencil stubs as markers. Distance A, between guides as wide as widest part of taper. Distance B, to coincide with diagonals at this point. By keeping the two guides always touching the sides of the spar and turning the gauge slightly as it is slid, the pencils will mark the true lines to which to cut the bevels

inch stroke, turn the paper about one-third the diameter, criss-crossing the stroke as you proceed. Then blot with warm water, allowing the soft grain to rise, and before completely dry, finish off with fine sandpaper. Give a coat of shellac immediately.

Booms and gaffs, contrary to popular illustrations, either should not be tapered at all or should be tapered *toward* the mast. The strain on these spars is at the center and is no greater at the tack than at the clew.

In the event that mast withes, bands, or other fittings shaped to a radius are to be used, they should be used as gauges as the work proceeds. The mast band, upon which is the downward strain of the shrouds when sailing, should be set on a slight shoulder

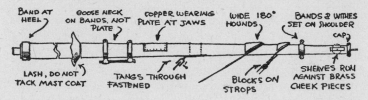

Some pointers on setting mast furnishings without weakening the mast

worked into the stick; one-sixteenth of an inch is enough in most cases. The heel of the mast should always have a band to prevent the tenon from starting a split.

The hollow mast, becoming more popular each year and certainly to be recommended for a real combination of strength and lightness, is not difficult to make. Spruce, preferably Sitka, is the only wood to use; but it is not absolutely necessary that it be in one length, and it is, therefore, perhaps more easily procured locally than the solid spruce spar.

Here is a method, lacking the clamps of a cabinet or boatshop, of clamping wood satisfactorily for the amateur. Use epoxy or equal glue mixed and applied strictly according to the manufacturer's directions; also be sure that the wood is thoroughly dry. It is not necessary to use screws for fastening at all, and only a few

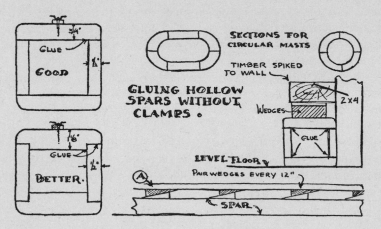

galvanized nails are necessary to tack the parts in place before gluing. Naturally, all doubling or inside blocking, cap, heel, etc., are glued in before the box is finally closed in.

In laying out the hollow spar, the afterside of the mast and the top of the boom are always made flat and without taper. This causes the sails to set absolutely perfectly, a thing not possible with the tapered round-mast or boom. Parts of the sparring—

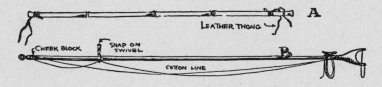

A. A *bamboo "whisker pole" for lightness. Leave inboard rawhide thongs long for adjusting the draft of the jib.* B. *A spinnaker pole rigged for duty as a boat boom or whisker pole*

though sometimes seemingly forgotten until ready to go overboard—are the various jib clubs, whisker poles, etc., needed on the average boat.

Jib clubs should be as light as possible and have a device by which they can be easily unshipped, the jib rolled about it and taken below, away from the hazard of handling ground tackle and being walked upon. A simple homemade device for the small sailboat is to knock the eye out of a swivel snap hook, then pin it into the forward end of the club, snapping it into one of the chain links which have been inserted between bow chain-plate and the lower eye of the head or jib stay. A similar snap on the jib sheet is fastened to a pad eye or wire grommet, and the whole assembly is thus quickly cast off for stowing.

The whisker pole, if it be a separate spar, is best made of bamboo for lightness, and rather than having jaws or heavy snaps, should be provided with merely a rawhide thong on each end for lashing to mast and jib clew. However, especially on the small boat, much gear of this sort is decidedly in the way, and a method of doubling up on uses is in order as suggested in the sketch herewith.

Most spar plans call for the use of spreaders. These can very well be made of either wood or metal. It is my belief that both types should be so hung as to be rigid and should not be permitted to slop about; also, that the ends which receive the shrouds should not be merely a notch but so designed as to securely grip the wire.

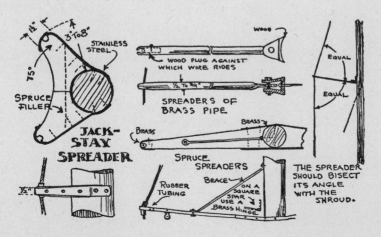

Most furnishings and hardware are very expensive and are hardly items on which to save money. I am conscious of the fact that I sound this warning too often as the book advances and that the reader, knowing this well enough, still must apply "expensive or not, I can't afford it and I want the next best thing."

Here, then, are a few drawings of standard items to be built and assembled for the mast. There is, unfortunately, no positive manner in which to recommend sizes and strengths. When I set about making one of these gadgets (or in building the spars them-

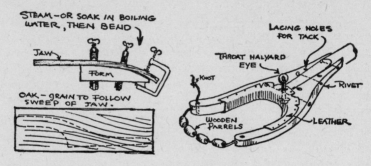

Making gaff jaws

selves for that matter), I turn to the builder's plans in the various yachting magazines and textbooks. Any plan of a boat of about the size and tonnage of my own will give me *about* the dimensions suitable. Another source are the catalogues of the ship chandlers; illustrations, sizes, and strengths are very conveniently noted there. This procedure is far from the exact science of engineering, I know—but few of us are willing to undertake a study of engineering in order to make a gooseneck for a simple little twenty-footer!

Since original publication of this work, the extruded-aluminum spar has come into full flower. It is a good shipmate. Any manufacturer building a few dozen or more boats a year has arranged to have his spars supplied by one of the aluminum fabricators. Look with great favor on a vessel so equipped, for you will be

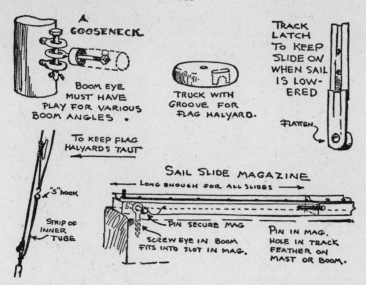

A GOOSENECK

BOOM EYE
MUST HAVE
PLAY FOR VARIOUS
BOOM ANGLES .

TRUCK WITH
GROOVE FOR
FLAG HALYARD.

TRACK
LATCH
TO KEEP
SLIDE ON
WHEN SAIL
IS LOW-
ERED

FLATTEN

TO KEEP FLAG
HALYARDS TAUT

"S" HOOK

STRIP OF
INNER
TUBE

SAIL SLIDE MAGAZINE

LONG ENOUGH FOR ALL SLIDES

PIN SECURE MAG

SCREW EYE IN BOOM
FITS INTO SLOT IN MAG.

PIN IN MAG.
HOLE IN TRACK
FEATHER ON
MAST OR BOOM.

Gadgets for spars

shipmates with an enduring piece of gear and have none of the trying upkeep of the wooden spar. Few custom boats, at least home-built custom boats, can afford a one-of-a-kind aluminum spar; nor can you, I'm afraid. However, it is quite possible to use a wooden mast and, because tapering is not necessary, construct booms, spinnaker poles, and whisker poles of straight aluminum tubing, which is readily obtainable at production prices. Usually the ends of these are capped with a wooden plug and conventional hardware is applied. Any fastening through the tubing must be backed by a wooden filler, driven into the tube.

In general, aluminum spars require no special treatment. There are various so-called "polishes" for exterior aluminum, but they are hardly necessary if the aluminum has been anodized. A dory-shop method of keeping aluminum bright is to rub down with ordinary diesel fuel-oil. The tube spar requires somewhat more staying than the wooden spar, and a good rule of thumb is to increase shrouds by 50 per cent. Large aluminum masts, of course, have webbing and bracing built inside and are plated rather than tube. These are jobs for engineers to specify and are somewhat beyond the skills of the tyro.

If you do have an aluminum mast, you can become popular in your local cruising anchorages by catharping all halyards and setting up the main halyard (which is often *inside* the mast) so you do not ring out like cathedral chimes all the night through. This slatting—like endless ringing bells—can drive your shipmates crazy!

Setting the Mast

Almost as important as the stays themselves are the hull supports of the mast.

Starting at the bottom, let the mast step be the keel itself. While this is not always possible, it is in most cases. If there is absolutely no way in which to mortise the keel member, an oak block may be built on, but *must* be most securely dry-bolted to the keel.

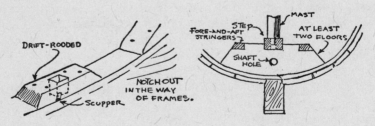

A *mast step scupper. One on each side leading aft*   Setting a *mizzen mast step in an auxiliary*

The next point of support above is the mast partner which is a heavy timber doubling under the deck. This should not be merely a butt block spiked between two beams, but a piece most carefully fitted to doubled or extra-heavy deck beams and braced to counteract the twisting which goes on at this point.

The hole in the partners should be about an inch greater in diameter than the mast at this point, in order to accommodate a set of real mast-wedges. While it may be punched out by boring a series of connecting holes about the circumference, the hole itself must be smoothed fair and true by sawing and rasping. The wedges should be shaped to the mast and should not be merely straight shingle slivers.

Very much easier than the round hole and wedges is an arrangement shown in the sketch below. The hole is cut square (an easy operation) and the U-shaped blocks of oak are permanent, being wedged to the mast by a flat, easily made, softwood wedge from behind. Both block and wedge are flush with the deck, and consequently a canvas mast coat is not required. The assembly can be caulked and painted in with the deck or, better yet, covered with a ring plate or lead collar.

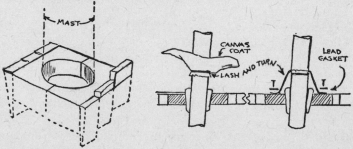

A permanent mast wedge set-up with common square wedges

Setting the mast coat. The seam is placed aft and hand sewn and the coat painted along with the deck

Old spars, as bought with the used boat, are sometimes found to be in very rough condition. Large cracks will have appeared, sometimes for half or more of the length. These, in themselves, are not necessarily dangerous. The great danger is that water and dampness have seeped into the crack and commenced their work of rot. Examine such a cracked mast carefully, digging away any of the punky wood encountered. If this wood extends below the

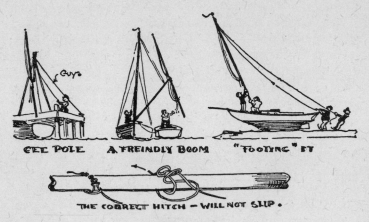

GEE POLE   A FREINDLY BOOM   "FOOTING" IT

THE CORRECT HITCH — WILL NOT SLIP .

Stepping spars

side walls of the crack or seems to extend into the heart, *discard the mast.* It is positively dangerous. Similar rottenness is sometimes found at the partners or behind the spreader fittings or around the sheave slot at the masthead.

A sound crack may be routed out, cleaned, and a dutchman very carefully fitted in. This should be a wood-to-wood fit, wedge-shaped, and driven into the crack beforehand, then smeared liberally with an epoxy type of glue and held there by clamps or a series of tightly-hove half-hitches. When dry, the dutchman should be faired off with the mast surface. Small cracks, after a cleaning and thorough drying, may be filled with one of the commercial crack-fillers, a marine-glue mastic, plastic wood, or a sparkle made of sawdust, whiting, and thick varnish. Ordinary putty should not be used as it is liable to squeeze, run, and will not keep moisture out for long.

The mast which has been broken is usually hopeless unless the break (or rot) is near the extremities. Such a spar can be "fished," as patching is called.

The spars so-far discussed have been those of sailing vessels. The straight powerboat owner, however, often ships a signal mast

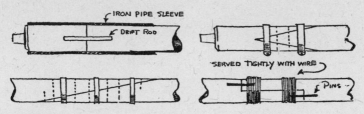

Fishing spars

that has evidently received too little attention from the standpoint of both design and utility.

Generally, such spars are merely a device from which to fly signals or carry the required white light at night. It is my personal belief that most such skinny and willowy spars would be better left off entirely. Both signals and lights can be carried on a short stub pole which does not require the staying of the tall mast—with consequent increase in room and safety on deck.

If the powerboat needs a mast at all, it needs a good one, well designed, placed in a position on board and at a rake to be in harmony with the general design, and above all, of some use beyond giving what is fondly believed to be a "shippy" look.

The powerboat mast of real use might include a short boom for hoisting the dinghy on board, doing away with the clumsy davits on average-size boats. For the fisherman, some form of perch or seat at the masthead is indicated with rattled shrouds or a series of footholds on the mast itself leading to it. It is important to keep such a feature light in appearance so as not to make the entire outfit look top-heavy and more or less ridiculous. I've never had the pleasure (if pleasure it is!) to sit in one of those office chairs spiked aloft which are sometimes seen on alleged offshore fishing cruisers. Somehow, I wouldn't want to get caught in one of them. I'm afraid my Grandfather Asa, who was a whaler and really knew what a masthead watch was, would come out of the rugged past and do some fancy haunting!

As a closing paragraph on spars, let us consider those smallest of all—the flagpole. First, the socket should always be of the flush

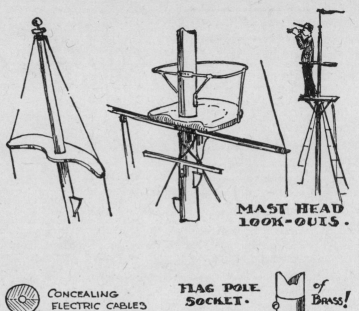

MAST HEAD LOOK-OUTS.

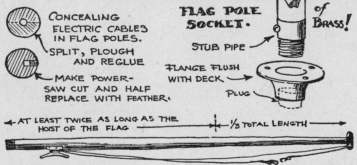

CONCEALING ELECTRIC CABLES IN FLAG POLES.

SPLIT, PLOUGH AND REGLUE

MAKE POWER-SAW CUT AND HALF REPLACE WITH FEATHER.

FLAG POLE SOCKET. of BRASS!

STUB PIPE

FLANGE FLUSH WITH DECK

PLUG

AT LEAST TWICE AS LONG AS THE HOIST OF THE FLAG — ⅓ TOTAL LENGTH

type, thus eliminating one more toe-stubber on our decks. The pole itself should be a neat, proud piece of gear—not a broomstick—and should be furnished with some device so that the ensign can be *hauled aloft*. No matter how small the pole, it should have halyards to which the flag is rove, and the pole should be kept standing while the vessel is in commission. Naturally, the poles should be removable for convenience while handling ground tackle forward or while sailing or trolling.

All flagpoles should be on the center line, the only exception being made in the case of an auxiliary. Here the ensign staff is placed slightly to starboard of the center to allow for the boom when in its crutch or on the gallows frame.

XIII *Rigging*

Rigging is divided into two classes, standing and running. Standing rigging is of wire and consists of the permanent stays and braces which support the mast. It remains standing, that is, does not run through blocks or hoist or trim sails. For these latter purposes rope, or a flexible wire cable, is used and is known as running rigging. Shrouds and stays are standing rigging; sheets, halyards, tackles, and lifts are running rigging. Backstays, which are temporary or emergency standing rigging, ought to be considered running rigging as their weakest parts are rope tackles, subject to the use of ordinary rope and needing the same care.

Rigging of any kind should be approached with the understanding that it is the most important single element of the whole sail and sparring plan. It MUST be good, strong, and adequate, and it is not an item upon which to cut corners. Only the best rope, the best wire, and the strongest furnishings should be tolerated.

The racing boat requires strong rigging, as small and as light as possible for the job to be done, in order to cut down the all important windage. Safety margins must necessarily be small, and this makes it especially important that splices, tangs, turnbuckles, etc., are of the best quality. The cruising vessel can and should err on the side of heaviness. The object here is not maximum speed, but maximum safety and reliability.

Standing Rigging

Wire ropes used for standing rigging are commonly of one of the following three types:

19-wire Standing Rigging:

Has greatest strength of any type, least stretch. Twelve wires about a 7-wire core. Difficult to splice but ideal with the socket type of wire ends.

6 × 7 Standing Rigging:

This has 6 strands of 7 wires each, is most commonly used, easily spliced, but has more stretch than 19-wire. Adequate (in the proper size) for cruising boats.

7 × 7 Standing Rigging:

Center core is of wire instead of fiber as in the 6 × 7 and is about 10 per cent stronger.

Following is a table of the strengths of the various constructions, also the metals in which they are manufactured. The plain galvanized iron, in addition to being the weakest of all types, is absolutely without lasting quality; its safe life is never more than one season. Galvanized plow steel should be the minimum standard of quality into which to put the considerable expense of splicing and rigging labor, with the stainless steels and non-corroding products much to be preferred.

Plans of new boats will have the size wire recommended noted on the sail plan. Rerigging jobs, however, might well be done with a size larger than formerly carried. A rerig job is indicated if, upon

COMPARATIVE BREAKING STRENGTHS OF VARIOUS TYPES OF MARINE ROPES

19-WIRE STRAND

Diameter, Inches	1/16	3/32	1/8	5/32	3/16	7/32	1/4	9/32	5/16	3/8	7/16	1/2	9/16	5/8	3/4
Galv. Imp. Plow Aircraft Strand	500	1,100	2,100	3,200	4,600	6,100	8,000	10,000	12,500	17,500	23,500	28,500	......	......	......
Best Quality	550	1,200	2,100	3,300	4,700	6,300	8,200	10,300	12,500	17,600	23,400	29,700	37,000	46,000	67,000

6 x 7 CONSTRUCTION

Diameter, Inches	1/16	3/32	1/8	5/32	3/16	7/32	1/4	9/32	5/16	3/8	7/16	1/2	9/16	5/8	3/4
Bronze	77	172	306	478	688	940	1,225	......	......	......	......	......	......	......	......
Galvanized Iron	236	459	711	980	1,220	1,580	1,980	2,400	2,720	3,900	5,280	6,860	8,640	10,600	14,200
Galvanized Cast Steel	......	......	......	......	......	......	3,500	4,300	5,600	7,800	10,600	13,600	17,000	20,800	29,600
Galvanized Plow Steel	......	......	......	......	......	......	4,200	5,300	6,570	9,270	12,400	16,200	20,300	24,800	35,600
Galv. Imp. Plow Steel	355	780	1,150	2,000	2,750	4,000	4,800	6,100	7,500	10,600	14,200	18,500	23,400	28,800	36,900
Best Quality	385	800	1,400	2,100	3,000	4,000	5,200	6,600	8,000	11,500	15,400	19,800	24,800	30,300	42,400

(Figures for Best Quality based on Hazard "Korodless" wire.)

bending the wire back and forth some of the individual strands spring out into whiskers. Look for weakness at the lower ends of stays and shrouds where the sea water has reached it; also, in the splices where splicing tools have flaked the galvanizing off. Rust is always an indication of weakness.

The piece of standing rigging with the ends gone need not be discarded. If the middle is in good, clean condition, use it for one of the shorter stays, buying new only for the longer stays. Jib stays should be carefully inspected as the constant wear by the hanks often expose bare metal for the whole length. Other points of wear are at the intersection of the spreaders, at light boards, and possibly where a gaff or boom has chafed. Sometimes, the wire which is just inches too short (and, mates, most of them seem to be!) can be made to do by inserting a few links of chain between the thimble and the turnbuckle. In fact, many deepwater vessels are so rigged to keep the spray and sea water below the wire. Chain can be painted and protected, the rust or weakening more easily spotted than in wire.

Be sure, however, in doing this that the chain is equal at least to the strength of the wire rope.

TABLE OF CHAIN STRENGTHS

SIZE INCHES	EST. WT. PER 100 FT. IN LBS.	PROOF TEST TONS	BREAKING STRAIN TONS
³⁄₁₆	40	½	1
¼	70	¾	1½
⁵⁄₁₆	105	1½	3
⅜	158	2	4
⁷⁄₁₆	210	3	6
½	275	4	8
⁹⁄₁₆	335	4½	8½
⅝	410	6	12
¾	580	8	16

The splicing of wire has ever been the bane of the amateur yachtsman. Some of the bird's nests offered as splices are frightful to see! However, a new and very simple method of grommet splicing has recently been developed for use with the preformed wire-rope which makes up most of the standing rigging used on yachts today.

All that is needed is a sharp snip and serving gadget (see plans) and some annealed serving wire. It can only be done with a preformed wire, one that does not fly apart when unlaid; it is quick and has been proven by tests to be just as strong as a tucked splice. Five minutes for the complete splice should be ample!

This is all that any amateur need know about wire splicing. The most important thing to remember in any splicing is to take pains, being especially careful that the wire surface is not scratched or its galvanizing chipped away. A fine finish and a durable job can be obtained by parceling and serving the splice. Parcel with light canvas, having the edge downward, like the clapboards of a house to shed water; paint with good lead paint; then serve with marling. Of course, rawhide serving can be used, sewing the seam with needle and palm, but this is not as much protection from weather as against chafing.

Racing boats, using light, strong wire, should have end sockets rather than hand-splices. These are of a great variety, some depending upon a mechanical compression screw to hold the spread wire-ends firmly; while others require hot lead to be poured and tamped between wire and socket. These are, however, very expensive and therefore unnecessary except with the *very best* grade of stainless-steel or other modern wire.

The connections of the rigging to the hull and spars are too often the weakest point in the complete structure. I am personally a great believer in the eye splice which goes completely around the mast, rather than a tang, eye, or mast band. Not only does this method make for simplicity, it also reduces weight aloft considerably. Such a splice should be served, of course, and the eye should rest naturally on a broad hound or backing piece.

On a square or hollow mast this practice is almost impossible, so

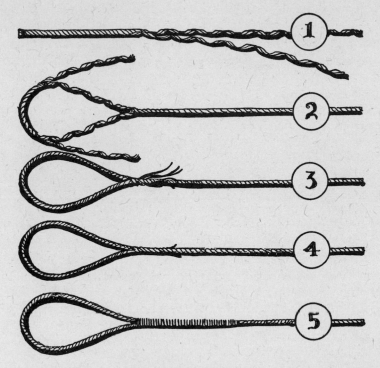

How to grommet splice

1. *Cut wire rope off clean. There is no need to whip the ends as pre-formed rope will not spring apart. Unlay, three strands on either side, carefully retaining natural curves, a length just twice the circumference of the eye to be formed. 2. Draw the two groups toward each other without unnatural bending and tie a simple overhand knot. The knot will form a small-size section of complete rope at the top of the bight. 3. Now lay each strand into the loop, letting the strands fall into their grooves. The fiber heart should be worked in carefully as the laying up proceeds. Bring the ends snug to the crotch and cut the individual strands off at varying short lengths from 1" to 2". 4. Work, by tapping with a wooden mallet, these ends into the lay of the standing part. 5. Serve the ends down tightly with stainless-steel annealed serving-wire, drawing it taut with a wire serving-tool. Properly done this splice is just as strong as a tucked splice and can be finished in one quarter of the time*

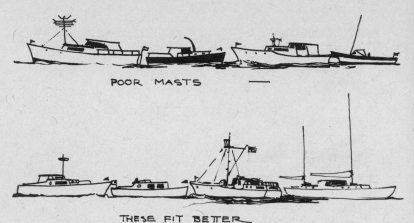

POOR MASTS —

THESE FIT BETTER

a tang had better be used. It is utterly essential that such a tang be through-bolted and not merely screwed into one surface of the mast. Doubling or filling should be present wherever a shroud or stay joins the mast. By far the best material is stainless sheet-steel with fastenings of the same material. The brass or bronze so often used here on the homemade tang is not strong except in excessively heavy weights and, further, weakens rapidly by seasoning or corrosion.

WIRE SPOOL

ABOUT 7"

FRICTION NUBS

MAKE OF SHEET METAL OR HARD WOOD

Make the grommet splice slightly larger than thimble, slip over, and draw tight with wire serving

Homemade serving board to lay wire. Keep tension on wire with fingers at handle while turning

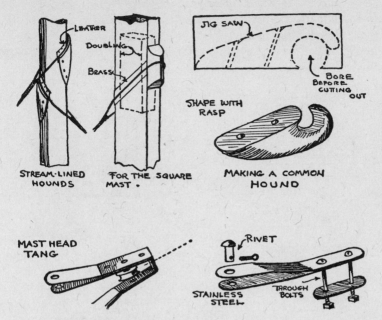

STREAM-LINED
HOUNDS

FOR THE SQUARE
MAST .

SHAPE WITH
RASP

MAKING A COMMON
HOUND

JIG SAW

BORE
BEFORE
CUTTING
OUT

MAST HEAD
TANG

RIVET

STAINLESS
STEEL

THROUGH
BOLTS

The turnbuckle end is simply a solid thimble, let into the forked end of the standard turnbuckle of a size to match the wire strength. Turnbuckles of the next size above the wire diameter are about right, thus, for ¼ inch, 6 × 7 galvanized steel wire, use a ⅜ inch turnbuckle. In the iron turnbuckles the pipe type are best as the threads which receive wear are somewhat protected inside the barrel. Pack with grease before assembling, and you won't be bothered by rusted-in screw fittings. (To get a rusted turnbuckle apart, apply heat from a blowtorch to expand the barrel and loosen the threads. Not too much heat, or the galvanizing will melt off.)

Bronze turnbuckles may be of the open type, though the cotter pins which are inserted to stop the ends from untwisting under strain are a hazard to deck mop, ankles, and sails. A hex nut on the thread, set tightly against the barrel, will do the trick much better and without the annoyance of projecting ends.

New wire will stretch considerably before the turnbuckles may be permanently set up for the season. If this stretch becomes too much, threatening to lock the turnbuckle because of lack of threads, cast off the wire and twist it *with the lay*, shortening it sufficiently to make it necessary to extend the turnbuckle again.

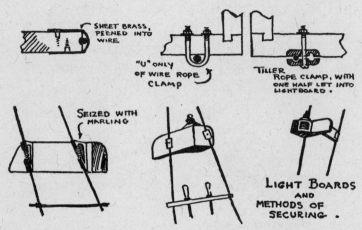

Be very careful in this setting up of standing rigging. The fore-and-aft rigging should be taut but equally balanced so as not to bend the mast either forward or aft from a true straight position. Shrouds should not be set bow-tight but should have slack to allow for slight thwartship movement of the masthead. The lee-ward shrouds, under press of canvas, should be almost (not quite) sloppy. Too much tightening here sets up a compression strain which sometimes causes leaks along the garboard in the way of the mast step.

By the way, the forward shroud is always the lower shroud; and the after shroud reaches to the masthead, possibly over a pair of spreaders first. The use of a jackstay on the forward side of the mast (or a pair of them) does much to stiffen lofty, hollow masts.

A light board should be carried at least five feet off the deck and should have a filler-piece of wood between it and the shroud to set it plumb. Here are some methods of fastening this trouble-some but necessary item to the shrouds in a no-slip, but still ad-justable, manner.

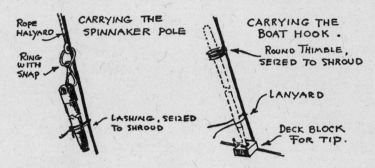

The shrouds, on a cruising boat at least, make an ideal place to carry the spinnaker pole, boat hook, or other light spars which usually must encumber the deck.

The annual care of standing rigging should always include a careful inspection of every inch of the wire. The slightest sign of rust or fraying should indicate replacement. All types of galva-nized wire will last longer if painted. Use, for this, aluminum paint as a primer and an engine enamel, one of the grays is best, for a finish. To assure the paint's filling the lay, stretch the wire out straight, a few feet above the floor, and untwist it slightly, spreading the strands, releasing it immediately after painting. Wire which has been flattened or pinched is suspect, even though not yet rusted or frayed. If the rigging has been removed from the mast, coil it carefully, with the lay, and store it *flat*, not hung in loops or festoons.

A word now about tiller rope-clamps and telephone clamps in place of splices. Nothing burns up a true boat-lover more than to see these things used on an otherwise trim little job. Actually there is no reason for it. Certainly the grommet splicing described be-fore is simple enough for anybody with brains enough to make the money to buy a boat. But if you cannot bring yourself to splice, at least use the next best and next strongest method. This is simply to turn the wire around the thimble, back along itself, and seize it with annealing wire for ten or twenty inches. Honestly, it's better than a clamp and, carefully done, might even be neat. Double serve it at the throat of the thimble; then continue, over the annealing wire, with marling.

For the small-boat owner who must go cheap (or perhaps not at all) there is a solid-plow steel galvanized-wire obtainable in various sizes which might serve for standing rigging. I have seen it used successfully in up to sixteen-footers of the light centerboard type, and I have no doubt it might prove quite successful, light, and inexpensive for the converted skiff or flat-bottomed boat. The neatest way is to shape the end as shown below, using a wooden mallet, then to serve it with marling and paint the entire assembly.

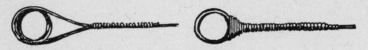

Single-strand rigging for small boats

Inside diameter to take pin of turnbuckle; three turns of wire; tightly seized with annealed rigging-wire. Painted

Served with marling, leaded, and painted gray. Serve at least 8". Eye splice similar and to fit mast snugly

Running Rigging

Any piece of rigging, wire, or rope which runs through a block or fair-lead or is movable is considered running rigging. It is, of course, usually of rope, and no part of the ship's gear is subject to more severe strains or wear.

Money saved on the purchase of rope is not money saved at all, but a risk of life and property. There are many kinds of vegetable ropes, but that made from the Philippine wild banana-plant called manila is the only kind of vegetable worth locker room on shipboard. It can always be recognized because it has a sheen and glossiness not present in other types. The fibers are smooth, round, and pliable, straw-colored, and about six feet in length. Sisal rope, sometimes passed off as manila at bargain prices, is by comparison dull, greenish instead of yellow, and has short fibers, averaging only two feet in length. Coir rope, made of coconut fibers, is red, harsh, and floats; and while sometimes used for large hawsers, does not stand well the fatigue of passing over blocks or through fair-leads.

Hemp, untarred, while very expensive, makes a fine mainsheet or jib sheet as it has all the qualities of good manila rope plus a great flexibility even when wet.

The main thing is to buy only well-known brands of rope, usually easily identified, or the same brand of rope which is being used by fishermen or commercial boatmen nearby. They have long ago learned the folly of using cheap rope, and their selection is to be trusted.

Today the synthetic ropes are in popular use, the dacrons being by far the best for yacht work. A tight-laid dacron rope, of somewhat smaller diameter than one of manila required to do the same work, is a joy. It will behave well—even docilely—and take usual deck-coil shapes readily. Even when wet, or iced, it "feels" comfortable when handled. Best of all, it will not rot. It may mildew or become soiled and gray, but its strength will remain intact until actual wear (as at a block or fair-lead) reduces the fiber and diameter. By all means, equip with dacron.

Now, there are so-called dacrons which *seem* similar but have fillers or are combined with nylon (which stretches too much for sail-setting) or are loosely laid. You can feel the difference or observe it by twisting against the lay (which is difficult in a hard-laid rope). Your best indicators are price—good line costs the most money—and the reputation of the manufacturer. The synthetics are made under license and are *not* all of the same quality.

Working dacron is a pleasure IF YOU KEEP THE ENDS SEALED AT ALL TIMES. If you fail in this, dacron will fly apart and will not readily relay. Seal the ends *before* cutting either by touching the line with flame (i.e., cigarette lighter, L.P. gas torch) or with a hot iron, or by wrapping it with two turns of one-inch-wide masking tape. Make the cut in the middle of the burn or the tape—and, presto, both ends are sealed and ready to work. The burning is usually used for strand ends as well when splicing, forming end knots, or in place of whipping.

From now on, dacron rope is worked exactly like vegetable fiber ropes, and no special techniques save one are required for splicing of all types. This is the special technique: Be sure to tuck ends at least twice as often as for vegetable rope, for dacron strands will slip. There is nothing against singeing the entire completed splice to give it slight abrasion before serving.

Included in the synthetics are the polypropaline types. This is all-plastic stranded line, for some reason made in the most garish colors and therefore an eyesore on a neat little vessel. It is fairly inexpensive but is positively not recommended for any running line. Possibly useful for an anchor line, a mooring pennant (for it is strong!), or a dinghy painter, the last being handy because polypropaline line floats and is less apt to sink and foul into your wheel(s). It stretches, it wears and frays rather easily, it coils poorly—and by and large should be left for lobster and crabtrappers. But it had to be mentioned.

The big enemies of rope are dampness and sand. Never stow a rope until it has been thoroughly sun-dried right to the heart. Sand can't always be helped, especially in rope used to handle ground tackle, but it can be washed off by trailing astern or sloshing down with sea water. Always coil it the same way, that is, right-handed or with the clock. When breaking in a new coil, start your rope by laying it flat on the deck, still in its burlap sack, with the inside end of the rope on the bottom. Now reach down through the center, draw out the inside end and coil right-handed. To do this any other way will form kinks which may become set forever in the rope and cause constant annoyance when passing over sheaves or being hauled.

Good rope, properly cared for, will last a long time and will always be in condition to do the job. These jobs are many indeed, but most of them fall to the lot of the running rigging.

In designing the running rigging of any ship, the first concern should be simplicity of rig, that is, a minimum of running rigging but enough to do the job adequately under any sea condition. Next, would be the proper block or sheave in the proper place. The smaller the sail to sheet or haul, the less reason there is for tackles or purchases. Following are some hints perhaps of use to you as you face the problems of rigging your own vessel.

Halyards

These are any lines which haul aloft, i.e., haul-yard.

Small boats, not racing, need simply a rope passing through a block or sheave aloft to change the direction of pull to hoist the sail. The weight of pull applied will set it up sufficiently for ordinary purposes. However, when racing, or with heavy sails and spars, some sort of tackle (pronounced *tayckle*) or power-multiplying device is needed. These are many. The rope tackle which is commonest is adequate but subject to much stretch because of the rope length. To overcome this, winches are often used, working a flexible wire halyard.

Such a winch is expensive and too often a cumbersome thing on the deck or mast of the small boat. If a winch is indicated, by all means select one of those with the handle on the bottom, leaving the barrel free to handle the rope. For the main halyard, the magazine winch which stores the wire on its own drum is best. Pictured here is a device which saves the cost of a winch, or avoids the generally unsatisfactory tackle with overmuch rope to be coiled and stowed. The track used must be of heavy bronze, what is commercially known as "Naval Track."

A shellback would call the operation "bousing down the tack." It is not seen often on the yacht, for some unknown reason.

The gaff-headed sail, if the area is anything over 100 square feet, should always have tackles on both throat and peak, espe-

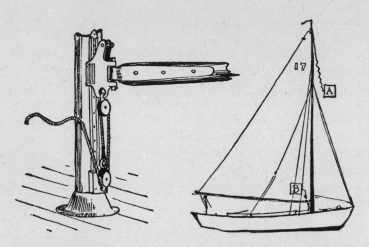

A method of setting a mainsail with the least possible "stretch" in the halyards. Halyard A is wire with a rope tail, set up hand-tight and belayed. Tackle B with its short parts is then hauled snug or "boused down." The boom fitting shown is a stock item, sliding in heavy Naval Track

cially the peak. Wherever possible, when the halyard (or sheet) hauls a boom or gaff, a flexible wire bridle should be its connection so as to distribute the pull in more than one place. A patent bronze bridle, having a locking device, must be used to permit the halyard to find the center of the bridle as it is hauled taut or slacked away as is sometimes desirable when sailing off the wind. Very much less expensive than this device is a simple lignum vitae lizard, for sale at any chandlery or easily turned on a small shop-lathe. The halyard is spliced around the scored groove and the wire bridle passed through the center hole.

Jib halyards on the size vessel with which we are concerned seldom need the power of a winch to set them up. A simple tackle is usually sufficient, for too much strain will merely bend the mast forward, slacking away the headstays and disturbing the balance of tension between the forward and after shrouds. Here, though, for expediency a simple, short gun-tackle or handy-billy on the

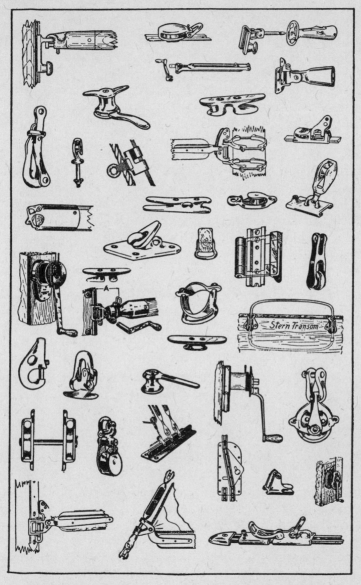

A page of modern yacht fittings. Courtesy Merriman Bros.,
Boston, Mass.

mast might be used when needed and the halyard set up as a single whip by hand and a good swig in ordinary airs.

These are the chief halyards on any simple yacht. Others may include the flag halyards, spinnaker halyard, etc., best made of braided cotton rope and belayed to a pinrail across the shrouds or on the back of the light boards in order to keep the base of the mast clear for the working halyards.

All halyards should have a stopper knot or crown on the deck end and a light screw-eye about two feet above the cleat so that it cannot whip aloft and through the block. A midseason inspection will usually show wear on the parts of the rope which have passed through the block or blocks. Reverse the entire halyard, top for bottom, and meet the fall winds with rigging almost as strong as when first rove.

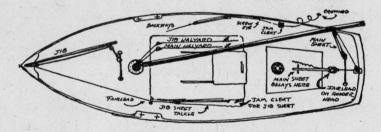

The deck of a small one-man boat

Sheets

No, gentle reader, sheets are not the sails! You do not (if you are at all salty) haul in the sheet; you sheet in the sail. The sheet is the rope or rope tackle which adjusts the sail in its relation to the center line of the vessel.

Most mainsheets are of too many parts for ordinary sailing in light or average summer winds. It takes a gale to overcome the friction in the purchase and stretch it out fully. Here are some ways to rig a mainsheet; and any one of them might be increased in power by the simple expedient of providing a latching snatch-block, where needed, through which the mainsheet can be rove in a blow or when real strapping-down is required.

Here is where a pliable rope is most appreciated. Hemp or linen, possibly four-strand construction, is better than manila. So is dacron. The mainsheet is a hard-working rope and should therefore be given special care. Always stow it hanging, where it can dry; and do not permit it to be kicked about the cockpit or remain coiled on the quarter, wet, under sun-mattresses, the

MAIN SHEET TACKLES

dinghy, or other gear. This sheet, like the halyards, can well stand a reversing about midseason to place its worn parts beyond further reach of the chafing of the blocks.

Jib sheets should be of the lightest possible rope so that they do not interfere with the fly of the sail. In fact, if a winch is required anywhere, it is in the setting of the jibs, especially large Genoas. With a winch to supply the power, a single sheet is sufficient, thus dispensing with the weight of blocks and fittings. These can be most annoying in light airs when a jib wants to fill and ghost but is prevented by its heavy tackle. Of course, a whisker pole will do the trick—if you carry a whisker pole. Sometimes even a single sheet is too heavy; and I have often rigged, especially for a Genoa or a spinnaker, a light piece of marling from the clew to any convenient part of the vessel. If a sail can't lift this, the wind isn't worth catching anyway!

In the one-man boat, where jib sheets are led aft to the tiller or wheel, the adjustment of the sheet becomes a delicate matter because of the friction of the various fair-leads and the deck or trunk top itself. If at all possible, run the sheet aft through fair-leads attached to the *side* of the trunk, letting the sheet festoon freely in air when slack. This will make it considerably easier to adjust. I have even seen the jib sheet run through the deck forward and

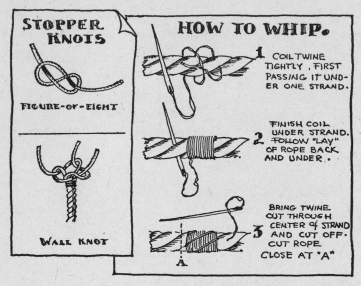

hung by fair-leads under the waterways inside, coming to the helmsman by way of the forward cockpit bulkhead. Certainly, this helps solve the friction problem as well as removes the sheet from the deck where too often it becomes jammed under some gear or lies ever ready to roll the careless hand overboard.

The overlapping jib has always been a problem when it comes to sheeting. There is no way of which the writer knows to make it self-trimming; the jib, lee and weather, must be trimmed independently after every tack. (It is rumored that Billy Spellman is the way he is from trying to figure this one out, even today babbling incoherently whenever he sees an overlapping jib.) The overlapping jib is a grand sail and worth the effort of trimming to get the last ounce of speed it gives to a boat, but for the single-hander or the cruising boat is not to be recommended. These types MUST be rigged so that when the tiller is put over, everything slops over and immediately draws.

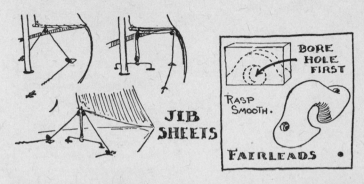

The ideal arrangement for sheeting the jib, needing as it does so many different "sets" for the various forces and directions of wind, would be a series of fair-leads studding the foredeck so that any could be used. However, we seem to have enough gadgets on our decks as it is, and this is hardly practical except in the strictly racing classes. Here is an adjustable jib horse which might help the man who is always fussing with the set of his headsail. It is self-trimming and therefore suitable for the cruiser.

Backstays

Backstays are midway between running and standing rigging; their upper parts, usually a single wire-rope from mast to a rope tackle. One is carried on each side, the one to the weather always being set up as the ship is tacked in any breeze which might severely strain the mast or shrouds. They are absolutely necessary on very tall Marconi rigs and with hollow spars. Yachtsmen hate them as necessary evils, and many types of securing them, releasing them, and setting them up have been devised (see cuts of marine hardware).

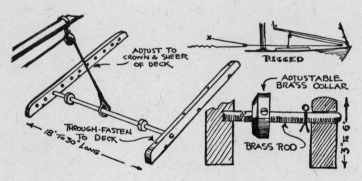

An adjustable jib "horse" permitting the shifting of the sheet lead. The traveler rod may be moved fore-and-aft by removing the cotter pin and placing the rod in any desired set of holes. Thwartship adjustment is obtained by shifting the sliding collars as desired and securing them with the flush set screw. Rod should be same diameter as the correct-size conventional traveler for the boat. Cleats to be made to accommodate sheer and crown of deck, allowing the sheet ring about 2" clearance between rod and deck

The simplest is a rope tackle, secured to a deck eye, which can be quickly slacked off. If the tackle is short and therefore not subject to much stretch, it is perhaps the best all-around type. But much better than backstays is what is known as a permanent backstay or Swedestay, these blessed gadgets having been first brought over by the Swedish meter teams back in the 20s. It is simply a wire stay from masthead to a short boomkin astern, out of the way of everything and always there. Naturally, it will serve only on boats with jib-headed sails.

Backstays must be handled quickly (oftimes by the girl friend or some other lubber!), and a jam cleat instead of the usual belaying cleat will speed up its handling and lessen the chance of fumbling. Unless the weather backstay is set up as the ship comes about and the mast stands without strain—just a few precious seconds—it will serve no purpose, and the boat will have to luff to get a good set. This is what loses races and makes for sloppy cruising.

It would be utterly impossible in this volume to discuss rigging thoroughly, or spar and deck hardware other than to mention that most boats are very poorly equipped. Somehow, too many boatmen fail to recognize the importance of the proper fitting for the job to be done, and in so doing they often spell the difference between joy and gloom afloat. I am fully aware that these are

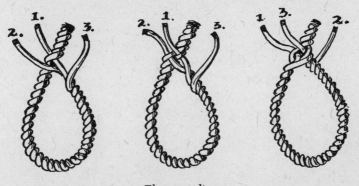

The eye splice

Unlay the strands and whip them temporarily. Then, opening the rope with a fid, tuck any strand under the opened lay. Arrange strands as in left-hand cut, tuck 2. and then 3. Continue around for three or four times, taper strands as in short splice, and roll

difficult things to obtain to *exactly suit your boat.* But, mates, much as this book has ignored advertiser slant, I am going to recommend that you write to Merriman Brothers, 185 Amory Street, Boston, Mass., get their general catalog, and use it as a handbook

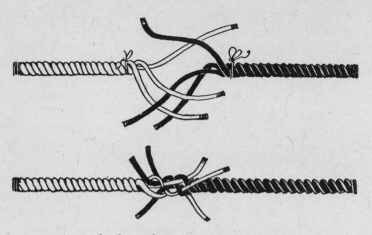

The short splice—for joining two ropes

First, marry the ropes as shown; then continue, over and under about three times each way from the marry. Cut strands in half, tuck again; halve again and tuck and cut strands off short. Roll under foot or beat into tapered, neat splice

with this chapter. It is free, and full to the 'wales with gadgets and devices which many of us have never seen or thought were manufactured for us. This book will solve most any rigging problem you might have.

Most boat books will include a great many knots and splices for the sailorman. I have been mates with thousands of miles of deep water and have yet to know of a knot situation of which one of the following five would not take care. I have made it my business to know these knots and splices backwards, to tie them one-handed or in the dark or with frozen and wet rope, quickly and strongly. Anything beyond them, as far as I am concerned, is for the rope trickster and of little use to me in getting my little ship from here to there in safety and comfort. Here they are:

These five knots, as well as the two splices, will prove quite sufficient for the ordinary rigging job. Splicing a rope-tail into a

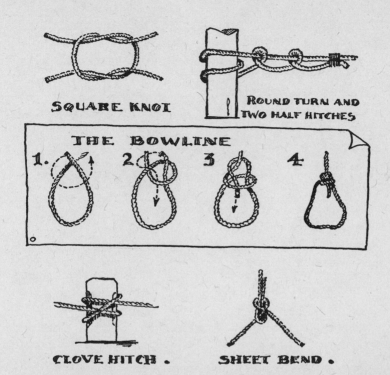

SQUARE KNOT

ROUND TURN AND TWO HALF HITCHES

THE BOWLINE

1. 2. 3. 4.

CLOVE HITCH .   SHEET BEND .

wire halyard is a good thing to know but very difficult to do without more practice and patience than falls to the lot of the average boatman. Just as good, and very much simpler and quicker, is to splice an eye into the ends and secure them in this way.

Every small boat should count a rigger's kit in its bosun's stores. This should include (of a size and strength called for by the particular rigging of the ship) the following at least:

TOOLS	SUPPLIES
Knife (ragged edge cuts best)	Beeswax
Close nippers	Marling and sail twine
	Annealed wire

TOOLS
Wooden mallet
Large wooden fid
Small steel marlingspike
Sail needle and palm
Cold chisel and anvil
Serving boards for marling
    wire.
Torch. Cigarette lighter

SUPPLIES
Canvas for parceling
Rope yarn and small stuff

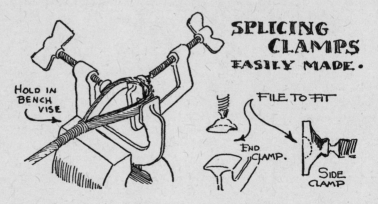

A splicing vise is useful and almost necessary for making the Liverpool or other conventional splices in wire. An ordinary bench vise can be easily converted for this purpose as in the drawing.

XIV *Dinghies*

"Animal or mineral?" asked the Bosun.
"Neither," replied Alice. "Guess some more."
"Bird, beast, fish, or devil?"
"D-devil," Alice admitted.
"I know," cried the Bosun, "it's a dinghy!"

—From Alice in Boatland

Our bosun was undoubtedly a yachtsman. Who else could better classify this nightmare, this nuisance, this low, sneering, cunning snake-in-the-wake, this devil—the dinghy?

There is only one satisfactory way to carry it: trussed up in davits like a bound tiger being borne to the waiting circus cage. But how many of us have davits on our little ships? Most of us must be content to drag the dinghy forever astern, spoiling an otherwise nifty outfit and ruining the cruise at the outset. But we must have 'em, of that there can be no question.

The only question allowed us is the one: What kind of a dinghy? And the answer is: the one best suited to your boat and needs. It's a vicious circle, mates!

Until recently, the average dinghy was merely any kind of a rowboat. Dinghies are today quite able little craft, sturdy, tight, light, and remarkably burdensome for their size. But no amount of intelligent design or construction can make them stay astern, at sea or at moorings. They want to be one of the party—to share bunk, galley, and every round of drinks.

277

Neither this book nor any other boik can be of any help in the matter. Experienced boatmen have discovered little tricks to help —but no cure-all. Under ocean conditions, when the dinghy seems bent upon perching on the taffrail, unbidden, some have found that a length of rope trailing the dinghy will slow her forward runs. Others drop the centerboard, or trail from the quarter, or fuss and fume to set her on the exact rump of a pet wake-billow. I know of no real solution—except inviting the dinghy aboard.

At moorings, the dinghy must caress its mother every so often. Nothing but a tide or a wind or both will discourage its affection. A bucket trailed astern or a brick hung over the transom has been known to make it harder for the dinghy, but probably the real solution is a boat-boom *longer than the dinghy.* These are not particularly salty on a small boat, but can be arranged.

The dinghy best suited to your boat should certainly be one that, if must be, can be carried on board. It is my personal belief that the scow or pram types are the best all-round dinghies. These will stow more easily than those with conventional bows and, length for length, give more carrying capacity.

The vessel large enough to ship regular boat skids forward, or on the trunk, has no particular problem. Any convenient halyard or tackle, leading to a yoke or the lifting eyes on the dinghy will

Boat booms

The spinnaker pole lashed to the main boom. Note the endless line to the block at the outboard end of the pole to which the dinghy is secured short

The spinnaker pole rigged against the rail at the shrouds, guyed with fore-and-aft stays and the spinnaker halyard as a lift

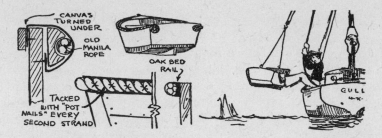

Left: *Rope-protected rubbing strakes for the dinghy. Use old, soft manila or cotton line. If canvas covered, tack with copper tacks and use about oo canvas or light fire hose*
Right: *Bringing the dinghy aboard singlehanded aided by the main halyards. Note how it is fended off with the feet until well above the rail and ready to swing inboard*

yank it on board in a jiffy. Such a dinghy should be of glass or of lapstreak or other construction which will keep it tight at all times. The plywood dinghies do the job beautifully and are as light in weight as can be found.

I would want these features in any dinghy:

1. Cushioned rubbing-strakes *all around.*
2. Oar locks attached to oars.
3. A moderately husky skeg (for good towing) and exterior bilge strakes (for beaching).
4. A transom sturdy enough to take the thrust of an outboard motor.
5. A bilge drain.

She would then do the job and might take her place with me as a fairly satisfactory utility boat. I think that she would be much more a source of enjoyment, however, for the inclusion of a simple sail rig that could be quickly shipped and unshipped.

Such a rig is easily made at no great expense. A single sail and pole mast is indicated unless you want to go in for dinghy racing —a grand sport but seldom to be fully enjoyed with the dinghy which must give both utilitarian and racing service.

In a dinghy of twelve or more feet it is quite practical to install a small air-cooled inboard motor. These are best installed well forward, balancing the live weight, and should be protected from the weather by a portable box or hood—to be removed or partly lifted when the motor is operating. A dinghy so equipped will take the same registration number as the parent vessel, but must carry its own complete government equipment. A folding canvas spray hood makes any motor-equipped dinghy a much more comfortable and useful craft.

There are on the market some small boats of folding canvas, rubber, or balsa. I have seen none which I would care to give the hard use demanded of the dinghy. These may be suitable for emergency use or for lifeboats.

Two plywood dinghy types

A 4' x 8' punt, weight about 75 pounds. Good carrier, stows on deck well; not such a good tower	*A 4' x 6' coracle, weight about 50 pounds. Tows well, stows well; but is strictly a one-man dinghy*

PLANS COURTESY OF CAPT. VICTOR SLOCUM

A word about the deepwater cruiser. In my opinion there is only one type of dinghy suitable for her—and that is a dory. In sheltered waters, she might ship one of the smaller compact types; but at sea, where the dinghy may also become the lifeboat, there is no type as safe and sane as a small Banks, Gloucester, Swampscott, Cape Ann, or other tried-and-true dory. It is well worth giving up valuable deck-room to this type. Not only will it withstand the weight and impact of boarding seas—which the dinghy won't—but it will live in seas utterly overwhelming to other small boats.

Dories will sail—and sail well. The secret is to keep the center of effort low. A tall rig makes a dory dangerous as there is a minimum of stability in the dory, increasing only as the dory becomes heavily loaded.

The repair and upkeep of the dinghy offers no new problems to the boatman. The skiff, sharpie, or other planked boat depends upon swelling to keep it tight. The leaks of this type are usually along the chine, especially astern (where you have jumped from deck on boarding). Caulking with cotton will seldom cure leaks here. As a first try, fill the open seam between lower strake and planking ends with a good liquid marine-glue after the wood is thoroughly dry. Then renail, setting the heads well. In the case of very open chine-seams, back off the planking first and lay a piece of paint-soaked cotton wicking around the lower edge of the lower strake; then renail securely.

Canvas-covered boats may be patched, using a heavy silk or light duck soaked in marine glue and smoothed on with a hot iron. Leaks in canvas-covered boats not actually punctured are most likely to be found under the keel, skeg, or bilge stringers. The canvas rots very quickly under these members, especially about the holes made by the fastenings. Plywood boats seldom leak. Marine glue, run in chine or where bottom joins the transom (or head shape), will usually seal them quickly. Punctures in plywood

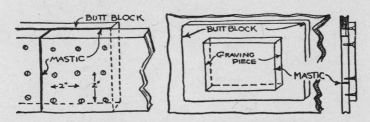

Patching the puncture in a plywood dinghy

Square up the puncture first, then fit in a graving piece neatly, backing this up with a butt block about 3" larger all around. Screw together from inside, apply mastic, and secure in place

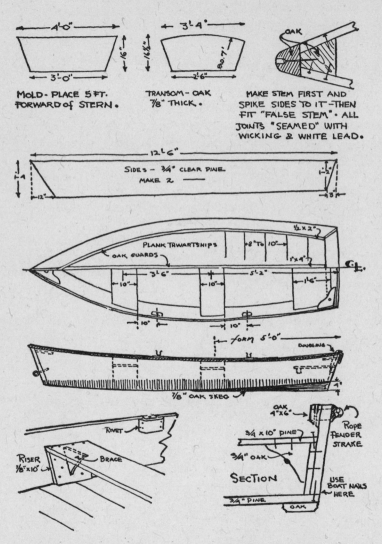

A 12-foot utility sharpie. A useful, easily-built, flat-bottomed tender especially designed for an outboard motor

are always localized. The hole should be cut out fair and even and a new piece of plywood its exact size and shape inserted; this, to be laid in marine glue and backed up by a butt block larger than the hole and securely fastened to the surrounding wood.

So much for our devilish playmate. She's very much like some other folks I could mention—a man can't live with 'em and he can't live without 'em!

XV Care and Storage
of Your Boat

It has been said that a boat suffers more in winter storage than afloat. While I do not agree with this thought completely, I do agree that *improper* winter storage may well be more harmful than actual use. Weaknesses and defects, only appearing under the strain of use, may well have been started during the long winter months.

Perhaps the greatest dangers of winter storage are: careless or inadequate blocking or support, exposure to the elements because of poor or no covering, and lack of provision for ventilation.

Blocking

The weight of the boat should be *entirely upon the keel,* never upon the bilge supports.

Depending somewhat upon the huskiness of the keel and vessel, blocking between keel and floor or ground should be spaced three to five feet along its entire length. Bow and stern blocks are first placed so that the water line will be approximately level (so that vessel drains well and no undue strains or stresses are created), then securely bedded, and the intermediate blocks placed, then wedged tightly between keel and block with *hardwood* wedges (not shingles, slats, crates, or conveniently-shaped stones!).

Block high enough for easy bottom painting. Wedge *all* blocks so that they can be easily slipped out, one at a time, to expose the complete underside of the keel. Use no blocks under rudder skeg,

 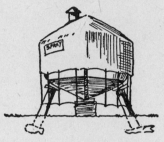

Incorrect laying-up. Too low, no protection, propped in a danger- ous and injurious manner

Correct laying-up. Blocked high, covered, propped safely, venti- lated

unless a wooden support is cut between it and the stern knee. Keelboats may rest entirely upon the keel casting; but for a boat with long overhangs, bow and stern supports to ground should be provided.

With the weight firmly on the keel blocking and the vessel lev- eled both ways, the weight on the port and starboard supports will not exceed a *few pounds*. These supports should never be hitched under a rubbing strake or into a porthole, but should be firmly *buried in the ground* and strike fair under the flat of the bilges, with a board inserted to distribute the thrust should set- tling, by any chance, occur.

The big danger is just this settling or shifting of blocking as freezing, thawing, washouts, or the careless knock occurs. Butt the side supports (a log, roller, or sizable timber) on a flat rock, eighteen inches or more in the ground; then tie from top to a keel block with a light batten.

Generally, it is not good to turn any boat over for wintering. As nearly as possible, arrange the support exactly as if the vessel were still water borne. For the centerboarder, don't forget to provide for the painting of this member by high enough blocking or by digging a pit directly under it.

With the vessel hauled and properly stored *before* you board her, the laying up may proceed. Check against this list:

1. Within two hours of hauling, scrub the bottom clean of grass, barnacles, and slime. (Saves much cussing next spring, mate!)
2. Knock out all plugs, drain engine block and fresh water tank —then sponge dry the bays between frames.
3. Empty any liquid liable to freeze; drain all plumbing (oil or kerosene in traps) and engine.
4. Systematically store or, better, remove to a dry locker or your home every loose article on board. Make a clean-up of old oilers, bottles, rags, condemned life-preservers, deflated swimming tubes, etc.—through the whole list of summer accumulations.
5. Remove from the boat all bedding, mattresses, cushions, and clothing.
6. Lay up engine in accordance with manufacturer's recommendations. This should certainly include removing batteries, magnetos, coils, etc. from the boat; putting a dab of light oil in cylinders and other moving parts; spreading a vaseline film over bright parts; and cleaning up of grease and oil on or near the engine. DO NOT COVER THE ENGINE.
7. Open every locker, porthole, bin, and hatch; remove as many floor boards as possible—*leave the boat wide open.*
8. *One month later,* dust and sweep all decks, cockpits, and canopies—and prepare to cover for winter. During this time additional protection can be given by varnishing and painting very raw spots.

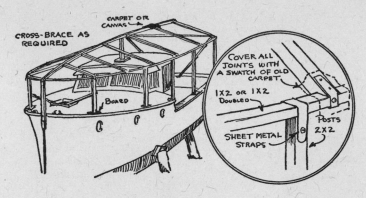

A winter cover

The sailing vessel should have her spars removed and stored inside, rigging carefully coiled and labeled, and sails taken to warm, dry storage (laundered first if necessary).

The boat should be covered whether stored inside or out. A light duck or sheeting over a 1″ × 2″ ridge will keep the boat free of the dust of inside storage. Exterior covers should be of durable *waterproofed* canvas or other weather-resistant material such as plastic sheeting, roofing, or composition board. In all cases, a supporting frame of light stuff should be erected (see sketch). This can be arranged to knock down easily for use again.

The cover should reach at least to the water line, hanging plumb from the rail, and should not be lashed against the topsides or hull. Chafing here might necessitate a major paint job on an otherwise good surface.

No matter what the covering, ample provision must be made for ventilation. The great enemy of the boat during the winter is dry rot and dampness induced by sweating. If a boat is thoroughly dry, inside and out, before covering, and is assured a circulation of air after covering, the boat will remain dry and sweet for as long as she remains hauled.

If you store in the southern latitudes, there are some special storage problems to lick. First, do not under any circumstances

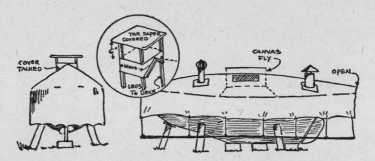

Ventilating the winter-covered boat

cover with a material of a black or dark color. It will invite excessive heat from the sun's rays and cause all manner of trouble. Fortunately, in the South it is possible to store *wet* (in the water), often under a shed. This is certainly recommended. However, you will still want a cover, even though light. If sun reaches the hull, turn the boat about several times during the lay-up period and, whenever possible, hose down the entire boat to keep it swelled.

Second, you must take very special care to guard against mildew and against insects, or, rather, those miscalled roaches, palmetto bugs. To treat against mildew, spray the entire boat and its parts—even those parts in storage at another location. Then hang "gas bags" about the boat, about one bag for every one hundred cubic feet. These bags release a noxious gas which deters the spores of mildew, yet is harmless to humans, fabrics, and materials and disappears into thin air. They are effective for from two to four months, whereupon you should replace them. You buy them in department stores and in chain stores—they are a common household article.

I have stored boats in Florida for many years with never a hint of mildew upon my return in the fall. These are the steps I take:

1. Remove all clothing, bedding, fabrics from the boat. Sun and air for a full day. Dry-clean and launder as necessary.

2. Wash down the boat, inside and out, with a strong detergent. Cut all grease, oil, and wax.
3. Spray—especially interior overheads, dark closet corners, and areas which appear to lack normal ventilation—with a mixture of water and ammonia (70–30). (I make this on board, using one of the spray bottles you buy with those tricky glass-cleaners.)
4. Replace all gear aboard, now cleaned. Much of it is wrapped in brown paper, or bagged. Clothing is hung carefully, with air spaces around and between. No food of any kind other than canned goods is kept.
5. Open every door, bin, locker, drawer, hatch, oven, refrigerator on the boat from stem to stern. Then open one (one only!) forward hatch or a pair of portholes or anything else that will give a few square feet of air passage to the exterior.
6. Somewhere amidships, construct a temporary baffle of light material (cardboard or craft boxes will do), dividing the vessel in two. Into the low center of this cut a hole and in the hole mount a 20 to 28 inch continuous-duty 110-volt a.c. fan. Hook this to a separate shore line, not to the ship's circuits, for these should be shut off. Now, in front of this fan hang several of the anti-mildew gas bags referred to.
7. Then open one (one only) after hatch or a pair of portholes or anything else that will provide about the same square footage as the forward opening you have rigged. *Inside* of this hang a few more gas bags.
8. As you have worked toward the after opening, you should have been placing little pellets compounded to lure palmetto bugs to their deaths and for sale at all grocery and hardware stores south of Georgia.

You now climb out of the boat, turn on the fan, and go home. The yardman will (for a fee) renew the gas bags once or twice, especially if you have been foresighted and have left him a stock; check the bilge, pumping with his own portable pump if required; and turn the boat several times during the summer—and, come

October, I promise that you will board a fresh, sweet, mildewless boat, *ready to live aboard* save for a few dead roaches here and there.

Now, I know there are such things as electric dehumidifiers. Bad cess on 'em. I've seen boats dried out to within four inches of the immersed hull so that you could see daylight through their plank seams. I've seen paint cracked all over the vessel and the entire interior smelling like an ancient tomb of stale, lifeless air. I do not in any way recommend them and advise that you keep away from them. Likewise, those who keep air conditioning on for long lay-up periods run the risk of excessive and destructive drying.

A hauled vessel will seldom start her shrinking until the March winds have come. The shade and protection of the full-length winter cover will retard this. An even better retardant is a coat of paint, topsides and bottom, about this time.

Visit the old hooker occasionally during the long winter. She kind of likes to see you, skipper—and a tuck in the cover here or a tap on a wedge there might make her wait for spring much easier to bear.

The lashing of the last holdfast on the cover does not necessarily mean the end of boating for you until May again rolls around. Any boat will yield an amazing list of needed items or repairs that can be taken care of during the winter months. A little ingenuity applied will permit even the building of built-in items, later to be scribed and set in place quickly. Paper or cardboard patterns of the receiving end will sometimes enable you to slip in a new locker, galley dresser, or chart case, completely painted and finished, with only a few fastenings necessary on the job.

One of the most delightful winter pastimes for the boatman is making the extras for his little ship—the little distinctive touches that makes this boat your boat, as different from another as your signature. I am a sucker for old-time tradition and even on the straight powerboat have added touches from the past which (to me, at least) have given me additional pride in my boat.

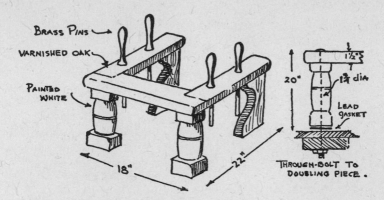

Old-time fife rail for mainmast, designed to be set against forward end of cabin trunk. Jib traveler may be attached to it, keeping deck clear

The exterior painting of even a small boat can be made to give out the flavor of the old wooden ships. Trail boards, scrollwork on the bows and quarters, and ornate transoms were some of the features which lent charm to the vessels of the past.

Bulwarks, or the inboard faces of even fairly low rails, were often painted white. Wales or strakes of contrasting color, not only give flavor but sometimes, carefully swung, add materially to the sheer of a boat. Any such color band running fore-and-aft tends to make a hull look longer and lower.

Down on the Chesapeake there is a fleet of miniature square-riggers. Small centerboard hulls sixteen to twenty-four feet have been rigged as perfect little brigs, barks, and ships, and to see them, reaching grandly across the bays, is to look deep into the past. For the man who loves the old days, I can think of no more delightful way to take his sailing. These boats not only perform beautifully but also teach the art of handling sail and working ship as no other small type can.

May your days with your little ship—outboard, knockabout, power cruiser or deepwater rag carrier—be as adventurous and

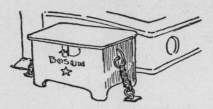

A DECK CHEST FOR TOOLS
AND SMALL STUFF.

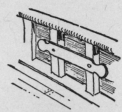

A CARVEL FOR
BELAYING.

A SEAGOING
SKYLIGHT.

PIN RAIL ON MAST.

COLORED WALE TO "LENGTHEN" A BOAT.

OLD-TIME STERN BOARD.

Some "wooden ship" touches for the modern yacht

brave as those of the sailormen of another age. There is no sport like it; no hobby in life, as complete.

There are quiet sunny days on azure-blue seas and quiet starlit nights in snug anchorages.

There are glorious days, with the whine of big wind in the rigging; and boisterous nights, sailing a storm-ridden course.

And these things end for most of us in the sadness of approaching winter with the brave little ship put to bed—and spring so distant.

But the joys of boating need not cease then. There are long snowy evenings ahead and long gray days to be made brighter by a thought for the good friend sleeping on a faraway shore.

And if, like Joshua Slocum in his beloved *Spray*, we can live again those sailing days, proud of the tight little, right little ship which grew under our loving hands—we have tasted of one of life's most abiding blessings.

Appendix

Useful Facts and Information for the Reader of This Book and Required for Naval Design and Planning

NAUTICAL MEASURE

1 league = 3 nautical miles
1 nautical mile = 6080.26 feet = 1.1516 statute mile
1 degree at the equator = 60 nautical miles = 69.16 statute miles
360 degrees = 21,600 nautical miles = 24,874.5 statute miles (or the circumference of the earth at the equator)

SQUARE MEASURE

1 square yard = 9 square feet
1 square foot = 144 square inches

CUBIC MEASURE

1 cubic yard = 27 cubic feet
1 cubic foot = 1,728 square inches
1 cord   = 128 cubic feet (usually 4 × 4 × 8 feet)

SHIPPING MEASURE

Internal capacity of vessel
        1 register ton = 100 cubic feet

Cargo measurement
> 1 U.S. shipping ton = 40 cubic feet = 32.14 bushels

MEASURES OF LENGTH

1 mile   = 1,760 yards = 5,280 feet
1 yard   = 3 feet = 36 inches
1 foot   = 12 inches
1 fathom = 6 feet = 2 yards
1 hand   = 4 inches
1 span   = 9 inches

WEIGHTS AND MEASURES

1 U.S. gallon = 0.1337 cubic foot = 231 cubic inches = 4 quarts = 8 pints
1 quart = 2 pints = 8 gills
1 cubic foot = 7.48 U.S. gallons
1 barrel = 31.5 gallons
1 hogshead = 2 barrels = 63 gallons

FLUID MEASURE

1 U.S. fluid ounce = 8 drams = 1.805 cubic inch = $\frac{1}{128}$ gallon
1 fluid dram = 60 minims.

COMMERCIAL WEIGHT

1 long ton = 2,240 pounds
1 gross ton = 2,240 pounds
1 short ton = 2,000 pounds
1 net ton   = 2,000 pounds
1 pound   = 16 ounces = 7,000 grains
1 ounce   = 16 drams = 437.5 drams

APOTHECARIES' WEIGHT

1 pound   = 12 ounces = 5,760 grains
1 ounce   = 8 drams =   480 grains

MEASURES OF PRESSURE

1 pound per square inch = 144 pounds per square foot = 0.068 atmosphere

1 atmosphere = 30 inches of mercury at 62° F. = 14.7 pounds per square inch = 2,116.3 pounds per square foot

MEASURES USED FOR
DIAMETERS AND AREAS
OF WIRE

1 circular inch = area of circle 1″ in diameter = 0.7854 square inch
     ″   = 1,000,000 circular mils
1 square inch = 1.2732 circular inch = 1,273,239 circular mils

MISCELLANEOUS

1 gross = 12 dozen = 144 units
1 dozen = 12 units
1 score = 20 units
A cubic foot of water contains 7.5 gallons, 1,728 cubic inches, and weighs 62.5 pounds.

ELECTRICAL EQUIVALENTS

1 kilowatt = 1,000 watts = 1.3414 horsepower = 44,260 foot-pounds per minute = 56.89 B.t.u. per minute

1 horsepower = 745.7 watts = 33,000 foot-pounds per minute = 42.41 B.t.u. per minute

SALT WATER

1 cubic foot = 64 pounds
35 cubic feet = 1 ton (long)
1 U.S. gallon = 8.58 pounds
1 Imperial gallon = 10.27 pounds

FRESH WATER

1 U.S. gallon = 231 cubic inches = 0.134 cubic feet = 8.33 pounds = 0.83 Imperial gallons = 3.8 liters

1 ton of fresh water = 35.88 cubic feet = 268.38 U.S. gallons

CONVERSION RATIOS

MULTIPLY	BY	TO OBTAIN
Diameter of circle	3.1416	Circumference of circle
Diameter of circle	0.886	Side of equal square
U.S. gallons	0.8327	Imperial gallons
U.S. gallons	0.1337	Cubic feet
Feet of water	0.4335	Pounds per square inch
Cubic feet	62.428	Pounds of water
U.S. gallons	8.336	Pounds of water
Knots	1.152	Miles per hour
Pounds	0.4536	Kilograms
Inches	2.540	Centimeters
Yards	0.9144	Meters
To obtain above	Divide by	Starting with above

Index: Including Reference to Illustrations